1759

The Battle for Canada

Laurier L. LaPierre

M&S

Canadian Cataloguing in Publication Data

LaPierre, Laurier L., 1929–
    1759 : the battle for Canada

Includes bibliographical references.
ISBN 0-7710-4699-5

1. Québec Campaign, 1759. 2. Plains of Abraham
(Québec, Quebec), Battle of the, 1759. I. Title.

FC386.L46 1990   971.01'88   C90-094528-1
E199.L46 1990

Printed and bound in Canada. The paper used in this book is acid
free.

McClelland & Stewart Inc.
The Canadian Publishers
481 University Avenue
Toronto, Ontario
M5G 2E9

To my sons, Dominic and Thomas.
This is also their story.

Contents

A Word Before You Start   xiii

Part One: The Siege   17

Les Anglais Sont Arrivés   19
Mired in the Mud   145
On the Move Again   211

Part Two: The Battle   241

On the Plains of Abraham   243
The Inevitable   273
Aftermath   299

Notes on Sources   303

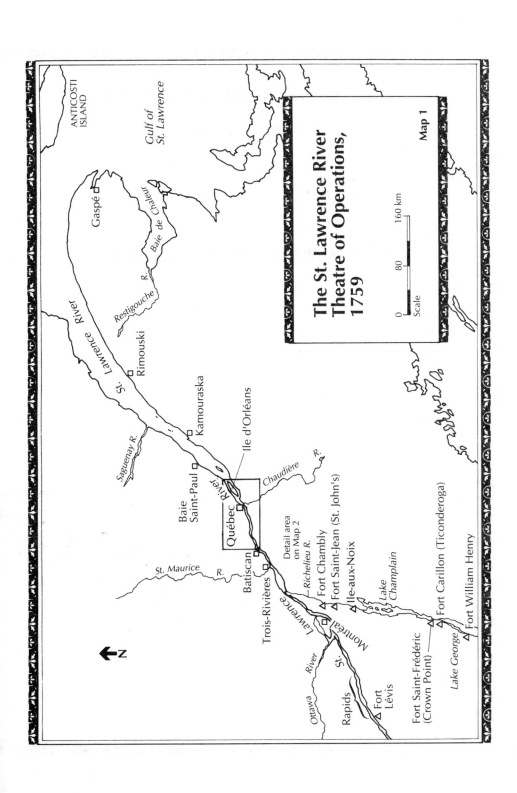

ANTICOSTI ISLAND

Gulf of St. Lawrence

Gaspé

Baie de Chaleur

Restigouche R.

St. Lawrence River

Rimouski

Saguenay R.

Kamouraska

Baie Saint-Paul

Ile d'Orléans

Chaudière R.

Québec

St. Maurice R.

Batiscan

Detail area on Map 2

Richelieu R.

Fort Chambly

Fort Saint-Jean (St. John's)

Ile-aux-Noix

Lake Champlain

Fort Carillon (Ticonderoga)

Fort William Henry

Trois-Rivières

St. Lawrence River

Montréal

Fort Saint-Frédéric (Crown Point)

Lake George

Ottawa River

St. Lawrence River

Rapids

Fort Lévis

←N

The St. Lawrence River Theatre of Operations, 1759

Scale

0   80   160 km

Map 1

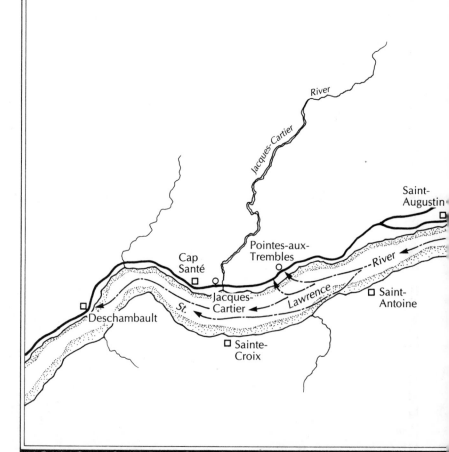

The Battle for Canada, 1759

British
encampments

French
encampments

- -·-→ Troop advance

Tidal flats

□ Village

○ Garrison

Road

Map 2

Jacques-Cartier River

Saint-
Augustin

Pointes-aux-
Trembles

Cap
Santé

Lawrence River

Saint-
Antoine

St. Jacques-
Cartier

Deschambault

Sainte-
Croix

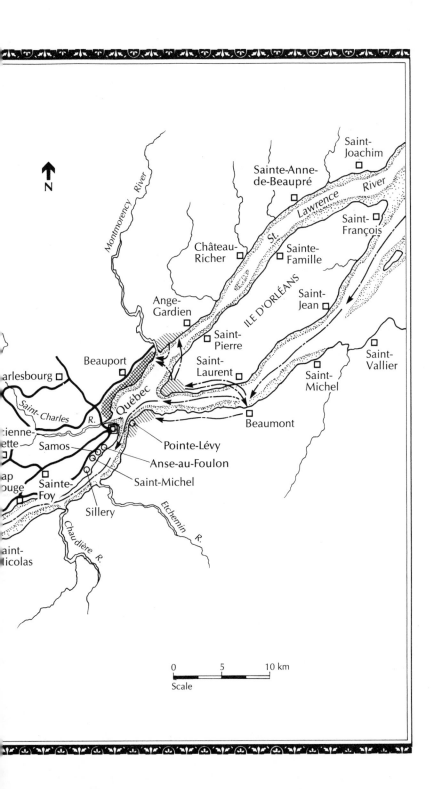

A Word Before You Start

Before I tell you the story of the Conquest of Québec in 1759, I must tell you something about myself and why I decided to tell this story.

As you saw on the dust jacket, I am Laurier L. LaPierre (the L. is for Lucien). I come from a little place in the eastern townships of Québec on the border of La Beauce and Maine called Lac Mégantic. You may have heard of Lac Mégantic as the rallying point of Benedict Arnold's army on its way to conquer Canada in 1775 during the American Revolution.

Until my forty-ninth birthday I lived in the province of Québec, with the exception of some ten years when I was studying in Baltimore and in Toronto. My studies culminated in a Ph.D. in history from the University of Toronto. Over the years I have been a teacher, a media personality, a failed restaurateur, sometime host of "This Hour Has Seven Days" – in its time the country's most popular television program – a defeated politician, a father, a gourmet cook, and a dabbler in poetry and in the New Age.

Now I am engaged in what I consider to be the most important task of my life: telling you the story of the events at Québec in 1759. I am a part of 1759. The happenings of that year place me where I am in the world; they define me and compel my spirit and my energies.

For most of my adult life, I have been puzzled by the fact that history does not seem to do for Canadians what it does for other nationalities. The Americans, for instance, seem to find in their history justification for whatever it is they are currently doing. It seems to allow the British to remember who they once were, the French to become boastful, the Germans purposeful, the Russians careful, and the Chinese watchful. It makes the Poles dissolve into tears and play Chopin, and allows the Greeks to keep the flame.

Canadians, on the other hand, spend considerable time in confusion about their history, wondering when it began and what parts of it they can identify with. In their dilemma they chop it up, generally into the English part and the French part, not knowing exactly what to do with the part played by those who are of neither French nor English heritage.

Historical heroes, who inhabit the national psyche and feed the imagination of most peoples of the world, are sadly absent from Canadian life. The few existing ones are apportioned to the two major linguistic groups and never fulfil a national mandate.

The same may also be said of our historical moments: They do not belong to all of us in the same way. They have occurred in Québec or in the West, or in Ontario or by the Atlantic, sometimes in the Arctic or in religious missions or battlefields all over the world, but never in Canada. And they seldom are accepted by all as belonging to all of Canada.

Canadians do not even share myths – those imagined truths that find acceptance because they illuminate the soul and galvanize the national will.

In other words, Canadians refuse to share a common history. And so history, the collective remembrance of moments past, is not an emotional act in this country. It is largely a political one.

I have decided to attempt to reverse that use of history.

The summer of 1759, culminating in the battle of the Plains of Abraham, which brought about the capitulation of the town of Québec and its adjacent territory, is perfect for my purposes. It is the most important moment in our history. It is neither an English nor a French moment. It is a Canadian one, and we are all a part of it.

A Word of Thanks

Jack McClelland threw this project at me a few years ago. I am glad he did. Steve Gable of Gable Bennett & Associates Inc., my business agent, made the arrangements with

McClelland & Stewart, my publishers. They are good arrangements. France Lapierre did the research with her usual flair and encouraged the project all along. Jim Oakes and Thomas LaPierre helped her from time to time. Many librarians and archivists helped me to locate books and pamphlets and documents and pictures. Maggie Hosgood put order into some of the English. Patrick Watson turned the whole project around. My literary agent, Lee Davis Creal of the Lucinda Vardey Agency in Toronto, was kind enough to take over representing my interests in the middle of this project, and not at the beginning, as is usually the case. My editor at McClelland & Stewart, Dinah Forbes, demonstrates once again that she is one of Canada's best editors. While the mistakes left in the book are all mine, she prevented many more from creeping in by her intense questioning.

I am grateful to all these people – and to many more besides, including Glenn Reiznar, Don Wells, and Mary Pawlus – and to you, the reader. I hope you enjoy this book and can find something of yourself in the story I tell.

A Word of Caution

There are hundreds of documents relating to the battle of the Plains of Abraham: letters, dispatches, memoranda, diaries, memoirs, and so on. Beyond the general outline of the siege, the battle and the aftermath, agreement as to what exactly happened is limited indeed. Often, only a sentence or two in these texts describes an incident or a moment. It was necessary for me to read between the lines in order to recreate for you what took place in and around Québec between June 26 and September 18, 1759. I am convinced that everything I tell you about really happened.

Also, please bear in mind that the word "English" or the expression *les Anglais* is used to denote all British forces and actions. The Canadians were not aware of the major differences between the Welsh, the English, the Scots, and the Irish. They were all *les Anglais*.

As well, you need to know that Québec in this story refers to the town of Québec and not to what is now la Province de Québec.

With apologies to the Native people of Canada, I have used the more traditional word "Indian" when referring to them and their role in my story.

Well, enough of that. Once upon a time, there was a land, a people, a town, a castle, many ships, and an old man. . . .

Laurier L. LaPierre
Vancouver
July 1, 1990

Part One

THE SIEGE
June 26–September 12, 1759

LES ANGLAIS SONT ARRIVES

June 26–July 15, 1759

June 26, 1759

(Day One)

On the ramparts of Québec
Early morning

The old man was thankful that it was at least a fine day. Not a cloud, not a wisp of mist marred his view from the ramparts of Québec. He could see clearly across the turbulent waters of the St. Lawrence River that – reversing themselves – appeared to be going in the wrong direction, past Pointe-Lévy to where the river divides for the Ile d'Orléans some eighteen miles away. From where he stood, he could even make out the difficult channel of La Traverse, through which every ship had to pass on its way upriver to Québec, the capital of La Nouvelle France – Canada.

But if neither cloud nor mist conspired to spoil his vista, something else did, and it contributed much to his agitation and annoyance. Glancing down on the promenade a hundred feet or so below him, the Governor General of all the North American possessions of his Most Christian Majesty, Louis XV, King of France – le Marquis de Vaudreuil – could see that others shared his anxiety. Grouped together in little knots on the large terrace built in front of his residence stood many citizens. Vaudreuil recognized the important ones: the chief of police, François Daine, Jean-Claude Panet the notary, Blaise Arnoux, the surgeon, with his brother, Joseph, the apothecary. He had entertained them often at dinner and he smiled as he recalled that the last time his wife had been most imperious with Panet, who bored her to distraction. He barely knew, however, two other men on the promenade: Jean Collet, the merchant who was now serving in the militia, and Colas Gauvreau, the cooper. Glancing nervously toward the Ile d'Orléans, they talked among themselves, filling and refilling their black stone pipes with strands of foul-smelling tobacco from seal pouches carried deep in their pockets.

A few feet away from them, women of different social ranks and various ages stood, panic showing in their eyes. Some had curled and powdered their hair; others, less vain, had put on sensible white bonnets. Most wore white blouses and short, straight skirts revealing half their calves, while a few were draped in long brown or blue capes that covered them from the top of their heads to their extremely narrow and high-heeled shoes. With satisfaction, the Governor saw Madame Mounier, the wife of a prominent merchant, lead the women and the children in prayer. He could faintly hear the *"Je vous salue, Marie"* "Hail Marys," the traditional Canadian prayer to the Virgin Mary.

Vaudreuil noticed a few seminarians from the Séminaire de Québec and students from the Collège des Jésuites further down the terrace. Among them were the two sons of a seigneur, André Couillard and his brother, Joseph, from Montmagny on the south shore. He was pleased that they were both dressed in their military uniforms. Of Jean-Marie Verreau, he only knew that his parents had a large and well-cultivated farm in Château-Richer, not too far from the parish of Beauport, where his army was encamped. But he remembered well the eighteen-year-old Pierre Mennard, whose father was an important businessman in Montréal who, in better days, had regally entertained the Vaudreuils when the vice-royal court took up residence there every year for the winter. However, Vaudreuil had heard that Mennard *père* had fallen on bad times. Near Mennard, Vaudreuil saw the fourteen-year-old Jean-François-Xavier Lefebvre, whose mother was *la plus dévouée des femmes*, a most dedicated person if the Bishop of Québec was to be believed, or an interfering busybody according to Madame de Vaudreuil. With them were two priests dressed in their black cassocks and wearing black broad-rimmed hats: Jean-François Récher, the French parish priest of Québec and Charles Baudouin, a Canadian attached to the Séminaire, whom Vaudreuil respected even though he often found the priest irritating.

"Les Anglais sont arrivés! Les Anglais sont arrivés! Les Anglais sont arrivés!" Vaudreuil heard the crowd repeating to each other, almost not believing what their eyes told them.

And what their eyes told them – as did Vaudreuil's – was that tall ships, with English flags flying high above their masts, were massed at the southwestern tip of the Ile d'Orléans, while others were stretched down the St. Lawrence as far as anyone could see. There seemed to be hundreds of them – gathered there to attack the people of the town of Québec.

When news had come in the spring that the English were assembling a fleet on the eastern shore of Canada, Vaudreuil had been convinced that the English could not reach Québec by way of the St. Lawrence because of the "impassable" barrier known as La Traverse. You have to understand that every ship that came up to Québec sailed close to the north shore as far as the Ile d'Orléans. In order to sail farther than the island, all ships had to pass from the north channel to the south channel, which would take them to the harbour. The passage between the Ile d'Orléans and the one closest to it in the west, Ile Madame, was the only place where the ships could cross to the south channel. And right there was La Traverse. For years French navigators and Canadian pilots had argued that the English could not bring warships through there without wrecking them. It was too turbulent, too shallow, too narrow. Many large French ships had been lost attempting it, and many French and Canadian sailors had perished.

Everyone had accepted that argument, or at least there is no evidence to the contrary. However, I found out that the commander of the French regular troops in America, le Marquis de Montcalm, had in his possession an old Jesuit map that showed La Traverse to be wide and deep enough to accommodate large ships. But nowhere is it mentioned that Montcalm corrected Vaudreuil or that he adjusted his defence plans accordingly. Nor did he do anything in May 1759, when the French realized that to block La Traverse would take more than forty of their largest ships.

The only conclusion I can draw from this grave miscalculation on the part of Vaudreuil and the other military and naval commanders was that French captains and Canadian pilots were incompetent.

By June 26, 1759, the English had managed to pass at least sixty big vessels, many of them warships, through La Traverse, where the French hardly dared risk a merchant vessel of a hundred tons.

On the Ile d'Orléans, François Martel, who had believed in the inviolability of La Traverse, had had a rude awakening when he saw the English captains navigating the "impassable" channel, and relatively easily at that. For almost a month Martel had watched the English tentatively approach La Traverse, sound it, zigzag their way through it, and finally conquer it. Since seven in the morning of June 26, one of the English ships, the transport *Goodwill*, had been anchored practically on his doorstep. For a long time he had stared at her through the trees that hid his house from the shoreline, about a mile away down a gentle slope. None of the English on board had ventured to shore, but he could see the sailors trimming their sails and the soldiers drilling on deck.

I am not making up François Martel. The records show that he was a fifty-four-year-old Canadian priest who had been ordained in 1731. A month after his ordination, he had come to the parish of Saint-Laurent, where he had been ever since.

No one has described him to me, but I will do so for you. Over the quarter of a century during which he had baptized, taught, married, and buried his parishioners, he had gained a great deal of weight, and had become almost totally bald and a little aloof. His people had grown accustomed to his plodding and punctilious ways and his boring sermons. They knew also that he was devoted to them.

At last, sensing that he had not much time left before the English invaded his parish, Farther Martel hurried to his garden and to the group of men digging by the stake fence that separated his garden from the large meadow in which his and his neighbours' cows and horses grazed peacefully. He paused to pray at the statue of the Virgin Mary, which one of his predecessors had placed in a small shrine with a fine view of the St. Lawrence. Like all the shrines to the Virgin Mary erected in almost every garden on the island, it was made of long thin laths and was covered entirely by vines.

Martel's prayer was short and consisted largely of a monologue, reminding God that He had allowed the English to come before, but that He or the Mother of His Son had always intervened with a miracle to save Québec. Accustomed to believing in the direct intervention of the Almighty, he hoped that God would oblige Québec this time as well.

It was cool and pleasant inside the shrine, and since the men at the end of his garden had not called him, Martel sat on the stone bench in front of the statue musing on the twenty-five years he had spent on the Ile d'Orléans, what it meant to him, and what the English would find upon setting foot on it.

If he had read modern spy novels – or had had more imagination than he did – Martel might have spun this scenario:

To prepare for the safe disembarkation of their troops, the English first send agents to interrogate the inhabitants of the village. Since he is the most senior resident, the parish priest is at the top of their list. They barge into his house, which is just like those of the farmers of his parish, made from stones the *habitants*, as the ordinary people are called, had gathered while clearing their fields. It is painted white, all the windows are glassed, and the inside consists of one large room with a stone fireplace, which serves as living room and kitchen, and two small bedrooms, one of which is equipped with an iron stove. The agents find no inside toilet but an outdoor latrine not too far from Martel's back door.

They settle in Martel's living room and quiz him in French.

Since the Bishop of New France, Henri-Marie Dubreil de Pont-briand, has ordered that his priests answer the questions posed to them, there is no need for the agents to use force.

Agent: "How many parishes are there on the island?"
Martel: "Five. Saint-Pierre and Sainte-Famille on the north side, and on the south, Saint-Laurent, Saint-Jean, and Saint-François. For a century we have occupied this land."
Agent: "How many people?"
Martel: "Two thousand."
Agent: "How do they live?"
Martel: "We are farmers. Our tools are rudimentary and our knowledge limited, but we manage to grow almost every kind of cereal, especially wheat and oats. We also plant peas, beans, and maize, a cereal the Indians intro-duced to us. When the demand of the breweries make it profitable, a few brave souls cultivate some barley."
Agent: "Are you a farmer?"
Martel: "Well, I only have a kitchen garden. I do not grow wheat nor any of the other cereals."
Agent: "Why not?"
Martel: "My parishioners supply these to me as part of their tithes."
Agent: "I see."
(Looking out the window)
            "You have an extensive garden, though?"
Martel: "Yes, I like gardening. I have a few apple, plum, and walnut trees. I grow cabbages, onions, and beets, along with lettuce, carrots, cucumbers, and various kinds of melons, gourds, and pumpkins."
(Martel stands, intending to go to his questioner, but a guard pushes him back into his seat. Somewhat put out by the unnec-essary violence, he continues:)
            "If you look at the other end of the garden on the right, you will notice that I have a vast quantity of turnips. It is the mainstay of my diet in the winter months."
(Here Martel hesitates, then adds shyly:)
            "All through the Island I am famous for my asparagus

and my pink and black radishes. The Bishop and the Governor honour me by serving them at their tables. I may also add that, unlike my neighbours, I have experimented with a few potato plants and Jerusalem artichokes, but without much success. As you can see for yourselves I am more lucky, however, with my tobacco plants. They are, of course, for my personal use. The only drawback to growing them, is that boys, some as young as ten or twelve, steal them."

(Here again, the priest hesitates before he adds sadly:)

"The garden is a total mess. Your coming up the St. Lawrence forced me to abandon it."

Agent: "Why?"

Martel: "The people had to be evacuated. They did not want to go. They wanted to fight you with their pitchforks and their rusted muskets."

(The agents laugh.)

Agent: "But they went just the same."

Martel: "They were forced to. The soldiers were pretty rough. I tried to defend them. But – "

Agent: "It is better not to mess with soldiers. Are they rich, your parishioners?"

Martel: "No. But when we had peace, we did well enough. However we've been at war a long time. Consequently, there has rarely been enough time for the men to till the soil. And there have been droughts. And the government didn't pay much for the wheat, so the people kept it."

Agent: "And we shall find it."

(Martel does not reply.)

The priest's knowledge of the English was limited. All his life they had been the enemies of France. They were Protestants. They were related to his numerous neighbours in the thirteen colonies to the south. These American colonials claimed the vast lands in the west of Canada as their own and competed with his people for the loyalty of the Indians, who had become indispensable to both sides. To add to his anxiety, he remembered that a visitor had recently told him that, in many colonies of the English in America, religious leaders were demanding that England undertake a holy war against the French Catholics. He feared that when the English landed in his parish, they would do much damage.

However, they would find nothing of worth in his house and nothing sacred in the church. All morning he had been busy removing the tabernacle, the three reliquaries that contained the relics of his favourite saints, the four silver candlesticks he had received as gifts, the two gold chalices from which he drank the wine at mass, the jewelled monstrance he carried around the streets of his parish on special feast days, the missal or prayer book he used all the time to say mass, and the much-decorated statues of the Infant Jesus, the Virgin Mary, and St. Joseph. He had carefully folded the ornate chasubles, stoles, and heavy copes, his altar garments, one of which had belonged to Samuel de Champlain, the founder of Québec. All of these he had packed in crates now waiting to be buried at the end of the garden. The church had been stripped bare, except for a few insignificant pictures of sundry saints.

When the men were through with their digging, he answered their summons. Placing a violet stole around his shoulders, he blessed the pit that seemed to him to be a grave. He watched as the men lowered the boxes gently and respectfully into it. After they had covered the grave with earth and had camouflaged it under grass and branches, Father Martel went back to his house.

In the small room that served him as a study, he wrote a letter addressed to the "Worthy Officers of the English Army." He knew them "to be human and generous," he wrote. "Therefore, I pray you, protect this church and its sacred furnishings, and also the house in which I live." He did not ask this favour for his own sake, "but for the love of God and as a manifestation of your compassion for my poor parishioners who have had to leave to you their parish and their farms." Before signing it with his name and title, he added, "I wish you had arrived a little earlier so that you might have enjoyed some of the vegetables from my garden, particularly the radishes and the asparagus. Sadly, everything has gone to seed by now."

Martel took one last look at his beloved garden, then carried the letter to the church, where he nailed it to the main door, unconsciously echoing Martin Luther's act some two hundred and fifty years earlier. His tasks done, he did not look back when, twenty minutes later, he walked with his companions to the north side of the island to be rowed across to Beauport and then driven by *calèche* to Charlesbourg.

After Father Martel's departure, the Ile d'Orléans belonged totally to the English. The sailor who had brought them there was Vice-Admiral Charles Saunders, commander of the English fleet. He was forty-four years old and had served in the navy some thirty years.

Saunders was the fourth Englishman to attempt to sail a fleet up the St. Lawrence River to Québec, but the first to try it with such large ships. In 1629, Daniel Kirke with his brothers, Lewis, Thomas, John, and James had done it and had conquered Québec, only to return it to France in 1632. Half a century later, William Phips had brought thirty-two small ships and two thousand militiamen to the French citadel. The French governor, Frontenac, had sent him packing. In 1711 another attempt had been made with ninety-eight sail and twelve thousand men. However, because of the blundering incompetence of the commanders, much of the fleet and hundreds of men had been lost.

And so for half a century the Canadians had lived with a sense of security and superiority and a feeling that God was on their side.

But now forty-six years later, Charles Saunders, with two hundred sails, was at the gates of Québec: forty-nine of his vessels were ships of the Royal Navy, some of them three-decker ships, and almost half had fifty guns or more. The rest served as transports, hospitals, sounding ships, or as tender, provision, and ordinance vessels. As it sailed up the St. Lawrence, Saunders' armada formed a line fifty miles long.

Upon these vessels were crowded 13,500 sailors and marines, 8,500 soldiers, and a scattering of camp followers, mostly women who, as sutlers, sold provisions to the soldiers, worked in the field hospitals, and provided sexual services.

It seems to me that a modern interviewer with a microphone aimed like a machine gun at Saunders could test his credibility in a rapid exchange. After all, the man had previously engaged in questionable practices and none of the independent commands he had held between 1746 and his appointment to Québec had been significant enough to warrant his being placed in charge of one quarter of England's navy. He may have been successful at his job, but he got it largely through pull. Had he not become a protégé of Commodore George Anson, with whom he embarked on a four-year voyage around the world in 1740, it is doubtful that Saunders would have amounted to much. In that voyage he became a pirate – one on the King's commission, no doubt, but a pirate just the same, and a well-rewarded one at that – and he continued this activity during the War of the Austrian Succession (1744–1748). This piracy was the foundation of his fortune.

In 1750, again due to Anson's influence, he became a member of Parliament, representing two rotten boroughs, which allowed him in time to acquire vast tracts of land. He also made money when he served as commodore of a squadron off the coast of Newfoundland, protecting the fisheries. He was able, as well, to acquire a large fortune as treasurer of Greenwich Hospital, a profitable sinecure to which Anson had him appointed. He made even more money as comptroller of the navy, a post Anson gave him in 1755. His fortune and influence, however, had already been secured when, on September 26, 1751, he had married a certain Miss Buck, the daughter of an immensely rich banker.

On January 9, 1759 – and again with Anson's influence – William Pitt, secretary of state to King George II, picked him to command the armada that sailed to Québec.

It is fair to say, I think, that Saunders had no extensive command experience to justify such an important assignment and certainly no claim to it. I relish the thought of what an interviewer on such a television program as "This Hour Has Seven Days" or "60 Minutes" could do with him.

Saunders had left England for North America on February 17, 1759. Crossing the Atlantic had been as tolerable as the time of year permitted, but when he arrived at Louisbourg on April 23, impassable ice fields, dense fog, and a steely cold that numbed his sailors' fingers when they were aloft so that they could not quickly make sail, prevented him from entering the harbour. He sought refuge in Halifax, which he reached six days later.

For the success of their expedition against Québec, it was imperative that the English blockade the St. Lawrence as early as possible in the spring to prevent the French from bringing supplies and arms to Québec. When Saunders reached Halifax, some twenty French supply ships were already waiting at the entrance of the Gulf of St. Lawrence for the ice to break so they could sail up the St. Lawrence, bringing with them news of the impending English offensive. Rear-Admiral Philip Durell, the commander of the English squadron of nine ships stationed at Halifax, was still in harbour, instead of cruising off the Gulf as he had been ordered to do. After a furious row with Saunders, Durell sailed out of Halifax on May 5 with half the fleet. By May 23 – thirteen days after the French ships had arrived at the capital – he was at the Ile de Bic, some one hundred and seventy miles below the town of Québec. From that date on, the English were in complete command of the St. Lawrence.

It was not until May 15 that the weather permitted Saunders to proceed to Louisbourg, where he spent the next three weeks assembling the vast fleet and stores intended for the conquest of Québec. During that time Rear-Admiral Charles Holmes arrived from New York with six battleships, nine frigates, and sixty-six transports.

Finally, on June 4, Saunders, with twenty-two warships and 119 transports, set out for the St. Lawrence and Québec, a distance of one thousand miles. The twenty-day journey to the Ile d'Orléans was difficult and taxing. The English had no accurate charts of the St. Lawrence, and except for one or two local Canadians who were lured or forced to assist the English fleet, no one aboard had firsthand experience navigating the waterway. The tides were high and the currents treacherous, changing erratically from one place to the next and continuously forcing the sailors to sound the depths of the turbulent, black water. Powerful storms would suddenly appear, endangering the safety of the smaller vessels and playing havoc with the orderly process Saunders had intended. But, since the French had no defence installations along the St. Lawrence, Saunders' fleet was not attacked, though once in a while a Canadian fired harmlessly at the passing ships. Saunders was aware that his progress was being charted and passed on to the authorities in Québec, for he could see the huge bonfires that relayed the news of the advancing English.

Dangerous and treacherous as the St. Lawrence was, it was also beautiful and majestic. The rivers that cascaded into it were as immense as seas and the hills that bordered it seemed to reach the sky and were covered with "tall and proud trees," as one of Saunders' ensigns put it. The dark waters were filled with fish and aquatic mammals of all sorts, and the sailors and the soldiers cramped on board the many vessels spent happy hours fishing and enriching their diet.

As the ships approached the Canadian settlements some fifty miles below Québec, the shore became unusually high above the level of the river. For the first time, the English saw the pleasant villages of handsome houses and imposing barns built on narrow strips of land giving direct access to the river. The valleys were dotted with vast fields and stark-looking wind- and water-mills. Presiding over all were the high steeples of churches saluting the heavens.

By June 14, Durell's advance parties, one of which included James Cook, the master of the *Pembroke* and the future "discoverer" of British Columbia, had unlocked the mysteries of La Traverse. The captain of the *Goodwill* transport, an old master by the name of Killick, found the channel easier than "a thousand places in the Thames" which were, according to him, "fifty times more hazardous than this."

On June 20, his pilots having conquered La Traverse and with Durell in command of the lower St. Lawrence, Saunders decided to keep most of the fleet under his direct command. He gave orders that the transports, followed by the smaller warships, cross La Traverse and anchor in the Québec basin. The larger ships, such as the ninety-gun HMS *Neptune* on which he had crossed the Atlantic, were sent downriver past the Ile-aux-Coudres to prevent the French from entering the St. Lawrence.

And so by June 26, 1759, Saunders, having transferred his flag to the seventy-four-gun HMS *Stirling Castle*, was floating gently a few miles from the fortress that was the object of what was known as the Great Enterprise. On the morrow, the army would disembark.

On the western tip of the Ile d'Orléans
Shortly before midnight

The wind, which had started to be a bother in the late afternoon, had completely subsided. In the darkness, the silhouettes of the English ships towered above the young man who was advancing slowly from the water's edge. He carried a lantern in one hand and a musket in the other and a couple of knives and a tomahawk hung from his belt. He was dressed all in black, but now and then the moonlight shone on the white buttons of his sleeveless jacket and on the solitary one of the short petty coat or kilt around his waist. Carefully avoiding the patches of light the moon created, he climbed the short escarpment from the shore.

He was Lieutenant Meech from a company of American "guerrillas" founded in 1757 by Major Robert Rogers, a farmer from New Hampshire. Recruited from most of the colonies, the Rangers, as they were called, followed assiduously Rogers' "plan of discipline," consisting of twenty-eight rules that had often saved their lives. The English, though, considered the American soldier a "dirty, most contemptible, cowardly dog" with an inclination to desertion and the Rangers as "the worst soldiers in the universe." Like the Canadians, the Rangers had their own way of fighting, and it had little to do with the European style. They scalped their enemies, as did the Indians and the Canadians.

After ascertaining that no one was around, Meech waved his lantern three times and crouched on the ground. As he waited for his forty comrades, he felt the dampness of the soggy earth seep through to his skin. But accustomed as he was to all sorts of conditions, he paid no attention. When his men reached him, he started on his mission.

Ordered to find out whether any settlers were left on the island, Meech's company advanced inland in small groups, zigzagging, crouching, and taking cover behind trees as they had been trained to do. They soon came to a clearing where they found a deserted log cabin. Meech left five men there to guard it and proceeded on his way.

Soon they saw shafts of lantern light in the distance. Drawing closer, they made out the shapes of four men digging. Thinking that these men were burying rifles and ammunition, Meech dispersed his company, ordering his men not to fire until he gave the signal. Helped by the flat terrain and the light of the moon, the Rangers advanced slowly and carefully. Before long Meech was able to see the four men more clearly. They were not soldiers, for they wore no uniform, and they were no longer digging. One of them stood in a hole and another one handed him various objects while their two companions stood by smoking their pipes, with lanterns at their feet and their muskets on the ground. Every now and then one of them pointed to the woods beyond.

When the Rangers opened fire, the Canadians threw themselves on the ground to retrieve their muskets and extinguish their lanterns. They quickly returned the fire and, while some of their comrades hiding there continued the salvo, ran for the woods. Fearing his party was outnumbered, and unwilling to risk his mission, Meech ordered a quick retreat to the log cabin where he barricaded himself with his men. But the Canadians did not follow him. Instead they rushed to the north channel, and taking to their canoes, they paddled towards Beauport. A few Indians, motionless in the undergrowth, had watched the fight impassively. When the field of action was cleared, they found the body of a Ranger who had been shot in the chest.

A few hours later, with the light of dawn, Meech resumed his mission, already feeling the warmth that heralded the heat of the day to come. Not too far from the cabin, the Rangers stumbled over the body of their dead comrade. He had been scalped. Birds or some animal had picked out his eyes and eaten his nose. A large bloody hole filled with ants and flies was where his cheek had been. A rat was eating his tongue and maggots crawled all over his body.

Not bothering to bury him, the company pushed on. Four hours later Meech reported to his major that the island was deserted. The army could disembark in peace.

Thus ended the first twenty-four hours of the siege of Québec. It is interesting to note that no one found it ironic that in this great English enterprise, the Conquest of Québec, the first to land on Canadian soil and the first to die were Americans from Connecticut.

June 27, 1759

(Day Two)

Aboard the HMS *Richmond*
3:00 A.M.

It was to be the most important day of his military career, and since he did not distinguish his professional life from his personal one, it was also to be the most important day of his life. He was thirty-two years old, a commoner from an ordinary family, a passionate but clumsy lover, and perhaps the ugliest man Charles Saunders had ever laid eyes on – Colonel James Wolfe, brigadier-general (his rank in the British army), major-general (his temporary rank in North America), and commander-in-chief of the troops of the expedition against Québec, which were now on board George II's ships near the Ile d'Orléans.

On the long voyage across the Atlantic Wolfe had made his plans. He would land at Beauport a few miles east of Québec, ford the St. Charles River, march up the Côte d'Abraham to the gates of Québec, and demand the surrender of the town. If it were refused, he would assault Québec and destroy it. By the end of July at the most – and with luck sooner – he would be on his way up the St. Lawrence to take Montréal. By the beginning of the winter, he would be back in England to reap the benefit of his bold daring. A grateful King would make him a peer of the realm. His mother, not to mention his fiancée, would indeed be pleased!

He walked out of his cabin onto the deck of the ship and saw a sailor light three lanterns and pass them one by one to a relay of companions who hung them horizontally from the mast of the vessel. It was the signal that he had given for the landing of the soldiers on Canadian soil. In an hour's time, the flat-bottomed boats, which were to take the troops to shore, would assemble at the frigate *Lowestoft*. Rowed by twenty sailors, each carried sixty-three soldiers. One seaman sat in the front of each boat with a swivel gun, an ensign in the back held the flag bearing the crosses of St. George and St. Andrew high in the sky, and a drummer in the middle beat out the orders as given or a tune as requested. As Wolfe walked back to his stateroom to wait for the landing to begin at six o'clock, the faint smile on his thin lips reflected both his accomplishment and the satisfaction of it.

It is important that you know something of Wolfe if you are to understand him and, consequently, his place in the history of our country.

Wolfe was born at Westerham in Kent, England, on January 2, 1727. His father, Lieutenant-General Edward Wolfe, was a respectable marine officer remembered for nothing in particular, but Wolfe found him "extremely upright and benevolent" and thought his "failings and imperfections were overbalanced by his many good qualities." He died while Wolfe was on his way to Québec. His mother, Henrietta Thompson, appeared to have been a limited, self-centred, melancholic person of frail health and with little capacity for love. She interfered constantly in his affairs, particularly those of the heart. He quarrelled with her frequently, one such fight occurring shortly before his departure for Québec. He was so angry with her that he did not visit her to bid her farewell. Instead he wrote her a cold letter addressing her, as he always did, "Dear Madam."

Wolfe's military career began in 1741 at the age of fourteen in his father's First Regiment of Marines. A year later he transferred to the regular army, and at sixteen he was under fire for the first time at the battle of Dettingen in Bavaria, where George II and his Hanoverian allies defeated the French on June 27, 1743. Three years later, on April 16, 1746, Wolfe was at Culloden in Scotland, where he helped put an end to the pretensions of Charles Edward Stuart to the thrones of England and Scotland. While Samuel Johnson was planning his *Dictionary*, and thousands of miles away Benjamin Franklin was inventing the lightning rod, Wolfe was wounded in the bloody battle of Laffeldt (July 2, 1747) while in Belgium during the war of the Austrian Succession.

In the eight years of peace that followed, Wolfe served in Scotland and in the south of England, and in 1757, a year into the Seven Years' War, he was appointed colonel of the 67th Foot Regiment. The following year he was a brigadier at Louisbourg and in charge of an élite corps of light infantry and grenadiers. According to all accounts, he was brave, efficient, and resourceful in battle and merciless in its aftermath. Ordered to destroy the Acadian settlements in the Gulf of St. Lawrence, he "gave orders for every thing being burnt," according to one of his aides, Captain Thomas Bell. Wolfe himself wrote to his commanding officer, Jeffrey Amherst, that he had done "a great deal of mischief - spread the terror of His Majesty's arms through the whole gulf; but have added nothing to the reputation of them."

He returned to England with some glory at the beginning of the winter of 1758 and was soon lobbying for another appointment in America "particularly in the river St. Lawrence." William Pitt, who was to all intents and purposes the leader of the government, recommended him to George II, who appointed Wolfe to Québec on January 12, 1759. One month later Wolfe sailed for Québec in Saunders' flagship, the HMS *Neptune*.

Saunders did not leave in his logs - and he apparently did not keep a diary - his impression of Wolfe, but he must have been amazed at his physical appearance. Wolfe was ridiculously unattractive. His face was shaped like a triangle, with a receding hairline of red hair coaxed awkwardly into a thin queue at the back of his head. His forehead was practically non-existent, and his chubby nose was turned up as if to catch the wind. He had no chin and his mouth was almost completely without lips, making his azure blue eyes the only interesting feature of his face. His entire appearance was made even more startling by his long frame, his gliding walk, and his normally moribund, pale complexion. When he was excited or angry, which was often, for he was quick to take offence and quite irritable, his face would flush a deep red, the line of his mouth would become thinner and firmer, and his eyes would bore mercilessly into whoever was annoying him.

His usual dress was a functional red coat and a waistcoat of the same colour. His breeches were blue and his gaiters had leather tops. He wore a cartridge box and a bayonet on a belt around his waist and, since his arrival in Halifax, a black armband tied in a bow on his left arm, in mourning for his father. In his right hand, he always carried either a light musket or a walking stick.

Most of the people who came in contact with him found him uninteresting, without a sense of humour, extremely pompous, arrogant, and obsessed by his own sense of importance, as that perfect eighteenth-century gossiper, Horace Walpole, wrote in his *Mémoires* of the last years of George II. There was no doubt in anyone's mind that Wolfe was strange, and it was even rumoured that he was mad. A distressing story made the social circuit of London about his behaviour at Pitt's dinner table. Towards the end of the meal, the commander-to-be of His Majesty's forces for the Conquest of Québec had suddenly jumped up from the table, grabbed his sword, and proceeded to destroy hundreds of imaginary enemies scattered around the dining room, all the while foretelling the great deeds he was to perform. Pitt was aghast and kept mumbling: "To think that I have committed the fate of my country and of my ministry into such hands." When the senile George II was told the tale, he is reported to have exclaimed to the Duke of Newcastle: "Mad is he? Then I hope he will bite some of my generals."

To add to the miseries of his appearance and personality, Wolfe was also a hypochondriac, complaining most of his life of his poor bladder filled with urinary crystals and his crippling rheumatism. Worrying constantly about his "tottering constitution," he became pessimistic that he would not be allowed to do great things, although he would "rather die than decline any kind of service that offers." His pessimism led him to ominous forebodings, and frequent visions of an early death danced in his head. Caught up in this vice, he often became cruel, obssessed by details, secretive, and erratic in behaviour.

But, when the occasion demanded, Wolfe could be charming and sympathetic. He was courteous and helpful and always animated in conversation. Katherine Lowther, whom he planned to marry, was touched by his love of children and dogs, and Saunders admired him for his solicitude about his men, who reciprocated with great affection. What Wolfe lacked in ability he more than made up for by his great diligence and his all-consuming sense of duty. He had once written to his mother: "All that I wish for myself is that I may at all times be ready and firm to meet the fate we cannot shun, and to die gracefully and properly when the hour comes." And he was a superb dancer.

Before coming to America, and between assignments on the battlefield, Wolfe was stationed mostly in Scotland, where he built roads and studied mathematics and Latin. Observing himself to be without social graces, he went off to Paris in the fall of 1752 so that "by frequenting men above myself and by discoursing with the other sex" he might learn "some civility and mildness of carriage." He stayed six months in the French capital learning the language, fencing, and good manners at the residence of the British ambassador; practising his social graces in the company of vivacious coquettes and transparent aristocratic ladies in the salons of Paris; being presented to the King and Queen at Versailles, watching Madame de Pompadour, Louis XV's mistress and the most influential of his advisers, doing her toilette in her boudoir; and familiarizing himself with the intricacies of the Gregorian calendar, which England had finally adopted in 1751, 169 years after Pope Gregory XIII had decreed it. Like everyone else in the English-speaking world, Wolfe had much to get used to: eleven days in September had been eliminated and 1752 began on the day after December 31 instead of on March 25. However, Wolfe had had an opportunity to study the complexities of the calendar while stationed in Scotland, where it had been in use since 1600.

While in Paris, his sex life was quite limited, if it existed at all. As such, it was no different from his experiences in England or Scotland. It is possible that he remained a virgin until his thirty-first year. Ugly, he was not popular with women and so was not invited to their beds. Clumsy, he was not capable of seduction and he avoided prostitutes. It is possible that he was a closet homosexual.

At the beginning of the new year of 1757, while visiting his mother at Bath, he met Katherine Lowther, the daughter of a former governor of Barbados. Though military matters did not give him much time to press his suit, the relationship was promising enough for him to seek her out when he returned to Bath in December 1758 to recuperate after his return from Louisbourg. In the short weeks before Christmas he spent with her in Bath, they became lovers. In January and February 1759, in the midst of his preparation for his expedition to Québec, they met several times and became engaged, despite his mother's strong objections. To mark their betrothal and, no doubt, her love for him, she presented him with a copy of Thomas Gray's *Elegy in a Country Churchyard* and a locket encasing an image of her smiling face. He promised to carry the locket on his person wherever he went.

His heart was beating against it as he waited to set foot on Canada, defeat his enemies and fulfil his destiny. He was about to have the surprise of his life.

Château Saint-Louis
11:00 A.M.

Wolfe's enemies were also preparing themselves to meet their fate as they assembled for a council of war in the main reception room of the residence of the Governor General. They were not too perturbed, however, for as they told themselves, the English had arrived before only to depart at the beginning of winter, and the mischief they had done had generally been settled with treaties that temporarily ended the hostilities between England and France. It never entered their minds that the English were in Québec to stay.

As they crossed la Place d'Armes, the ceremonial centre of Québec, to enter Vaudreuil's château, the officers could admire, if they felt so inclined, the fine, large, stone houses with their broad chimneys and superb gardens, which bordered the square. On their way to the meeting, some of those who came from the Upper Town, built high above the escarpment, as did le Chevalier François-Gaston de Lévis, the second-in-command of the regular troops, and his aide-de-camp, had to pass the beautiful church of the Récollet friars where Frontenac and other governors general were buried. Others reached Vaudreuil's residence from one of the finest houses in Canada. It was on Rue Saint-Louis, which led to the gate of the same name, and it boasted a living room made of glass and covered with fine works of art.

Three officers who had been ordered to attend came from Rue des Jardins, named after the gardens attached to the convent of the Ursulines. A couple of Canadians in the *troupes franches de la marine*, however, entered the city by the Porte Saint-Jean and walked by the imposing Collège des Jésuites, the most beautiful building in the town, and the Place de l'Eglise, on which was built the cathedral. The Bishop and his companion used Rue du Parloir, which led to the Séminaire de Québec, a large compound of buildings and chapels. Just one official came from Rue des Pauvres where presided the Hôtel-Dieu, which was still being rebuilt after a disastrous fire.

The Intendant, François Bigot, along with his cronies, was driven by carriage from his palace outside the walls of the town and through the Porte du Palais. His grandiose enclave housed not only his magnificent residence and his beautiful *salle de bal* (where he entertained the best of Québec society and where, from time to time, he permitted some of the habitants to look down from a gallery on the revellers and gamblers, including their bishop, amusing and gorging themselves below), but also the executive, judicial, and legislative offices of the colony. His gardens gave onto the east bank of the St. Charles River where wooden palisades equipped with cannon and defended by guards had been erected. Close at hand were the prison and the warehouses of the Grande-Société, the name given to the band of crooks and entrepreneurs chaired by the Intendant, who manipulated the entire Canadian economy for their benefit.

For his part, the French colonel Louis-Antoine de Bougainville, the twenty-nine-year-old aide to the commander of the French regular troops, had come from his headquarters at the house of his cousin, François-Joseph de Vienne. It was situated at La Canardière, not too far from Beauport and the Intendant's palace. The place was so named because it was the nesting grounds of a great number of ducks.

In their *calèches*, the officers whose duties stationed them in the Lower Town rode past the three- and four-storey wooden houses built close together on narrow and stony streets that were almost always wet. The dwellings all faced the well-protected harbour, where close to a hundred ships could anchor safely.

Usually when they went up to the château, the officers in charge of the harbour would stop at one of the taverns where the ordinary people gathered for companionship, to meet a wearied traveller who had found lodgings and a meal there and to eat – when times were good – pâtés of all sorts, pies, stews or ragoûts, fricassées, tourtières (so called after the dish they were baked in, following recipes as numerous as there were cooks in Canada), crêpes, *beignets* (fritters), and cakes and *galettes* (biscuits). Above all, they came to drink, among other things, an alcoholic beverage known as *eau-de-vie* (water of life) or *tafia*, which was concocted from molasses and a syrup made from sugar cane and was not unlike the rum the English consumed in vast quantity. What they particularly liked, however, was beer – a *bière d'épinette*, also called *petite bière*. It was powerful stuff made from spruce, molasses, ginger, peppers from Jamaica, and yeast, which was fermented for at least twenty-four hours. Of course, the officers could not have this *petite bière* on this second day of the siege of Québec for the taverns were all closed. In fact, they would have to do without it at the château, since the Governor, bowing to the pressure of his French peers, would serve only wine imported from France.

On their way to the Château Saint-Louis, they also passed the Magasins du Roy, a series of dilapidated buildings housing the governmental stores, and the Place Notre-Dame with its ancestral church, Notre-Dame-des-Victoires, and the square where, before the arrival of the English, the weekly market was held and where criminals were executed to the delight of the inhabitants.

To reach Vaudreuil's residence, the officers had to go up the Côte de la Montagne, the only access suitable for carriages and carts from the Lower to the Upper Town. It was a wide, winding, steep road full of potholes and bordered on both sides by large houses. At the top stood the imposing – but much too large for his purposes – Bishop's palace. Built of stone, it had two wings of two storeys each, with a facade of columns falling in ruin. From its dormers there was a fine view of the St. Lawrence. Like all the houses of the Lower Town, it was boarded up and would be used as a military installation after the Bishop had left Québec to take refuge, like Father Martel, with the parish priest of Charlesbourg.

From the Bishop's palace, the officers drove along Rue du Fort which led to their destination, the Château Saint-Louis, a meandering two-storey stone building erected on the spot where Samuel de Champlain had built his fortress in 1620 after the destruction of his "Habitation." Sitting 160 feet above the St. Lawrence, it dominated the city and its approaches.

The last to arrive under escort and accompanied by his secretary, Monsieur Marcel – whose first name is totally unknown – was Louis-Joseph, Marquis de Montcalm, seigneur de Saint-Véran, Candiac, Tournemine, Vestric, Saint-Julien and Arpaon, Baron de Gabriac, lieutenant-général and commander-in-chief of the French regular troops in North America. He had ridden on his favourite black horse from his residence on Rue des Ramparts.

Having crossed the guarded courtyard, all those invited to the council of war walked along a large, well-kept alley to the main entrance of the château. From there they were escorted to the main reception room, where the council was to be held. It was a splendidly furnished room, with many works of art adorning the walls and dominated by a huge fireplace. In the middle of the room was a large, rectangular pine table surrounded by a throne at one end and twelve chairs to be occupied only by the most important people; the others would remain standing throughout the meeting, unless the Governor General ordered otherwise. As they waited for him to arrive, they drank some excellent wine imported from France in May and made small social talk. Ordinarily the

Canadian wife of the Governor General, the seventy-five-year-old Jeanne-Charlotte de Fleury Deschambault, would have presided over this part of the gathering, but she had left for Montréal earlier, making a stop in Trois-Rivières to replenish her stock of *eau-de-vie*.

Many in the room had doubts that the council of war would accomplish anything. From past experience, Bougainville knew that the two marquis – Montcalm and Vaudreuil – would argue with each other, the officers of the regular troops would find fault with everything, the colonial officers in the *troupes franches de la marine* would be miffed, and the Canadians would be obliged to feel insulted at anything the French said. He did not think that even the presence of the English so close at hand would bring reason to the gathering.

At exactly twelve-thirty, the Canadian secretary to the Governor General, who was also his nephew and whose father was reputed to have sired thirty-two children, came to inform the members of the council that the Marquis de Vaudreuil was on his way.

The first to enter the room was a Canadian relative of the Governor General and the captain of his guard. He took his place behind the throne while the Bishop, who soon followed, sat in his usual chair at the right of it. A few minutes later, Pierre de Rigaud de Vaudreuil de Cavagnial, Marquis de Vaudreuil, Grand-Croix de l'Ordre Royal et Militaire de Saint-Louis, Governor General of New France and of Louisiana, swept into the room followed by the black slave he had acquired while serving as Governor of Louisiana.

The council of war began with the Bishop asking the Holy Ghost to grant them all wisdom and begging the Virgin Mary to make possible the harmony that always escaped them in their deliberations. Vaudreuil then administered the oath of fealty to the King and opened the meeting to discussion. For close to two hours they argued relentlessly, and tempers flared as the officers jockeyed for recognition and position. The room became unbearably hot as the two marquis lost themselves in flights of rhetoric. François Bigot pleaded for cheaper foodstuffs to buy so he could resell it to the army at vast profits, the commander of the town of Québec went on and on about the defences of the town, the Bishop thundered at the sinful ways of the habitants, and Vaudreuil almost wept.

The only point on which all agreed was that the Canadians had responded overwhelmingly to Vaudreuil's call to defend their country. In the census Vaudreuil had taken prior to the arrival of the English, it had been determined that there were a little over fifteen thousand men of military age in Canada, that is, between the ages of sixteen and sixty. But many more had volunteered. Out of a population of barely seventy thousand souls, over sixteen thousand Canadians, boys, some as young as twelve years, and men, even a few in their seventies and eighties, had answered Vaudreuil's summons. It was a remarkable mobilization. Most of them, of course, had no experience of the European style of warfare.

Through the cacaphony of the council, some conclusions did emerge. The most important one was that the French were not as ready to face Wolfe as they should have been. The St. Lawrence had been left unfortified, particularly around Cap Tourmente, thirty miles below Québec, and Pointe-Lévy, across from the town on the south shore, had been more or less abandoned to the English. However, bridges had been built where they were most needed: over the Cap Rouge and Jacques-Cartier rivers west of Québec, in case the army had to flee. The access to Québec by the St. Charles River was protected by an hornwork – a sort of bastion – on the east bank and by a pontoon bridge thrown over the river for easy transportation and communication. Wooden palisades equipped with several field guns had been built around the Intendant's palace, and a boom with a battery of twelve guns closed the entrance to the St. Charles to barges of any kind.

Another conclusion, over which Vaudreuil and Montcalm argued passionately, was that the fortifications at Beauport would have to do. Had they been started two years earlier as Montcalm had recommended, the French would have been in a better position to defend themselves. At that time most of the officers of the High Command had asserted that if the English came up the St. Lawrence – a feat that Vaudreuil found inconceivable – Beauport was the only possible landing place from which they could attack Québec. The south shore, with its dense woods and turbulent rivers, was considered impractical, and everyone was convinced that the enemy would not land above Québec because of the height of the cliffs there and the guns of the batteries in the Lower Town, which could blast English ships out of the water as they sailed past Québec into the upper St. Lawrence. So Beauport it had to be.

There the Beauport shore extended eastward about six miles from the St. Charles River. The tides were high and left wide, slimy tidal flats behind when they retreated. Above the coastline, the ground rose gradually before rearing in high cliffs to the plateau on which the village of Beauport was built. The whole landscape was dominated by the Montmorency Falls, which cascaded over the cliffs to the shore below and into the St. Lawrence.

But no barricades had been built at Beauport until Montcalm and Bougainville arrived from Montréal on May 22, 1759. By that time the English were already in the St. Lawrence, and the French had therefore had to act quickly. It had not been easy. The rain had been almost constant. The 10,800 men, mostly Canadian, who dug miles of trenches, built dozens of redoubts and other fortifications, and erected campsite after campsite, were often almost buried in mud. The few times the sun showed itself, its heat broiled the men and made the earth as hard as rock. They had to transport timber a long distance, and too often there were no carts. Their shelter was inadequate, their rations meagre, and the flies almost unbearable.

Yet in the space of five weeks, under the command of Bougainville, they had built a line of defence winding almost fifteen miles from the St. Charles River in the west to Montmorency Falls in the east. Entrenchments zigzagged across the heights of Beauport and guns were mounted in strategic positions, particularly near the shore of the St. Lawrence. Row upon row of tents and a few wigwams dotted the landscape. In the middle of it all stood the parish church of Beauport and, not too far away, the de Salaberry family's manor house, which had been fortified to serve as Montcalm's headquarters and those of the cavalry and the light infantry. So advanced were the fortifications that, at the council, Montcalm ordered the two thousand regular soldiers and the eight thousand militia to leave their temporary headquarters behind the Hôpital Général and proceed to their Beauport encampments.

When it came time to discuss the defences of the town of Québec, the debate was interminable. Montcalm, Bougainville, and other French officers believed the town's fortifications were crumbling, and useless. In the late fall of 1758, Montcalm had told the Court at Versailles that "Québec is without fortifications and is not capable of being fortified... If the enemy reaches the foot of its walls, we must capitulate."

Others at the council pointed out that the fortifications, built to protect the town from the raids of American colonials and Indians, were still formidable, nature having helped greatly. Québec sat on a promontory like an immense amphitheatre, protected in front by the St. Lawrence, the St. Charles River to the north and the east, and the cliffs of Cap Rouge and the Chemin Royal, the road to Montréal, on the west. Two thousand men under Jean-Baptiste-Nicolas-Roch de Ramezay had been assigned to defend the town along with about fifteen hundred sailors. On the ramparts guarding the west approaches were fifty-two unidirectional cannon, and forty-two more faced the St. Lawrence and safeguarded the harbour, which was also protected by floating batteries and boats mounted with guns. In addition, six-foot-high palisades, armed with three batteries of eight cannon each, had been built to the north and others with sixteen cannon to the southeast and southwest. To complete the defences of the Upper Town, two of Québec's three gates were closed, leaving only the Porte du Palais opened.

In the Lower Town, where every house was a possible redoubt, and where all but one of the streets leading to the Upper Town had been barricaded, there were four great batteries, the Saint-Charles, the Dauphine, the Royale, and the Construction, with guns of various sizes. Finally la Côte de la Montagne was fortified with two batteries of four cannon each.

But Montcalm was not satisfied. He had wanted the Lower Town destroyed. Vaudreuil had refused, contenting himself with closing it to the usual traffic and moving out the inhabitants, most of whom had taken refuge in the Upper Town. By the end of the discussion Montcalm had to be satisfied with what there was, although he repeated for the record what he had so often stated: The capital of Canada could be defended only outside its gates.

Another contentious matter was food and other supplies, the argument taken up by the Intendant and his partners on one side and, on the other, the Bishop and Montcalm. For two to three years prior to the coming of the English, food had been a crippling problem. There had been major crop failures and the increased militia had quickly drained the available resources of the purveyor. During those years the Canadians of Trois-Rivières, Montréal, and particularly Québec, and the soldiers either on campaigns or billeted in these three towns had fared badly. The Intendant had cut their bread rations drastically and had ordered them to eat horse meat, which most of them found repugnant because of their dependence on and fondness for horses. Most people living in the surrounding countryside, however, had had plenty of food but had refused to sell it to the government in return for paper money of little value.

To meet the emergency, more and more food had had to be imported every year and 1759 had been no exception. Now with the English controlling the Ile d'Orléans and some of the villages, seigneuries, and farms to the east of Beauport, food would be more scarce. The potential for famine would even be more menacing should the English occupy the south shore.

In May the purveyor general, the Canadian butcher Joseph Cadet, had arrived from France with about sixteen ships to replenish his empty stores. Now Bigot and Cadet informed the council that they had enough rations for the army in and around Québec until September 10. The soldiers and militia at Fort Carillon (Ticonderoga) would have to fend for themselves after August 10, while those on Lake Ontario and in the posts further west could be fed until September 1st. As for the civilian population, Father Récher and the nuns at the two hospitals would be given some food to distribute, and the Sieur Dupont, the butcher, would continue to receive rations for the poor. Since Vaudreuil, supported by the Bishop, was not prepared to take the measures necessary to force the habitants to sell their goods to Bigot and Cadet, the matter rested with the arrangements made and the hope that the English would not stay past September 15.

And Vaudreuil had a plan to hasten them on their way. But before he was able to announce it, a messenger burst into the room to announce that Wolfe had been seen on the northwest end of the Ile d'Orléans. With that announcement, a fierce wind threw open the windows giving onto the terrace and rain pelted down with unusual fury.

———————

I can see them clearly: Vaudreuil, a huge, affable, courteous man, born in Québec on November 22, 1698, where his father was then the Governor General; Montcalm, a forty-seven-year-old portly little aristocrat with a lively face and alert eyes and as passionate as befits one born in the south of France. While Vaudreuil was irresolute, mean, and had little insight, Montcalm was vain, tactless, and opinionated. An optimist, Vaudreuil saw a way out of practically every difficulty, even if he had to rely on miracles. A pessimist, Montcalm perceived only disasters, disasters for which he would be accountable and which could ruin him.

Vaudreuil and Montcalm had two characteristics in common, however. The first one was a strong inclination for hyperbole. I can hear Vaudreuil dictating a letter to the King before the siege. Pounding the desk for emphasis and his voice rising with emotion and loyalty, he solemnly declares, "The zeal with which I am animated in Your Majesty's service will enable me to overcome the greatest obstacles. There is no trick, no expediency, no means which my enthusiasm does not suggest to set traps for our enemies and when necessary to fight them with a fervour, and indeed a fury, which exceeds the scope of their ambitious plan." He is adamant there will be no capitulation for "there is no doubt in my mind that it would be sweeter for my people to be buried under the ruins of Québec than to be the subjects of the English."

Sometimes I think I know Bougainville so intimately, I *am* Bougainville. As I (as Bougainville) walk with Montcalm, he confides in me. Later, Montcalm's words become paragraphs in the letters he sends to his minister at Versailles. "Against the English," he once whispered dramatically, "I have only my zeal, my courage, and my stubborness. I am telling you, Monsieur le Colonel, that I intend to save this colony or die in the process." After statements like this, he makes a little bow and walks away. Talk about hyperbole!

The second characteristic Vaudreuil and Montcalm shared was procrastination. As a man who never did anything impetuously or spontaneously (he had married late in life a woman fifteen years his senior, whom he had courted for almost ten years), Vaudreuil was constantly buffeted between conflicting views. He generally took the easiest way out. But he acted.

Montcalm, on the other hand, never seemed to follow through with anything. He made plans but left them to others to implement. In private he expressed his opinions freely, particularly to Lévis and Bougainville, but asked them to burn his letters. He seemed obssessed by the nightmare that the decisions he made would come to haunt him. So he contented himself with telling Vaudreuil that this and that should be done, but never insisting. It left him a way out.

In 1759, the fate of Canada depended on these two men – and they disliked each other from almost the first moment they met in the spring of 1756: Vaudreuil because he saw Montcalm as a potential usurper of his military authority, and Montcalm because he recognized Vaudreuil as a civilian playing at war. The fact that the Governor General was a Canadian of recent lineage

51

and Montcalm a Frenchman of old and noble ancestry had much to do with their antipathy. In time, abetted by his wife, Vaudreuil's prejudice became more pronounced. He found Montcalm pompous, arrogant, and inclined to have an infallible belief in his own ability. Montcalm came to see Vaudreuil as ignorant, corrupt, and, most damning of all, too Canadian.

The command structure set up by the ministers four thousand miles away at Versailles did not help to cement good relations between the two men. Vaudreuil was commander-in-chief of all forces in Canada, the direct commander of the *troupes franches de la marine* (the colonial troops), of the militia, the guardian of the Indians (if I may invent that title), the chief strategist and planner, and the general whose orders had to be obeyed. Montcalm was the commander of the *troupes de terre* (the regular troops) and led in the field. They argued relentlessly, they accused each other of bad faith and intrigue of all kinds and they bored to distraction their respective ministers (Vaudreuil's, the minister of marine; Montcalm's, the minister of war) about each other's lapses, fearing all the time that one would supplant the other or receive a better hearing in France.

There are two other considerations I want you to bear in mind. The first one has to do with Vaudreuil and the second with Montcalm and the two together made for a volatile situation.

In my view, the simple fact that Vaudreuil was a Canadian explains his moods, his relationship with Montcalm, and much of his behaviour during the events of the summer of 1759. Canada was his country, his land, and its people, his children. Their interests and their fate were his own. During the battle for Canada, he was a man torn between his duty to his royal overlord and his duty to his people. From the King, whose creature he was, he received honour and prestige; with the people he was bound in a common cause to save as much of Canada as possible, for he was an integral part of it. I think the old man lived a terrible nightmare.

Knowing what was good for his people, he had a hard time accepting the intervention of foreigners. Yes, I did say foreigners. Vaudreuil was a Canadian. The French were French. He may not have called them foreigners, but he certainly saw them as expatriates and exiles who came to Canada only for a short time. Their single ambition was to advance their careers, do their best not to dishonour themselves or their families, and return home decorated and pensioned. Having no permanent interest in Canada, they lived as luxuriously as possible, exhausted colonial resources for their own pleasure and advancement, and made battle plans without regard to the interests of those whose permanent home was Canada. So fed up was Vaudreuil with them all that he wanted to be rid of them totally once the Seven Years' War was over. He had already asked for Montcalm's recall.

If Vaudreuil was too concerned with his prerogatives and was obsessively jealous, Montcalm was essentially defeatist and devious. After the battle of Carillon, which he had won in 1758, he had come to lose all faith that Canada could and would remain in French hands. When Bougainville went to Versailles in November 1758, Montcalm sent with him plans for the possible flight of the French army to Louisana via the Ottawa River, the Great Lakes, and the Mississippi. At his bidding, Bougainville requested only a few recruits and reinforcements to be sent to defend Canada. And Montcalm agreed with Bougainville's plan, relayed to Madame de Pompadour, that only a minimum effort be made in Canada so that an invasion of the Carolinas might be undertaken.

Towards the end of February 1759, Montcalm had written to Lévis: "The colony is lost unless peace comes. I can see nothing that can save it." As the English came up the St. Lawrence, Montcalm had personally drafted the Articles of the Capitulation of Québec and had sent his supplies to Batiscan, some fifty miles above Québec, no doubt to pick them up on his way to Louisiana. I think he was already defeated before Wolfe arrived at the Ile d'Orléans.

To save his reputation and honour, to avoid the personal ruin he saw constantly on the threshold of his private life, to have a good conscience when facing his autocratic mother, and to ensure the prosperity of his heirs, he had to be given a second chance to save the honour of France, as he would say. And Louisiana was to be that second chance. He must have been terribly disappointed, if not totally dejected, when Bougainville ciphered to him shortly before leaving France for Canada in May 1759, "Plan of retreat to Louisiana thought well of, but not accepted." This must have added considerably to Montcalm's distress and general pessimism.

In light of this, Montcalm's strategy at Québec in 1759 may be better understood. It was simple: wait for the English to make the first move. Should they attack, he would defeat them in one engagement; should they not attack, he would wait it out. After all, they would have to go home with the coming of the winter. It may have been the only possible military strategy, but it had little to do with saving Canada.

It is very important in assessing Vaudreuil, whom most English-speaking historians have turned into a blundering idiot, and Montcalm, who is their darling, to remember that Montcalm was, by the time of the siege of 1759, the commander-in chief of all the armed forces of the King of France in his empire in the new world. The instructions to Vaudreuil that Bougainville had brought back from France to Québec in May 1759 were quite clear on the matter: Vaudreuil was to defer to Montcalm in all matters that pertained directly or indirectly to the war effort and the Governor General was not to interfere in Montcalm's plans in any way, shape, or form. The old man was not even allowed to be present on the battlefield without Montcalm's approval. Montcalm was in total command.

Think about that as you read on. And to allow you to do that I must find Wolfe. He is on his way to the north channel separating the Ile d'Orléans from the Beauport coast.

Ile d'Orléans
Noon

While his enemies were deliberating but were still not taking his presence too seriously, Wolfe was disembarking on Canadian soil. He had 8,500 men with him, some 3,500 fewer than he had been promised. It was a consolation of sorts that they were professional and seasoned soldiers drawn from England's regular regiments, some of which had been stationed in America. Other than the six companies of Rangers who came to Québec with him, Wolfe had few Americans in his army and no "colonial" regiments.

As he stepped from the longboat that had brought him from the HMS *Richmond*, he could not help thinking that the soldiers under his command looked more like toy soldiers than real ones in their uncomfortable and tight-fitting uniforms, which wrenched whenever they stooped or bent down. Wolfe was glad that he had ordered the uniform modified so that the coats were now freer and shorter, the lace cuffs abolished, and the hat of the light infantry soldiers transformed into a cap with black cloth under the chin "to keep him warm when he lies down." Because of his orders his men wore their knapsacks high, fastened with webbing over their shoulders, *à l'indienne*, making them lighter to carry when walking. He had added extra pockets to their coats for musket balls and flints and had decreed that the cartridge boxes be hung under their left arms and powder horns under their right, while their bayonets, knives, and tomahawks were to be suspended from their belts. He had not been able, however, to redress the complaint of his officers that rats and mice sometimes found refuge in their powdered and plaited hair.

Now his troops were all over the place setting up their tents (five men to a tent), storing their gear, building latrines, digging trenches, and setting up fortifications, while the sutlers prepared the kitchens and the hospital. He saw soldiers foraging for firewood and straw, and in the distance others were corralling cattle, hogs, and fowl. He immediately gave orders that such a "dishonourable" practice as looting end forthwith under pain of severe punishment both for the men involved and the officers who allowed it. He wanted his army professional, well-disciplined, and always ready to march or fight.

As Wolfe walked among the soldiers, John Knox, a lieutenant in the 43rd Regiment, approached Wolfe with Father Martel's letter, which he had found on the door of the church. From where he was standing Wolfe could see the elegant stone building with its lofty steeple and its white spire. He read the letter but declined Knox's invitation to go to the priest's garden to see the radishes and the asparagus that had gone to seed.

Since it was a perfectly glorious day without a cloud in the sky and with the sun shining bright and warm, he dismissed the horse-drawn carriage that was to take him to the northwest end of the island, a distance of about two miles from the parish of Saint-Laurent, and decided to walk instead. He took with him an escort of light infantry and Major Patrick Mackellar, the chief engineer who had been a prisoner in Québec in 1756–57. While there, Mackellar had studied the topography and defences of the town. The map he had prepared was now the only concrete information Wolfe had about the capital he had been sent to capture.

Wolfe was happy to be off the ship and walking briskly in the fresh air. The flowers were in bloom, and he could hear the bees buzzing and the crickets chirping. A few rabbits or squirrels scurried out of his path, and the flies that had been most troublesome coming up the St. Lawrence now left him in peace. He was in a good mood as he approached the north end of the island, from where he hoped to find out for himself what his enemies were doing to protect Québec and from a safe distance inspect the beach on which he hoped to land. He was appalled at what he saw.

The French were already there and in force. He saw their trenches, their batteries and redoubts, their camps, and their tents, and everywhere he looked there were cannon and guns and thousands of men engaged in making their position impregnable. By his frowns and mutterings as he surveyed the Beauport coast, it was obvious that he had not expected what he saw. In fact he had counted on quite the opposite. The strategy he had developed while crossing the Atlantic now was unworkable. From the information available to him then, he had reckoned that Montcalm had at his disposal less than five thousand professional soldiers in either the regular or colonial troops, in addition to between eight and ten thousand militia and one thousand Indians. He had supposed that as the English would be attacking the French on three fronts at once (at Québec, Montréal, and Niagara) Montcalm would have to divide these forces, leaving him at Québec with a number of soldiers roughly equal to Wolfe's.

Wolfe had therefore decided to land on the Beauport coast, cross the St. Charles River and attack Québec, which Mackellar had told him was badly fortified. It would not be easy, but it could be done, with luck, early in the summer so that he could carry on to Montréal to assist in finishing the job of conquering Canada. But it was obvious from what he now saw at Beauport that his initial plan was totally unfeasible. Québec was too well defended. He would have to devise another, and quickly at that.

Dejected, he returned to the main encampment and retreated to the safety of his stateroom aboard the HMS *Richmond*. As soon as he set foot on the deck of the ship, he experienced for the first time the erratic nature of the Québec weather. A fierce storm coming from the west broke without warning.

The soldiers were fortunate. In their looting they had found a good deal of straw and hay to lie upon in their tents while waiting out the storm. The fleet, however, did not fare as well. In the official logs of the Royal Navy, some unknown scribe reported with the usual economy of words that "every position is precarious." While many vessels were anchored far offshore, there was a considerable number of ships cramping the shoreline. The ground tackle was poor and the ebb stream strong. Disaster was inevitable in spite of the dispatch with which the sailors struck yards and topmasts and manoeuvred their ships to a good length of cable. Seven vessels lost their anchors, nine went aground, and two had to be abandoned. It would have been worse, though, had it not been for the prompt and disciplined seamanship of the crews and their officers.

Wolfe, however, was critical of the navy and directly of Admiral Saunders. He wrote in his journal, "Multitude of Boats Lost & strange neglect of the Men of Wars crews." Montcalm, who watched from the safety of Beauport, was more appreciative of the English seamanship. He told Bougainville, "It is quite probable that in the same circumstances a French fleet would have perished."

Shortly after four, the storm ended, having spent itself over the mountains in the northeast. Under the canopy of a colourful sunset, the English soldiers lit their campfires, ate supper, and prepared to bed down for the first time on the soil of Canada.

June 28, 1759

(Day Three)

Beauport, Montcalm's headquarters
Early morning

Shortly before the Récollet chaplains began their religious services, Bougainville rode from La Canardière to accompany Montcalm on a tour of inspection. The weather was murky but it was not yet raining. The soldiers were already up, some in the trenches, some standing outside their tents, and others lined up at the canteens for their daily ration of meat (this day it was *porc salé*) and of bread. Those already served were dipping their bread into a thick syrup of molasses, or sharing a fruit or a turnip or a radish with friends. Some lucky ones who had won eatable luxuries at the all-night gambling sessions the soldiers organized were now selling them for an exorbitant price. Soon thousands of Canadians would be puffing on their pipes, filling the air with a pungent odour unpleasant to Bougainvile's refined nostrils. As they ate, a dark cloud began to loom over the encampments.

In my fantasy as I write this story, Bougainville, this intelligent, handsome, dedicated young colonel, visits me. It is a delightful fantasy at my advanced age. Let me tell you about him and how I see him.

Louis-Antoine de Bougainville was twenty-nine-years old at the beginning of the siege of Québec. He was an orphan, the son of a notary still living in Paris and the neighbour of the famous mathematician and *encyclopédiste* d'Alembert, who instilled in Bougainville a life-long passion for mathematics. By the time he was twenty-two Bougainville had already written the first volume of his *Traité de calcul intégral*, which was published in 1755. In the meantime, at the insistence of his father and brother, he had been admitted to the bar. He also became an exquisite swordsman and a superb horseman.

But the life of a scholar and the predictable career of a lawyer could not possibly satisfy Bougainville's temperament. He needed adventures, the romance of danger, and a wide variety of experiences. So he joined the army, first as *aide-major* in the Picardy militia and then as a lieutenant in the *mousquetaires noires*, an élite regiment favoured by the King. When he was twenty-four he was sent to London on a diplomatic mission during which he learned English, was elected to the Royal Society of London, and met and became friendly with some of the officers who were in the English army attacking Canada in 1759.

Bougainville knew nothing about navigation or about botany. I mention this because you might have heard of him as the first Frenchman, I think, to have circumnavigated the world, as an explorer who made the romance of Tahiti part of the literature of the planet, and as the "discoverer" of the beautiful tropical vine with brilliant red or purple flowers now known as bougainvillaea.

Picture him, if you will, as a relatively handsome man, but short and with a tendency to stoutness. By all accounts the women of Québec found him attractive. He had dreamy, soft eyes, a straight nose, and "full and inviting lips," as Madame de Beaubassin, Montcalm's mistress, once described them. He was powerfully built, with broad shoulders and strong thighs, which the women tried to brush against as they passed. I am sure he felt confident that, in a room full of other officers, everybody who mattered would notice him, for he always stood as straight as he could. In that way he managed to dominate even those taller than he, except for Lévis.

Bougainville met Montcalm towards the end of February 1756, when both were at Versailles engaged in the seemingly interminable pursuit of securing their commissions, instructions, and orders for their mission to Canada; Montcalm as major-general and commander-in-chief of the regular troops, and Bougainville as his aide-de-camp.

Montcalm was immediately taken by the young man, whom he found, as he told his wife, a "man of parts – pleasant company."

He envied Bougainville's intellectual pursuits, his sense of plea-sure, and his impressive abilities. He envied above all Bougain-ville's astonishing connections. The Marquise de Pompadour called Bougainville's uncle "Boubou"; the Comte d'Argenson, then the minister of war (and to whom both Montcalm and Bougainville reported), was his protector; his adoptive mother, Madame Hérault, was the daugher of the comptroller of the finances of France and the sister-in-law of the the official who was minister of marine and responsible for the French colonies while Bougainville was in Canada. In the pecking order of the French court, these were extraordinary connections.

Perhaps the only times these connections failed him was in the winter of 1758–59 when Vaudreuil and Montcalm sent him back to Versailles to urge the King to make a small effort on behalf of Canada. He returned to Québec with few reinforcements but with many honours and promotions (Montcalm to lieutenant-general, Lévis to major-general, and Bougainville to colonel). "Tri-fles!" Montcalm had called them, but "Trifles are precious to those who have nothing," he had added in his crisp, precise voice.

As Montcalm and Bougainville waited to start their journey to Canada in 1756, I imagine that they had many conversations in which they exchanged information and, as they came to like each other more, confidences. I am sure Montcalm told Bougain-ville then that he was born in the south of France, at Candiac, on February 29, 1712, and would add something like this: "We were first of the nobility of the robe but in the seventeenth century we became soldiers and, I think, we did very well at it. My family has always been fiercely determined to serve the King."

He smiles shyly, looks at Bougainville, and adds: "My wife and I had doubts about my accepting this commission. But my mother is a strong-willed woman. She told me in no uncertain terms that never in the history of our family had a Montcalm refused the King's commission. After that it was impossible to say no. So here I am! But it is not easy leaving my wife and children for a com-mand so far away and so fraught with danger."

In scouting for information about Montcalm, Bougainville had already found out that Montcalm had married Angélique-Louise Talon de Boulay in 1736.

"Mon cher Monsieur de Bougainville, she too has connections. Her father was a marquis and colonel of the Régiment d'Orléans – *ça aide!* After all, the Montcalms are not rich and powerful, and we live far away from the centre of power. Did you know we have five children: two sons and three daughters? How am I to look after my sons' careers thousands and thousands of miles away? And my daughters? Marriages to arrange! Dowries to pay! I tell you there is much to worry about."

After a pause, he adds, "She knows a little bit about Canada, Madame de Montcalm, *ma femme*. She is the grandniece of Jean-Baptiste Talon who went to New France twice as Intendant in the last century."

There was no need for Montcalm to instruct Bougainville on the usefulness of connections, and the younger man understood quite well: Montcalm's rise in the military had been assured and rapid because of his connections. Having joined the army at age twenty-one, Montcalm spent the next thirty-one years serving his King faithfully, participating in eleven campaigns, and being wounded five times. In 1753 he was duly rewarded with a pension.

"You should come to Candiac in my beloved Provence. It has all that a man desires. Unfortunately, I have only spent seven consecutive years there, uninterrupted by war. I have magnificent olive and almond trees. They need constant supervision, as do the children. And now, I will not be there."

Bougainville could read the pain and the anxiety in Montcalm's eyes. But the King had to be obeyed – and His Majesty paid relatively well. As major-general or *maréchal de camp*, Montcalm received a salary of 25,000 *livres*, a 12,000 *livres* moving allowance, a living allowance of over 16,000 *livres* and a 6,000 *livres* pension upon his return to France. Bougainville was not paid anything close to this, but as an officer, he had enough to live quite comfortably and to bring substantial baggage and a couple of servants with him to Canada.

Montcalm and Bougainville sailed from Brest on April 3 at five o'clock in the afternoon. Upon learning that Madame Hérault's health had deteriorated, Bougainville had written of his sadness and anxiety to his brother and had asked him, "Speak to her sometimes of me, dear brother, and maintain the friendship which she has been kind enough to bestow on an unhappy child who would never have parted from her had he foreseen how things were to turn out." In the same letter he had chanted the praises of Montcalm, "He is friendly, witty, frank and open minded . . . He hides nothing from me and pays me the honour of consulting me, an honour I repay by not advising him."

After a thirty-eight-day voyage on the *Licorne*, sometimes battling waves higher than the vessel, being thrown off course and held up six days by ice floes, they finally reached Québec on May 12, 1756.

Under Montcalm, Bougainville fought three arduous campaigns between 1756 and the one in which he was now engaged. In all of them he served diligently, was duly wounded, and negotiated truces and capitulations with the English.

"You Canadians live in a cruel country," Bougainville says to me, "and certainly an uncomfortable one. But, what can you expect? Your natural surroundings, as I once wrote *ma chère maman*, are 'apt to engender and maintain a melancholy temper.' My moods whilst in your country were always sad and sometimes hideous – even horrifying."

He laughs and then adds, "What a field for misanthropy your country is, what a setting for regrets and fond desires. When I thought of quitting this exile, I cheered up, but was soon faced again with the stern reality that I might not have a future."

"But you learned something? Something important?" I ask.

"Yes, I learned something: that I could stand almost anything. The vastness, the ruggedness of the land, and the hardships it exacted may have ruined my health but I was exhilarated. I waded waist-deep in freezing and turbulent rivers, I slept on hard ground with a rock for a pillow. I was able to do that, and, I must tell you, I found some interior peace and serenity, but only now and then. Your people didn't help, you know. I wanted to like them and I did, but I needed much patience. Their disposition was not welcoming and they were pleased to feel an aversion for us, the French."

"You wrote that to your brother. You also added 'All I can say is that when the time comes to leave this country, we shall sing with all our hearts, '*In exitu Israël*.'"

"I suppose I went through a crisis of sorts. In Canada I became a rather peculiar creature, sometimes philosophical, sometimes not, with the same passions as before, but with more frequent flashes of wisdom, a stronger tendency to think up fine ideas, but with no great capacity to carry them out. In the long run, Canada taught me that, to overcome, I had to acquire *une âme à plusieurs étages*."

"A stout heart."

"Yes, a stout heart!"

Between campaigns Bougainville recuperated by reading, writing, talking endlessly with the Jesuits in Québec and the Sulpicians in Montréal, and thinking. He pursued his scientific studies and learned much of the language, the customs, and the way of life of the Indians. Dividing the long months of winter between Montréal and Québec, he attended elaborate balls, gorgeous dinners, and in the summer, splendid picnics and outings. All year long there were scandalous soirées of all sorts. Even when famine threatened New France, such extravagance did not stop, and Bougainville came to accept horse meat disguised under such gourmet names as *petits pâtés de cheval, filet de cheval à la broche avec poivrade, semelles de cheval au gratin, langue de cheval au moroton, frigousse de cheval, langue de cheval boucané* (which Bougainville liked better than moose tongue) and *gâteau de cheval* (more appetizing than *gâteau au lièvre*).

He was shrewd and clever at Bigot's gaming tables, never losing more than honour or politeness made obligatory. He flirted recklessly with all the pretty women around him. He found them attractive, well-proportioned, intelligent, and good conversationalists. They were also ardent flirts, too often contenting themselves, however, with small favours that definitely were no more than venial sins, as Montcalm once remarked. Yet there was much gossip in Montréal and Québec about this or that lady whose caresses with Bougainville had indeed been mortal sins. It was said that in the vast country to the west, an Iroquois girl had given birth to his child. The Iroquois of Saint-Louis had adopted

Bougainville and had made him a brother. The name Garoniatsi-goa, meaning Wraths of the Great Heavens, was given to him because of the fury of the war songs he used to make up on the spot. Over the years he often visited his Iroquois brothers and their families in the small village in which they lived and where they grew their crops, watched over their flocks, raised their children in the Catholic religion, traded with the French, fought the English, and broke in horses.

He had learned much from the Iroquois: not only how to survive and fight in the bush, but also about their spirituality which he found compelling.

"Did you know, Monsieur LaPierre," he asks me, "that their dreams contain their hidden desires, which their holy men or women explain to them. They see spirits everywhere and their intention is always to be in harmony with the Manitou inhabiting all things. I was overwhelmed by the power of their visual imagery and enchanted by the way they tell interminable stories about their past and the sacredness of their myths."

Over the years they were together, the relationship between Montcalm and Bougainville intensified, each developing a profound attachment to the other. In time Bougainville came to regard Montcalm as a father from whom he had no secrets. Montcalm reciprocated, and found in Bougainville a dear son to whom he entrusted personal and confidential missions.

Bougainville knew that Montcalm had many enemies, influential ones at that, and that he was often difficult to deal with. But he was grateful for his friendship, compassion, passionate temperament, and his enthusiasm at serving his country. They shared dreams of glory and mighty achievements that would bring them honour.

In my fantasy, Bougainville tells me, "We were both family men, deeply attached to the families we had left behind. Not a day went by that we did not mention them; not a day went by that *Mon Général* did not worry about the financial situation of his family and the future of his children."

"Is that why he was always anxious about his relationship with the authorities at Versailles? Was he concerned that his behaviour might endanger the welfare of his children?"

"Yes. In the world in which we lived, losing good connections could prove fatal. Without influence in the proper circles, it could be an hostile world. I think my presence calmed him. I listened to him, I shared his anxiety, and while I was in France in the winter of 1758–59, I was able, on his behalf, to make arrangements for the marriage of one of his daughters. But I had to bring him sad news. Shortly before I left to return to Canada at the end of March 1759, news reached me of the death of one of his daughters. I could not even tell him which one of the three. We cried together, just as we had wept when I found out that my friend Hérault had died at the battle of Minden."

And with this, Bougainville salutes and leaves me to get on with the story.

Before they went on their tour of inspection, Bougainville informed Montcalm of the Governor General's plan for this third day of the siege. Vaudreuil had ordered the English fleet destroyed. If the weather held out, then it would take place that night.

Harbour of Québec
Late evening

The wind was fair and the sky dark but with just enough starlight to illuminate the water between the harbour of Québec and the English fleet resting near the Ile d'Orléans. The instruments that Vaudreuil had chosen to destroy the English fleet were six fireships equipped and ready in the harbour. The French placed great faith in the destructive power of the fireships, and the Canadians were confident that God would grant them the miracle they had been praying for over the last two days.

The fireships, made from vessels that Cadet had sold to the Crown at vast cost, were all armed in the same way. Quantities of five-inch timbers had been hollowed out into troughs, laid around the decks, and connected by cross-troughs leading to the ships' portholes, which were meant to blow open in the intense heat. The troughs also led to barrels of pitch, which, when lit, would spread the flames up the masts and the rigging. Melted resin had been spread everywhere. Between the decks large funnels would create an up-draught to feed the fire. Finally, boxes of grenades, obsolete muskets, and old cannon covered in gun powder and loaded with bullets and cannonballs were scattered on the decks.

For the safety of the men operating the fireships, a small landing platform had been built onto the hull of each ship. From that platfrom stretched an additional trough filled with gunpowder and attached to one of the cross-troughs. Each platform had a longboat, which the sailors were to board shortly before igniting their respective fireships.

Originally there had been eight ships: the *Ambassadeur*, the four ships known collectively as the *Quatre Frères*, the *Américain*, the *Angélique* and the *Toison d'Or*. However, one had exploded on June 8, almost causing the entire Lower Town to go up in flames, and another was unusable.

Vaudreuil's orders were clear. The fireships were to leave the harbour of Québec at eleven o'clock. Since they had to travel six miles before making contact with the English fleet, they were not to be lit until they were about one mile from the enemy.

An hour or so before the ships were to leave on their momentous journey, Vaudreuil was driven from his château to the Beauport church. Laboriously he climbed the rickety stairs to the steeple of the church with his secretary, his aide-de-camp, and his slave. Montcalm, Lévis, Bougainville, and other senior officers stood on the steps. The army watched silently from their trenches. In the darkness they could just make out the English armada anchored in the basin of Québec.

Everyone in the town who could be there – priests and seminarians, officials and merchants, off-duty officers and soldiers and sailors, elderly folk, women and children – was on the ramparts and the terrace of the Château Saint-Louis, and a few people had sneaked down by the harbour and the shore. Only the nuns had stayed in their convents. The men puffed away on their pipes, and the women and children recited the rosary. All hoped for their miracle.

The young English soldier in the sentry trench at the west end of the Ile d'Orléans was tired. All day the weather had been unpredictable with sudden gusts of wind and cold rain. For hours he had waited for the electrical storm that threatened. Then, with thunder and lightning, it had fallen upon him and his companions for the second afternoon in a row. The storm had lasted several hours, delaying his supper and soaking him to the bone. Offshore it had fouled the anchor of some of the ships near his observation post. They had rammed into each other and many smaller boats had been smashed on the rocks. Even though the storm had passed and the night was now clear, he was wet, tired, and hungry.

At precisely eleven o'clock, the Sieur de Louche, the commander of the fireship fleet, gave the order to sail forward. Nothing eventful happened as the vessels covered the first three miles. Aboard the fireship the *Ambassadeur*, Captain Dubois de la Militière was making good time. In the distance he could just make out the masts of the English ships silhouetted against the sky. Around him were the other fireships with de Louche in the lead.

Suddenly and unexpectedly, de la Militière saw de Louche's ship explode in a torrent of flames. Soon, four others were also burning and their captains and sailors vaulted into their longboats and rushed for the shore. De Louche had panicked and set his vessel on fire too far from the English ships.

De la Militière remained calm and led his craft on. The other fireships, engulfed in flames, floated aimlessly. Most of his men abandoned ship and threw themselves overboard, but two sailors remained with him. About a mile or so from the first English vessel that he could clearly discern, de la Militière ignited his own ship. There was a tremendous explosion as the flames raced along the troughs and up the riggings.

De la Militière stood the intense heat, the billowing smoke, and the acrid stench as long as he could, then he leaped into the rowboat his men were holding alongside. A short distance from their burning vessel, they collided with one of the other fireships. The impact hurled them into the inky blackness of the St. Lawrence. The burning *Ambassadeur*, de la Militière's ship, sailed on.

Out of the darkness the young English soldier first saw black objects floating towards him. He stared at them for a moment, then summoned the closest soldiers in his trench to do the same. They peered and listened. They heard noises breaking the silence of the night. In terror they waited.

Suddenly, a torch! Then another! The sound of explosions rent the calm of the night. The St. Lawrence was ablaze, covered with floating fires. Jets of flames rushed up to the sky. Cannon roared, grenades burst. And all of this inferno was coming straight towards him, his post, his fleet, and his friends. As smoke engulfed him and burned his eyes, he rushed out of the trench, screaming with fear and followed by his mates.

As soon as the lookout aboard Wolfe's ship saw the exploding fireships, Wolfe was informed. Quickly he set about putting an end to the panic and confusion that followed the desertion in the sentry trench. Fearing an attack from the French stationed at Beauport, he dispatched a detachment of light troops to the north side of the island and called the rest of the army to arms. He then directed his aide-de-camp to ascertain the name and rank of every man who had panicked.

Admiral Saunders, in the HMS *Stirling Castle*, was alerted by the guns of the HMS *Centurion*, the vessel closest to the oncoming inferno. He rushed to the deck to see the fireships coming towards his fleet. He ordered the sailors into their boats. With some enthusiasm, they first rowed proudly towards the fireships, but soon the sailors recoiled as the flames seared their hair and the smoke choked them. The size of the burning ships approaching from all directions frightened them, and many saw the job of saving their fleet a hopeless one. However, in response to the tongue-lashing of their officers and their own instinct for survival, the sailors and the marines who had joined them threw their cables and grappling hooks and towed the inferno to shore on the island. There the vessels burned themselves out without having touched a single one of Saunders' ships. Soon the admiral heard the familiar "All's well!"

From the security of the rear of the line, Knox also watched the burning of the fireships. "They were certainly the grandest fireworks (if I may be allowed to call them so)," he wrote in the journal he was keeping of the campaigns in America, "that can possibly be conceived, every circumstance having contributed to their awful, yet beautiful appearance."

Vaudreuil was in no mood to be entertained by the fireworks, however. The English fleet was safe. The mission had been an utter failure.

As if nothing out of the ordinary had happened, de Louche arrived on the steps of the church with the other captains to make his report. He bragged about his exploit and refused to accept any responsibility for the fiasco, complaining that the Intendant and the commander of the Artillery had forced his hand. How, he never explained. Someone asked what had happened to de la Militière. De Louche did not know, but Montcalm replied: "Maybe he lost his head!"

Montcalm would later explain his disparaging remark in a confidential memo to Lévis. He felt that de la Militière, who had two brothers serving in America, wanted to surpass them in bravery. He had therefore remained too long aboard once he had lit his fireship. "Somme toute," Montcalm wrote, "de vous à moi, à cause de ses frères, la tête avait tourné à la Militière." In his usual devious way, Montcalm asked Lévis to burn his letter.

To the amazement of many of the soldiers, Vaudreuil and Montcalm did not rebuke de Louche nor did they severely reprimand him. They accepted the fiasco calmly.

Wolfe, on the other hand, was not calm. In fact he could hardly contain his fury. He was first of all angry at himself for he knew that the French had fireships, which they regarded highly as offensive weapons. But he had paid no attention to this important detail, which he had found in Mackellar's reports. Nor had he communicated the information to his officers. It could have prepared them and their men for the terror they faced. He was also furious with the sentries and particularly with their officer. He reprimanded the men severely and ordered that the officer be arrested and court-martialled. "I hope he hangs," he told one of his aides.

Among the dozens of people still on the terrace of the Château Saint-Louis was Madame Lefebvre, the mother of the seminarian Jean-François-Xavier. All through the eventful night, she had watched with her son, his friend Pierre Mennard, and Father Baudouin. When the fireships were lit, they could not tell if the ships were close enough to do any damage to the English fleet. They just hoped they were. Later, after Vaudreuil had returned to the château, the guards told them that the fireships had failed in their mission.

I do not know much about Madame Lefebvre, or about her son. When I think about her, she appears to me to have been a short, chubby woman in her early fifties with an ample bosom, a reddish complexion, and a ready smile. She was a kind person, devoted to the church, with a particular devotion to the Virgin, whose church, Notre-Dame-des-Victoires in the Lower Town, was her special responsibility. She cleaned it, put flowers on its altars, and spent hours there talking with the Virgin, St. Joseph, and the child Jesus. Like many families who had relatives upriver, she had sent her children to her sister who lived in Sorel, a few miles east from Montréal. Only Jean-François-Xavier stayed behind, after begging her to be allowed to remain in Québec. Her husband, a stonemason by trade, was with the French army in the Lake Champlain district.

The only information I have about Jean-François-Xavier is that, at the time of the siege, he was fourteen years old and a student at the Séminaire, and that the priests there gave him a bursary. I am sure he was a tall lad with flaming red hair, which his mother knew he hated. He was relatively handsome and well-built, and the girls in his neighbourhood found him attractive, but awkward, while their mothers could not help thinking that in time he would make a fine husband should he change his mind about being a priest.

I consider him a prototype of all the teenagers who were involved one way or another in the siege and in the battle for Québec. I intend to use him that way, along with his friend Pierre Mennard, who was in his late teens but already tonsured (the first step to the priesthood), shorter and fatter than Lefebvre, with jet black hair and already smoking a pipe. I also intend to make Madame Lefebvre and Father Baudouin represent their generation.

As she made her way home from the terrace, Madame Lefebvre was overcome with grief. God had not allowed the destruction of the English fleet.

"Where is God?" she asked her son. "He is where He ought to be," he replied simply. Between her sobs he heard her say, "There will be no miracle this time." He tried to soothe her: "Maybe in the long run! In the long run, Maman." He walked her home and both sensed that more, much more, was yet to come.

An hour later, Jean-François-Xavier met with Pierre Mennard and Father Baudouin. The two young men told the priest of their decision to join the army. The priest did not attempt to dissuade them; however, he did point out that if they bore arms they would have to obtain an absolution from Rome, known as a *gestione armorum*, before they could be ordained. They did not understand exactly what that entailed, but they were determined that the next day they would go to the King's stores and be fitted, equipped, and sworn in as soldiers of the King of France. Their adolescence was over.

June 30, 1759

(Day Five)

Beaumont on the south shore
7:00 A.M.

During the early hours of the morning, the English rowed three thousand men from the parish of Saint-Laurent on the Ile d'Orléans to the village of Beaumont on the south shore of the St. Lawrence.

The officer commanding this brigade, Brigadier-General Robert Monckton, was Wolfe's senior brigadier and second-in-command. An Englishman from Yorkshire, he had been in the army since he was fifteen, coming to Nova Scotia in 1752, where three years later he had supervised the deportation of the Acadians. Not content with merely deporting them, Monckton had destroyed their houses, their barns, and their crops. This kept him busy in Acadia for four years before he came to Québec with Wolfe in 1759.

Beaumont was a village consisting of four seigneuries: Beaumont, the oldest and owned by the Couillard family, Vincennes, which had fallen into the hands of Joseph Roy, Vitre, belonging to Marie-Louis Bissot, and the most recent one, Livaudière, which was owned by the Péan family. Beaumont was also the gateway to the south shore.

Four hundred people lived in the hamlet on pleasant and productive farms. Their parish church, dedicated to Saint-Etienne, was an imposing stone building with a tall steeple. Built in 1733, it had an ornate interior with a finely chiselled main altar and beautifully carved woodwork especially in the small Sainte-Anne's Chapel. It was the pride of the Canadian parish priest, Gaspard Dunière, who at this time, was so ill that the bishop had sent him an assistant, Pierre-Bernard Dosque, a former missionary in Acadia.

Wolfe had ordered Monckton to the south shore to occupy Pointe-Lévy, a point of land which jutted into the St. Lawrence, not too far east of Québec. Saunders was worried that the French would build a battery on the point, which could do irreparable damage to his ships in the basin.

In the late afternoon of the previous day, Monckton had sent a company of light infantry troops and a few Rangers, under the command of Lieutenant-Colonel William Howe, to Beaumont to secure the place. Finding themselves unopposed, Howe and his men had spent the night in the church.

(Howe's unannounced arrival at Beaumont caught Vaudreuil's official envoy, Gaspard-Joseph Chaussegros de Léry, unawares. He had to rush out of the house in which he was writing a report for Vaudreuil, leaving his papers and his sword behind. Later Wolfe returned the sword but kept the papers, which constituted a sort of diary of Léry's activities on the south shore. The whereabouts of this diary was unknown for close to a century after Léry's death. Then, in 1900, an English collector donated it to the Canadian archives.)

When Howe and his men came out of the church at dawn, they were accosted by a party of Canadians and Indians. In the short battle that ensued, the Canadians lost eight men: three were killed and scalped by the Rangers, two were injured, and three taken prisoner. Only two English soldiers were wounded.

After the skirmish, the English retreated to a farmhouse situated on top of the steep hill that led down to the shore. No one was about, and on entering the house they discovered a fair quantity of provisions and some good furniture. While they walked about the main floor and the attic, expropriating all the moveables they could, some soldiers heard muffled sounds. After a thorough search, they found no one, but to be on the safe side, Howe had the house burnt to the ground. As he returned to the church, only his rearguard heard the frightful screams of the farmer's wife and children, who had taken refuge in the shallow cellar under the house. After a frantic and unsuccessful effort to save them, the soldiers watched helplessly as the woman and the children burned to death. They were the first civilian casualties of the Conquest of Québec. No one knows their names.

Shortly before ten o'clock, the troops assembled in the square in front of the church. With drums beating and much ceremony, Monckton marched solemnly to the main door of the church and nailed there the Proclamation to the Inhabitants of Canada that Wolfe had written in French three days earlier. When the Rangers reported that all was clear, Monckton and the soldiers marched up the serpentine path to Pointe-Lévy, leaving two hundred men to guard the church. An hour and a half later, he withdrew them.

Once the English had disappeared from view, some of the villagers emerged from the woods at the other end of the village, a scattering of women and children marching with the men. On the door of the church, they found the parish priest holding Wolfe's proclamation. Father Dunière read it to them:

"By His Excellency James Wolfe, Esq.; Colonel of a Regiment of Infantry, Major-General and Commander in Chief of his Britannic Majesty's forces in the River St. Lawrence, etc." the proclamation was addressed to the Canadians. In it, Wolfe stated that he had come to Canada to check the insolence of France, revenge the injury done to the English colonists in America, and conquer New France. However, as the priest read on, Wolfe meant the Canadians no harm as long as "the wisdom of the people of Canada" prevailed and they remained neutral "in this great dilemma." But should they assist the French in any way, Wolfe warned them that they "must expect the most fatal consequences; their habitations destroyed, their sacred temples exposed to an exasperated soldiery, their harvest utterly ruined." Thus "the wretched natives" would perish from the most dismal want and famine during the forthcoming winter.

The Proclamation was only *pro forma*. Wolfe had decided to destroy Québec and the country around it as he was sailing to America in the winter of 1759. En route to Canada he had written to Amherst: "If by accident in the River, or by the

Enemy's resistance, by sickness, or slaughter in the Army, or, from any other cause, we find that Québec is not likely to fall into our hands ... I propose to set the Town on fire with Shells, to destroy the Harvest, Houses, & Cattle, both above & below, to send off as many Canadians as possible to Europe, & to leave famine and desolation behind me; *belle résolution, & très chrétienne!"*

After the reading, the priest knelt down and together with the people around him recited three Hail Marys. Then the men took up their guns and followed the English up the path to Pointe-Lévy. The parish priest sent a farmer to Québec to give Vaudreuil the proclamation and, with the help of his assistant, Dosque, the women carried the bodies of the dead militiamen to the cemetery, where they buried them. That done, instead of hiding in the woods as Vaudreuil had ordered them, the women and their children went back to their farms. Wolfe, apparently, had not frightened them.

Château Saint-Louis
Early afternoon

Vaudreuil was not amused. Events had not turned out as he had expected. He was also lonely; his wife, to whom he was devoted, was at their château in Montréal. So there was no one reliable to look after him, and his household was in chaos as his servants packed furniture (including his bed), crystal chandeliers, and *objets d'art*, special rations of food, his collection of fine imported wines, and his favourite outfits for his stay at La Canardière, two miles east of Québec.

The news of Monckton's landing on the south shore and his march to Pointe-Lévy had interrupted Vaudreuil's noon meal. That the English brigadier had encountered no regular or colonial troops there was no surprise to Vaudreuil. None of his advisers had believed that the English would land anywhere on the south shore: the terrain was far too difficult, the rivers too many, the gorges too deep, and the woods largely impassable. Furthermore, the French engineer had assured both Vaudreuil and Montcalm that the distance between Québec and Pointe-Lévy was too great for English cannon located there to fire on the town. Consequently no battery had been built on the "elbow" – Pointe-Lévy – and no troops had been stationed there. Montcalm had thought of doing both but had preferred the option of concentrating all his manpower at Beauport, a policy to which Vaudreuil had not objected.

As soon as he was told of Monckton's landing, and before eating the cheese course his slave was serving him, Vaudreuil acted. Without waiting to reach Montcalm at Beauport, he sent the seigneur of Pointe-Lévy, Etienne Charest, with a small force of Canadians and Indians, to drive out the English. Next he ordered a floating battery into the basin to harass the barges ferrying baggage, armaments, and supplies to the south shore.

The thought of the English occupation of the south shore exasperated Vaudreuil. He was convinced that Montcalm would hold him responsible and write to Versailles accordingly. And there would also be reproaches for his inability to remove the eight thousand people living on the south shore between Ile du Portage and Beaumont. Vaudreuil had tried but failed.

When news of the English presence in the St. Lawrence had first reached him, he had sent three Canadian officers of the *troupes franches de la marine*, including Léry, to carry out the evacuation. They had been badly received. Like most of the people on the north shore, the habitants of the south shore, particularly the women, simply refused to take refuge in the woody concessions above the St. Lawrence as Vaudreuil had ordered. Instead, when they saw the English ships, they gathered their children and a few belongings and took to the nearby woods. But as soon as the English had passed, they came back to their villages and farms. They argued with Léry that they did not wish to be disrespectful of the Governor General but they had encountered the English before and had been able to hold them back. They would do so again.

Vaudreuil had also had little success with the militia of the south shore. Most of them stayed home in spite of his

threats. Some of the seigneurs even encouraged the recalci-
trants, particularly that blackguard Gabriel-Jean Amiot, seigneur de Vincelotte (a seigneurie around Saint-Ignace) who
was exhorting the militia of his district to defect, arguing
that they were needed to protect their homes. A few, however, had heeded Vaudreuil's command and had begun their
march to Québec with Léry. But they had done so at their
own pace, protesting all the while.

The Canadians of 1759 were a stubborn people, and the
militia of the south shore gave ample proof of that once
again. They went with Léry, but they exacted a price and
annoyed Vaudreuil and Bigot no end. They refused to eat the
pigs and the sheep Bigot had ordered butchered and complained that the two pounds of bread allotted to each one of
them was not sufficient to sustain them. Bigot sent more
bread. Then they protested that they could not go on
because they did not have adequate shoes, so the Intendant
sent a hundred pairs to placate them. When it came to
ammunitions, Vaudreuil was deluged with requests. One day
it was the captain of the militia of Islet wanting powder, the
next it was Capitaine Gabory from Saint-Vallier insisting on
a large quantity of bullets, following closely upon the
requests of Capitaine Jerber of Saint-Roch, who along with
other captains of the militia had developed an insatiable
hunger for guns.

Vaudreuil had finally lost patience, closing his eyes to
those who went back home to get food but never returned
and telling the others that they would be fully equipped
upon their arrival at Beauport. When Léry reported that they
were firing on the English, the old man gave up.

The English arrival on the south shore, however, interrupted the militia's march, and most of the recruits went
back to their homes. Vaudreuil was not as angry as he might
have been. At least now they could be used to chase the
English out of Pointe-Lévy and prevent further landings. If
that happened it would help to soften any criticisms of his
leadership to the King. But in other areas, he felt himself
quite vulnerable.

For instance, he had not been able to evacuate totally the civilian population of Québec. A few had gone, but the rest of the inhabitants had remained and were all over the Upper Town getting in everyone's way. And he had not enough food to feed them all adequately. Also, he knew that he would be criticized because he had done nothing about the corruption all around him. There is no evidence that he partook in Bigot's thievery, but he had tolerated it, fearing that exposing the Intendant would weaken his support at Versailles.

———————

I do not know how much the defence measures he took made him vulnerable to Versailles' criticism. But I do know that he had been ordered to concentrate the defence of New France within the smallest periphery possible. Nevertheless, he had a frontier of some twelve hundred miles to defend. He had spent the winter of 1759 arguing furiously with Montcalm about what to do; Montcalm wanting to abandon the West and Vaudreuil insisting that the French empire could not be relegated to the St. Lawrence Valley and the provincial towns of Montréal, Trois-Rivières, and Québec. To Vaudreuil – and to many Canadians of his day – the West was the key to the French (and for that matter, the Canadian) presence in America. Before the arrival of the English, they had compromised. Vaudreuil kept a small detachment on the Ohio, and sent another to Niagara at the other end of Lake Ontario and still another to the head of the rapids where Lake Ontario ends and the St. Lawrence begins its long journey to the Atlantic. François-Charles de Bourlamaque, the third French officer in the line of command, went to Carillon (Ticonderoga) at the beginning of May to protect the Lake Champlain route. In the event of an attack, he was to destroy that fort and the one at Saint-Frédéric, a few miles away, and make his stand at Ile-aux-Noix at the door of the Richelieu River.

There was another area of vulnerability for which I have no direct evidence, but which I think he experienced nevertheless. He was disappointing his people. He felt responsible for the failure of the fireships because he had entrusted them to that incompetent de Louche. More than anyone else in the higher echelons of command, he was aware that the habitants of Canada had made a supreme effort to defend their country; they would expect no less from their leaders. There could be trouble should he and Montcalm not live up to the expectations of the people. The Canadians, after all, were not an easy people to govern.

Vaudreuil had experienced their unruliness often. The most popular view of these early Canadians, a view fostered by a succession of historians whose only evidence was their own prejudice, and, I must admit, also fostered by some clerical apologists, is that my ancestors were a docile people, priest-ridden and tied to the land. But I'm sure that Bishop Pontbriand, Montcalm, and everyone else in authority would disagree with that assessment.

My people's life in Canada began with Samuel de Champlain when he landed in Québec in 1608.

Over the next century and a half, 8,527 French immigrants came to the St. Lawrence valley, and by 1759, 70,000 people of French descent called this land home.

On the shores of the St. Lawrence, where most of the Canadians lived, they founded three towns: Québec in 1608, Trois-Rivières in 1634, and Montréal in 1642. Fifteen per cent of the population lived in these towns (about eight thousand in Québec, eight hundred in Trois-Rivières, and five thousand in Montréal) and enjoyed a life similar to that of the provincial towns of France. Class distinction, dominated by the French officials, high military officers, and the important Canadian merchants, was rigid. Most people earned their living as tradesmen, labourers and servants, administrative officials and clerks, priests and nuns.

The townspeople were not as well off as their rural counterparts. This was largely because massive French colonial interference had ruined the Canadian economy by the time the English arrived to conquer us. In every conceivable economic sector, edicts from France confronted and weakened colonial initiative, with the result that the French authorities stymied the development of indigenous industrial and mercantile enterprises. The fisheries, when not operating for the benefit of the mother country, were at a standstill. The fur trade, which had employed thousands, had become centralized and benefitted only a few chosen monopolists. And the forty or so Canadians who grew wealthy from their control of the economy lacked the entrepreneurship of their southern neighbours. Clothed in the latest fashions from France – which helped prevent the formation of a Canadian textile industry – they wanted to live like French nobles, in the wilderness of America. It is no wonder that the bulk of the population lived in poverty.

The other 85 per cent of the population lived in 140 rural parishes, villages, seigneuries, and missions where they tilled the land – about two hundred thousand acres. The farms of the habitants were long and narrow, fronting onto a river or a public road for easier transport and communications, and close to their neighbours.

At the beginning of settlement, life was difficult. The land had to be cleared, the soil tilled, and houses and barns built. Know-how was limited, skilled labour largely unavailable, and tools crude. And the Indians were everywhere, fighting to hold on to their territory. In time, however, the Canadian habitant came to enjoy a life of relative comfort and economic self-sufficiency, particularly in the first fifty years of the eighteenth century.

The focal points of that rural life were the family and the Roman Catholic church. The family provided order and continuity. The work was hard, particularly for the women to whom it fell since their husbands and sons spent much of their time either fighting or scouting for furs in the West. But there were many feast days and holy days which provided merriment and joy.

The habitants took their religion seriously – at least in public – and were obedient to the dictates of their bishop and priests, as long as these did not interfere with their economic stability and influence. But their lives were not priest-ridden, not in the manner of nineteenth-century Québec.

There in the countryside of the St. Lawrence Valley, European ways changed to Canadian ways. In the process, a new identity was born, traditions were shaped, and Canada came to be.

About three thousand other Canadians lived among the Indians in the lands west of Montréal, along the Great Lakes, the

Ohio, the Illinois, and the Mississippi rivers, and in large sections of the plains. After lengthy and dangerous voyages that often exhausted them and ruined their health, the Canadians built trading posts, missionary stations, and military forts there.

These descendants of the French were so intrepid and so good at empire-building that by the time of the Conquest they occupied a territory that stretched from the shores of Hudson's Bay to the Gulf of Mexico, and from the Atlantic Ocean almost to the foot of the Rockies.

One factor in the geography of the continent helped considerably in their rapid expansion: a splendid, interconnected system of rivers and waterways. The dominant waterway was, of course, the St. Lawrence River. Paddling up and down the river and on its tributaries they invaded the continent. The St. Lawrence was their lifeline.

The second part of the waterway system nature had provided was the Great Lakes: Ontario, Erie, Huron, Michigan, and Superior. Together with the St. Lawrence they formed a navigable system penetrating five thousand miles into North America. The many rivers that flowed from, into, or around them assisted that penetration: the Ohio, the Illinois, and the Mississippi being three of the most important.

To hold the vast territory they occupied for France and for themselves, the Canadians spent most of their lives fighting the Indians (less so after 1701), the American colonists (mostly in the first half of the eighteenth century), the English (from 1754 to 1760), and the French autocrats (almost constantly).

In almost every aspect of colonial life, the interests of the French clashed with those of the Canadians. *Coureurs de bois*, traders, and merchants challenged the French for the lucrative fur trade; townspeople and farmers fought each latest edict by circumventing it; parishioners often vehemently questioned episcopal and clerical authority; and the militia outdid themselves to force the French to conduct their battles *à la façon du pays* – the ways of the country – a sort of guerrilla warfare, which would have led to a different result had the French adopted it during the 1759 English expedition.

There is ample evidence that in time the French came to recognize us, the Canadians, as a people different from themselves. They found us haughty and boastful, with a tendency to exaggerate. They complained that we were too independent and undisciplined, unwilling to obey orders and disrespectful of authority. But they did see that we were indefatigable hunters, swift runners, conscientious explorers, and excellent at fighting à l'indienne. They also could not deny that we had a zest for life, which probably accounted for our being not too competent at farming – it is as if our spirit could not be confined to a small acreage. We played hard and for keeps, were generally good-looking and charming and pleasant to be with. When the French compared us with the peasants in their own country they concluded that we were more intelligent and better educated.

I believe that by the time of the Conquest, the French were beginning to regard us as belonging to a nation different from their own. In some ways we thought of them as our natural enemies. "The second venial sin for the Canadians," one exasperated official once declared, "is to be French." It is no wonder that by the middle of the eighteenth century, some observers in France – and maybe in Canada for all I know – predicted that the day would come when new states would rise in the vast lands of France in the new world. So why, these critics asked, should the French government spend time, money, and men to delay the inevitable?

For their part, the Canadians came to resent the imperiousness of their French masters, the menial tasks and roles they were given or allowed to perform, and the harsh way in which they were treated. They complained that the French living here only temporarily contributed little to the development of the land, while they, who had no place else to go, made all the sacrifices, only to be abused by the French.

When the English arrived in the spring of 1759, several factors intensified that struggle and left the majority of Canadians terribly disenchanted: years of poor crops, limited food rations, the high style of living of the oligarchy, the struggle for control of the western lands, and battle plans that had little regard for how the outcome would affect those who had to remain. Many of my people came to feel betrayed. When the final betrayal came, the Canadians gave up on their French masters. This does not mean that the Canadians did not try to defend their homes, their villages, and their country, *our* country. They did. And they paid dearly for it, as you shall see if I let you return to Vaudreuil's woes.

In the early afternoon of June 30, 1759, Vaudreuil had to face facts: the English were practically in the harbour of Québec. There was much to be done. However, he was not in command. Montcalm was.

Saint-Joseph de Pointe-Lévy
Late afternoon

Etienne Charest was the seigneur de Lauzon, which included the village of Saint-Joseph de Pointe-Lévy on the south shore. The son of one of the richest men in Canada, Etienne and his younger brother, Joseph Dufy, had inherited his father's vast holdings when Etienne was just seventeen. Over the years, with Joseph Dufy concentrating on the riches of the sea and Etienne on those of the land, they had managed their affairs with acumen and had increased considerably the holdings they had inherited. They ran the family's store on Rue Sault au Matelot in the Lower Town – one of the best stocked shops in the colony – and they managed cod and seal fisheries in Labrador. As well, Etienne controlled over thirty thousand acres on the south shore, on which lived fifteen hundred land-owners grouped in the parishes of Saint-Joseph-de-Pointe-Lévy, Saint-Nicholas, and Saint-Henri. The brothers did most things together. They married sisters on the same day in the same church. Etienne had thirteen children, and it is recorded that all of his sons settled in Saint-Domingue or Hispaniola.

Earlier in the day, Vaudreuil had sent Charest to Pointe-Lévy with forty of his habitants and three hundred Indians to attack the English. For part of the afternoon they had shadowed their enemies, hiding behind trees and crouching in the bush. The English regulars had had a hard time of it. Their silly uniforms made ducking to avoid bullets and arrows almost impossible. The baggage army regulations stipulated they carry also made walking quickly difficult.

(The baggage or the "impedimenta" of the English soldier of the day weighed about sixty-five pounds. He carried a week's iron ration, a cooking pot, three shirts, two pairs of white socks, one pair of black socks, three pairs of oiled linen stockings [oiled to prevent sores], one pair of leg coverings that came up to the knees and were buttoned on the side, two pairs of black linen leggings and one pair of woollen ones, one pair of drawers, a red cap, a rosette, a cloak, a knapsack, a haversack, one pair of shoe buckles, one pair of garter buckles, two pairs of shoes, twenty-four rounds of ammunition kept in a supposedly waterproof pouch, two flints, six ramrods, three priming pans and a "bullet mould with iron ladle to make his own bullets out of a pound of lead," a blanket or two, and a fifteen-pound musket known as Brown Bess.)

Unlike the American Rangers, the English regulars were unaccustomed to bush warfare. In their predicament, they became an easy prey for Charest and his men. Throughout the day the Canadians and the Indians killed, wounded, or scalped over thirty of them.

As soon as Monckton reached Pointe-Lévy, he made for the church, but for some unknown reason he soon came out, leaving it unprotected. Charest seized the opportunity, made a rush for it, and barricaded himself inside with a small contingent of Canadians, leaving the others and the Indians to deploy themselves behind the rocky mount on which the church and the presbytery stood.

When Monckton was notified that the Canadians had occupied the church he sent light troops to dislodge them. For the next three hours both sides fought repeated skirmishes, taking turns occupying the church. The English did not forget the proprieties of war: every time they held the church, they flew their colours from the steeple. The Canadians, when their turn came, took them down. In between one of the scuffles one of the Abenakis Indians, whom I call

Mascou, brought Charest a prisoner, an ordinary soldier who had been caught literally with his pants down. Charest sent them both to Vaudreuil.

By six o'clock, Monckton had had enough. He felt inept at being rebuffed by an enemy he outnumbered at least five to one. Taking most of his troops with him, he stormed the church from three different directions. The Fraser Highlanders attacked from the woods, the light troops surrounded the mount and drove the Canadians and the Indians who were there into the outskirts of Pointe-Lévy, and Monckton with the Louisbourg Grenadiers advanced boldly from the front. The Canadians inside resisted for a while, but finally fled by the back protected by Indian fire as Monckton entered through the shattered front door.

After that, the English set up camp while the Canadians and Indians fired at them without causing too much damage. As the evening crawled into the night, both sides observed an uneasy truce.

Château Saint-Louis
Early evening

There was no easy truce, however, at Vaudreuil's château. The Governor had spent all afternoon receiving conflicting reports about the size of the English forces at the Pointe-Lévy and about the occupation of the church. Since Charest could not be expected to hang on forever, a decision would have to be made about what to do.

As Vaudreuil pondered what he was empowered to do, Montcalm, who had ridden from Beauport, burst upon him with the demand that a detachment of regular troops with proper supplies and arms be dispatched to Pointe-Lévy to rid it of the English. Vaudreuil, who was only too happy to be consulted, had only one objection: no regular troops should be used, only a few detachments of the militia under Canadian officers with as many Indians as could be gathered. There followed their usual confrontation, Montcalm arguing that it was a matter for professionals since the English were professional soldiers, and Vaudreuil waxing eloquent about the Canadians and Indians being best suited for the kind of warfare the woody terrain required. The argument was still raging when Mascou and his prisoner arrived at Château Saint-Louis.

The young soldier Mascou had taken was shaken but not afraid. After his capture, he had kept his head and no harm had come to him. On the beach, as he was about to board a canoe for the trip to Québec, women and children had hit him with their fists, but Mascou had stopped them. During the short trip to the Lower Town the prisoner was blindfolded. In Québec he was more or less hauled up the Côte de la Montagne to the château. There he was brought to a small waiting room. When his blindfold was removed, he was astonished to be in a fine place with brocade and furniture that shone like gold, paintings on the walls, vases of flowers on the tables, and good-looking gentlemen in elaborate uniforms milling about. He was left standing next to Mascou and a few Indians until Vaudreuil, Montcalm, and their aides arrived.

Without looking at the prisoner, Vaudreuil dismissed the Indians and sat on a high chair behind a table his slave had placed in the middle of the room. After admonishing the soldier to tell the truth or else to be turned over to the Indians, Vaudreuil interrogated him through an interpreter.

When questioned about the prevalent opinion in the English camp about the size of the French troops in and around Québec, the prisoner said that Wolfe believed that all of Montcalm's regular troops had been sent to Fort Carillon to face the English army on its way there. According to Wolfe's intelligence, Montcalm had at Beauport only seven thousand militia troops, including residents but no Indians. When queried about the size of the English army, he guessed its strength to be at ten thousand men, mostly Irish Catholics like himself. When examined about the landing at Pointe-Lévy, he described it as a diversion with the purpose of making the French divide their forces by sending a strong contingent there. And when asked about Wolfe's plans, the young Irish soldier told Vaudreuil that Wolfe had ordered the troops to be ready to attack the French at Beauport shortly after ten o'clock that night.

The announcement of the imminent battle stupefied Vaudreuil and stunned Montcalm. Without a moment to lose, Montcalm rode furiously back to Beauport to place the troops on alert. He reckoned that Wolfe would concentrate his assault in the middle of the French line, but closer to the St. Charles River than the Montmorency Falls. He ordered Lévis to fall back somewhat to be closer to the regular troops in the centre of the line. He brought some of the Canadian militia to the shore by the St. Lawrence and left the rest to guard his right, and he directed the cavalry to La Canardière to act as couriers. Then he waited.

After sending the prisoner to the guardhouse where he was to be kept in custody, Vaudreuil sent Mascou back to Charest with orders to abandon the Pointe and return to Beauport immediately with his men and as many Indians as he could persuade. Turning the town over to Ramezay, he said to the Canadian commander of the town of Québec: "We are in your hands." Then, he walked slowly and sadly through the château, not knowing when he would see it again. At the main door he met his secretary, servants, slave, and his escort. Before leaving, along with vast quantities of food and wine and coats of many colours, he told an officer to fetch Father Récher, the parish priest, to hear the young soldier's confession. And without looking back, the Governor General of Canada was driven quickly to La Canadière. It would be the first time in his career that Vaudreuil was in the centre of an armed camp.

Not long after Vaudreuil's departure, Intendant Bigot also left his palace outside the walls to take up residence in a small farmhouse. His escort and servants, horses and *calèche*, were to be in constant readiness to leave Beauport and seek refuge elsewhere.

After their departure, the gates of Québec were closed.

Ile d'Orléans
That night

On their way across to Beauport, the three Indians made a detour to the northeast end of the island. Noiselessly they entered the English camp. Seeing two grenadiers standing talking quietly at the entrance to their tent, the Indians jumped upon them, dragged them into the woods, and killed and scalped them in revenge for their brother whom the English had killed that afternoon at Pointe-Lévy. They left their mutilated bodies to be discovered the next morning.

Across the north channel at Beauport, Montcalm, together with Bougainville and an escort, inspected the whole line and conferred briefly with Lévis. After making adjustments here and there and moving a few cannon, Montcalm returned to his manor-house at the centre of the village of Beauport to await the enemy.

Five hours later, the English had still not come. The men were tired and bewildered. Montcalm felt foolish and humiliated. He ordered the soldiers back to their encampments with the warning to remain on the alert. He sat down with a cup of tea and waited again.

Suddenly at four o'clock in the morning, the alarm sounded.

"Alerte au camp des Canadiens, à la droite!" Montcalm was told.

He rushed to the right of his line, where he found a few Canadians firing in pitch darkness towards the St. Lawrence. It was soon apparent that it had been a false alarm. Dressing down the soldiers, he sent them back to their tents and returned to the de Salaberry manor to wait out the night. On his way there, he had to dispatch a courier to Ramezay in Québec. The Canadian musketry had been so loud that Ramezay, believing the army at Beauport to be attacked, had sounded the general alarm. After a while everyone and everything was quiet.

By six the following morning, it was obvious that Wolfe was fast asleep and, by the fires burning at Pointe-Lévy, that

Monckton was still encamped there. The young soldier had lied. Montcalm rode to see Vaudreuil at La Canardière to arrange again for troops to be sent to the Pointe. However, he found Vaudreuil in no mood to make decisions at that ungodly hour of the morning. Instead, and at a decent hour, the Governor would return to Québec and interrogate the prisoner a second time. In the meantime he would go to bed, and he advised Montcalm to do the same.

To end this strange tale, suffice it to say that the prisoner stuck to his story, arguing that the attack must have been postponed for reasons he certainly did not know. He was certain that it would now come on the night of July 1. For the second day in a row Vaudreuil and Montcalm believed him. That night the troops at Beauport, fully armed, waited once more for the English. They, of course, never came. Nowhere is it recorded that Vaudreuil ordered the prisoner executed or turned over to the Indians.

By seven o'clock on the morning of the sixth day of the siege of Québec, Wolfe and his army were still on the Ile d'Orléans, Saunders and his fleet were still in the St. Lawrence, Monckton and his brigade were still at Pointe-Lévy and Montcalm and his troops asleep, at Beauport. Father Baudouin, though, was on one of the quays of the harbour at Québec watching intently for activities on the south shore. When he was told of the Irish soldier's deposition to Vaudreuil, he was quite surprised that the Governor and Montcalm had attached any credence to his tale. As he glared in the darkness at the fires at Pointe-Lévy, Baudouin was certain that the English intended to stay there. "No good can come out of that!" he said to himself. He shivered in the cold, but he continued his vigil.

All I know for sure about Charles-Louis-Marie Baudouin is that he was forty-two years old, a Canadian and a priest who had come to live at the Séminaire de Québec in 1752. I see him as a man of independent character and means. He is learned, has travelled extensively, and he knows a couple of priests in the Catholic state of Maryland. Even though he tends to be sceptical about the motives of men, he is kind and generous, spending much of his time helping others and making himself useful as best he can in spite of his bad health, which has forced him to abandon the regular ministry. At the Séminaire, he helps as a spiritual counsellor to the students and teaches them the history of their land and people. His pupils like him, particularly Mennard and Lefebvre, whom he considers to be his protégés. He is outspoken and never misses an opportunity to state his opinions, a trait that does not endear him to the civil, military, and clerical authorities. He and Bougainville get along quite well, however. Over the years his tall and skinny frame, his deeply set eyes, his bald head, his ready smile, and his constant wheezing have become familiar to everyone.

Six days into the siege, he was beginning to wonder what was going on. He was not alone in that feeling, which would intensify as the days dragged on.

July 2, 1759

(Day Seven)

Ile d'Orléans
7:00 A.M.

The two last days had been terrible for Wolfe. The weather had been foul and his bladder painful, a combination of circumstances that made him impatient, obstinate, and easily annoyed. Monckton and the soldiers at Pointe-Lévy were the recipients of his bad temper as he complained about the location of their encampment and about their ignorance. However he had found the time to sympathize with the soldiers on the island, who had been without fresh provisions for days, cheering them up with "things would improve in time!"

Wrapped in a large, warm cape with several scarves twisted around his neck to muffle him from the cold, he found the dawn the seventh day of the siege to be no improvement at all. In fact all signs pointed to another gloomy day. It was cold and it was about to rain. His bladder was still giving him trouble, but, thank God, not as much as the day before. Soon the longboat was ready and he was rowed across to Pointe-Lévy.

As Wolfe was approaching Monckton's camp, Major George Scott, the commander of the Rangers, was preparing to leave on a mission. Scott was a professional soldier married to a woman from Massachusetts. He had been in the army all his life and had come into prominence at Louisbourg, where he had become an expert at laying waste the countryside. With the Rangers he commanded, he had been merciless and thorough in his work, leaving no one and nothing in his wake. At the same time he had become an expert in intelligence work. He could scout a large area undetected, infiltrate enemy lines and positions as if they were hardly more than an inconvenience, and no prisoner could remain silent under the pressure of his interrogation.

While carrying out his duties, he had encountered a kindred spirit, Captain Joseph Goreham. Goreham was a fearless and ferocious American in his early thirties, who had learned his trade of terror protecting English settlements in Nova Scotia against Acadian and Indian raiders. He came with Scott to Québec and both were about to march up country to the Chaudière River to find a prisoner who could inform Wolfe about the French ships that had been sent above Québec for safekeeping.

Scott, Goreham, and the Rangers came to attention when Wolfe arrived at Pointe-Lévy. The General did not waste much time. He greeted the troops and complimented them on the fine redoubts they had built. The officers, whose baggage had not yet reached them, looked less gloomy than they had on his visit the day before. Wolfe attributed their new mood to the arrival of fresh provisions from Boston. Before marching off with Mackellar and a company of light troops, he admonished Scott to avoid scalping anyone unless it was a Canadian disguised as an Indian.

In spite of his physical discomfort Wolfe walked briskly to another point jutting into the St. Lawrence west of Pointe-Lévy, known as Pointe-aux-Pères. Since it was barely four thousand feet across the river from Québec, he had a splendid view of the town.

Major Mackellar pointed out to him the Château Saint-Louis, the cathedral, the Séminaire, the Collège des Jésuites, the Hôtel-Dieu hospital, the Bishop's palace, the convent of the Ursulines, and other important buildings of the Upper Town. Through his telescope, Wolfe could actually see soldiers, sailors, and a few civilians walking along the narrow streets of the Lower Town or manning its batteries.

To the west of the town, Wolfe saw a long line of cliffs high above the St. Lawrence. Moving his gaze slightly to the east, he noticed a large plateau atop a bluff rising above the St. Lawrence. Mackellar told him the place was called the Plains of Abraham, sometimes known as the Heights. They were named after an Abraham Martin, who had come to Canada in 1614 and had remained there during the Kirke's occupation of Québec a quarter of a century later. Martin never owned the Heights, as far as Mackellar knew, but he had gone that way every day to water his animals in the St. Charles River. In 1759 the Plains were now the property of the Ursulines, whose convent Wolfe had just admired.

From the Intendant's palace outside the walls, Wolfe's eyes travelled to the Hôpital Général on the banks of the St. Charles River. His eyes followed that river to the St. Lawrence where he had a good view of the channel between the Ile d'Orléans and the cliffs of Beauport. He concluded that his fleet could not get close enough to bombard the Fench positions there. Furthermore, the French encampments made an attack from across the Montmorency Falls – east of the long French line of defence – difficult if not impossible.

As he stood there peering at the north shore both east and west of the town, another plan began to form in his mind. Could not a landing be made above Québec instead of below it? He remembered that he had mentioned such a possibility in the letter he had written to his uncle while crossing the Atlantic. Looking over Mackellar's charts, Wolfe found a spot on the north shore three miles west of Québec called Saint-Michel. About half a mile east of it was a place known as Anse-au-Foulon, a cove from which apparently a most difficult path led up to the top of the cliffs. The Foulon was situated in the bay of l'Anse-des-Mères.

Ignoring the pain in his bladder, Wolfe paced up and down while he asked himself again if he could land at Saint-Michel. He did not know. Saunders would have to be consulted, some reconnaissance work would have to be carried out, and he would have to arrange a diversion around Beauport to confuse the French.

In the meantime, while he gathered the necessary information, he could amuse himself by bombarding Québec. Before leaving Pointe-aux-Pères he chose the sites for the batteries the English would build to bombard the town Wolfe meant to capture.

East of the French line, Beauport
2:00 P.M.

The prospect of deciphering yet another of Montcalm's handwritten letters, with its small, almost illegible characters, dismayed François-Gaston de Lévis, the tall, handsome forty-year-old officer who was second-in-command of the regular troops. Fortunately for his disposition, Monsieur Marcel, not Montcalm, had written the message Lévis had just received.

Lévis came from one of the noblest and most ancient families in France. One of his ancestors had fought in the third crusade (1190). Unfortunately for Lévis, though, his family was also one of the poorest in the nobility. But Lévis had wits, tact, and courage. In his teens he had joined the army and had risen steadily in rank, in part because of his family ties and in part thanks to his commitment. At the time when he should have led a regiment of his own, he had been too poor to afford one. Consequently when in 1756 Louis XV offered him the post of second-in-command to Montcalm in Canada, he had accepted. He was the third Lévis to serve in New France: Henri de Lévis, Duc de Ventadour, and François-Christophe de Lévis, Duc de Danville, had been viceroys in 1625 and 1644 respectively. In accepting the King's offer, Lévis had been conscious that the beleaguered colony, besieged by France's traditional enemy, could offer him many opportunities to advance his career. Also the pay and the supplementary allowances were more than adequate to cover his expenses, even allowing him the luxury of bringing five servants to Canada.

Even though both he and Montcalm came from the south of France, those who saw them together were often struck by the differences between them. Lévis towered over everyone, not only physically but practically in every other aspect. He was a natural leader, even-tempered, diplomatic, and self-assured. He seldom changed his mind, and once a decision was made he never reopened the question. He had taken no part in the intrigues that stormed around the French establishment in Canada, but at the same time he had never missed an opportunity to

remind his superiors in France of his existence and accomplishments. Versailles had always obliged by giving him additional
pensions and promoting him regularly.

Montcalm, on the other hand, had to work hard at being
accepted as leader and most of the time he was not taken
seriously. His pessimism made him unsure of himself, he questioned the decisions he had taken over and over again, and he
perpetually needed confirmation that he had done the right
thing. Unlike Lévis, who never uttered one more word than was
necessary, Montcalm babbled almost incessantly, with little tact
and diplomacy.

Perhaps the only trait Lévis and Montcalm had in common
was their all-consuming ambition for glory, which brought
wealth to Lévis and useful contacts to Montcalm. It is doubtful
that either of them cared much about Canada; to them it was
nothing more than a battlefield on which they would obtain their
commissions, earn their medals and titles and find *la gloire*.

Upon first meeting Lévis, Vaudreuil had liked him and they had
become fast friends. Vaudreuil, though, shamelessly used Lévis in
his feud with Montcalm, never missing an opportunity to praise
Lévis publicly, to defer to him and to take his advice while ignoring Montcalm's, and to promote him at Versailles as a more suitable commander than Montcalm. But Lévis took no part in
Montcalm's humiliation. Montcalm was his commanding officer
and Lévis' career would not be served if he forgot that. Furthermore, he had a genuine respect and affection for Montcalm. For
his part, Montcalm was grateful that Lévis allowed him to dis-
close "all my weaknesses and the innermost secrets of my heart."
Lévis never betrayed these confidences.

During the three years he had passed in Canada, Lévis had
participated in three major campaigns. In all of them he had
fought valiantly and bravely but without great distinction.
Between campaigns he lived in Montréal, where he had a most
active and splendid social life. He had no qualms about that: it
was a perk of command.

In this, Lévis was less of a hypocrite than Montcalm, who
piously disapproved of balls and fine dinners while food was
scarce for the inhabitants of Canada, yet did not have the cour-

age to refuse any of the invitations he received and did all he could to make the gatherings successful.

For instance, this is what he said in a letter to Lévis on January 17, 1759. Montcalm had been invited to a picnic for the following day. The organizers, Madame Gauthier and Madame de la Naudière, had invited fifty-two people. "They count on me," Montcalm wrote. "I can never be an ordinary guest. I have to supply the lights, the violins, as much wine and beer as I can, the food for twenty-six of the sixty-six dishes to be served, the two tables needed and the chairs." Even though, "I do not amuse myself much" at these affairs, he had to go so as not "to embarrass anyone, particularly the charming ladies." And this at a time when he knew the English were coming and the population and the soldiers under him did not have the wherewithal to prepare one dish, let alone sixty-six.

When Lévis attended balls and soirées he was usually accompanied by his mistress, Marie-Marguerite Pennisseaut, the beautiful wife of Louis Pennisseaut, a merchant in business with Bigot. They would be escorted by the most handsome of the young officers in Lévis'command, as both Lévis and Montcalm admired fine-looking young men. Once, in writing to Lévis about an event he had just attended, Montcalm said: "I swear to you that you would prefer him [the young soldier who had come with Montcalm] to La Naudière [one of Lévis' favourites]." As usual, Montcalm, not wanting to be caught, ended his letter with, "But *Motus*; burn my letter."

As Lévis read Montcalm's letter dated July 2, he sensed the general's panic. "I am alarmed at our position," Montcalm had dictated, "and I beg you to think it over openly and without reservation."

The "position" Montcalm was referring to was the French line of defence at Beauport. It was a meandering one of some fifteen to eighteen miles long, most of which was defended by the Canadian militia. Montcalm, being of the opinion that the English would attack him in the centre of his line, (where his regular troops were) wanted to strengthen it further by shortening the left flank which Lévis commanded, even though this would make Lévis' rear vulnerable to attack.

Lévis was responsible for this meandering front. He had persuaded Vaudreuil that the Montmorency was a natural barrier the French should use to good advantage. So Lévis was not prepared to make any changes to the line except peripheral accommodations in an emergency. He was convinced that Montcalm would accept his opinion. After all, Montcalm had written: "I write to you frankly, but will defer to your advice. Let us, however, try to be of only one mind, my dear Chevalier, for friendship and a common interest should lead us to do so."

Monckton's camp, Pointe-Lévy
Early evening

Mercifully the day was over. The Canadians and the Indians seemed to have disappeared, Wolfe was safely back aboard his vessel, and the officers and soldiers appeared content as the sutlers prepared their evening meal. Monckton could therefore sip his tea quietly.

No sooner had he begun than Major Scott arrived from his excursion to the Chaudière River. He reported that he had not found anyone to satisfy Wolfe's demands for a prisoner. The Rangers would have to try again another day.

Scott had had one casualty. A young Ranger was missing, and in spite of a thorough search he had not been found. Where the man was from and who he was, Scott had no accurate information, nor did Goreham. Monckton sent both of them back to Saint-Laurent to report to Wolfe. (No one knows who the Ranger was and what happened to him. Let me tell you what I imagine happened.)

The young woman had watched the English soldiers walking along the Chaudière River. She had not moved from the security of the woods bordering the opposite bank of the river, though she had had great difficulty controlling her dog. She saw the arrow fly out of nowhere and hit the last soldier in the column. As his companions marched on, unaware of his plight, he had tumbled into the river and had been carried away by the current. When the soldiers had come back to search for him there was no body to be found, and they had retreated in the direction from which they had first appeared.

Now that they had disappeared from view, she left her hiding place and, followed by the dog, she hurried downriver towards her village. Soon the dog stopped and barked furiously, staring intently at the water. Afraid but curious, the girl searched in the underbrush on the edge of the water and found the body of the soldier, his shoulder pierced with the arrow. Mumbling a prayer to the Virgin Mary, she went to him. His body was caught in the bushes. She tried to dislodge it with her foot, but it would not move. Not knowing what to do next, she studied the body closely. Death did not frighten her. She had seen too much of it. However, when she heard his moan and he turned his head towards her, she almost fainted. She quickly blessed herself, a gesture that seemed to inspire her. Making certain he would not float away, she ordered the dog to stay and rushed home to fetch her grandfather.

An hour later, she came out of the woods on horseback followed by an old man riding a horse almost as ancient as himself. The dog, wagging his tail, went to meet them. Quickly she dismounted and rushed to the bank. The soldier still lay half in the water.

The old man followed her more slowly. "*Mais Elisabeth, c'est un Anglais,*" he said with disgust. Of course she knew he was English, she told him. Still, he needed their help.

"*Mais ce sont nos ennemis!*" he reproached her urgently. The French authorities would certainly not take kindly to what she proposed to do. They could be arrested, even hanged, he went on. As he was over seventy, death was not a problem for him, but she was seventeen. "*C'est mieux de le laisser mourir.*" They could say a prayer though.

"*Non!*" she said. They could not let him die. Had not the old man taught her to be kind, especially to strangers, she argued. Did not the teachings of the Church state that caring for the sick and the dying was an act of mercy that God would certainly reward? She carried on at length, piling every social and religious argument one on top of the other until she clinched it all with, *"Maman serait d'accord!"*

He knew that. Her mother, who could never leave well enough alone, would carry on just like her daughter. Having lived with both of them for most of his grown life, he realized that if he did not do what Elisabeth wanted, she would find some other way of doing it herself. Giving up, he walked down to the soldier. The man was breathing slowly and with difficulty. His heartbeat was uneven. Fortunately the cold water had prevented a tragic loss of blood. But it would not do to tarry.

"Il faut faire vite," he commanded. Using all their strength, they dragged the Ranger out of the water and hoisted him as best they could on the old man's horse. She jumped on hers as she had seen the Indians do, and the three of them, followed by the dog, moved into the shelter of the woods. They followed the path that led to the hut deep in the woods. It had not been used since the spring when they had tapped the maples, boiled the sap, and reduced it to a sweet syrup and slabs of brown sugar. The process had been learned from the Indians.

The *cabane à sucre* was a sacred place to her and her mother. Both took refuge there often to talk and exchange confidences. And it was there that – for the first time – a boy had kissed her, awakening so deep a desire in her that she blushed every time she recalled the incident. In that secret and safe place, she would make the soldier well. Why? She did not know. Her grandfather was a wizard at preparing teas and potions of all sorts with herbs and leaves and whatever was at hand. The Indians had taught him well when he first came alone to this land, their valley. She knew he could not refuse her anything.

When they arrived at the cabin they lifted the soldier gently and laid him on old sacks piled high in a corner. Afraid of being detected, they could not light a fire, so she placed more sacks on top of him for warmth. The old man left to fetch water and blankets and his healing remedies.

While he was gone, she undressed the soldier. His shoulder pack proved no problem, nor did the green Indian leggings that he had fastened at his ankles and below the knees. She removed his moccasins, and unbuttoned his green jacket, cutting it carefully around the arrow still implanted in him. With difficulty she removed the jacket and his undershirt. She deliberated about his breeches. However, they had to come off, they were all wet. She did not mind his nakedness. In fact, she realized for the first time how handsome his muscular body was. Before her admiration led her into mortal sin, she thought to herself, she had better cover him up.

As she waited for her grandfather to return, she went through his pockets and pack. There was nothing of much interest to her: a few good short knives, a small pouch with money in it, some tobacco, a pipe, a rubber sack she did not know the use of, a little food, and some ammunition. There were only two pieces of paper. One was a letter, the other, a document. Both bore the inscription "James Montague," which she presumed was his name, and both came from a place called Virginia. On the document she found a date on the same line as his name: September 17, 1740. His date of birth, she thought. "*Comme tu es jeune, Monsieur Montague,*" she said out loud. He would be nineteen this coming September. She also found a locket containing the picture of a woman, older than he, quite beautiful and kind-looking. Glancing at the unconscious soldier, she recognized the resemblance. "*Sa maman,*" she said and placed the locket in his hand.

Half an hour later, her grandfather returned with blankets, clean towels, and an assortment of pots and pans containing water, herbs, and hot bricks. She admired him; the old man certainly knew how to survive. He placed the bricks on the stove and told her to heat up some water and a few of the rocks he handed her. Also she was not to look at what he was doing.

While she busied herself at the stove, he took some mud from one of his pouches, the large knife he had tied to one of bricks to keep it warm, and some leaves. Standing on the right of the American, he opened the soldier's mouth, placed a piece of wood between his teeth and tied his mouth shut in case he screamed. Then the old man made a large hole around the arrow so that the head of it would come out more easily. He knew that the pain was hardly bearable but there was no other way. Bracing himself against the table, he gave a mighty pull. The soldier's head jerked back in pain and his eyes opened wide with horror, but the arrow was out. Feeling his way into the wound as best he could, Elisabeth's grandfather checked how far the arrow had penetrated. It had gone in deeply. He stopped the bleeding with mud packs and leaves and then called to Elisabeth to bring him the hot water and the rocks. He washed the wound thoroughly and seared the flesh with the rocks, causing the soldier so much pain that he fainted. Elisabeth did not flinch. She held the soldier's hand and wiped his brow. The old man finished his task by filling the wound with leaves and bandaging it.

"Il va vivre," he told his granddaugther. She knew. Few ministered by him ever died. Before leaving – for both together could not be away from the settlement for any length of time – he gave her his instructions. In about an hour and every hour thereafter, she was to give the soldier a drink of one of his tisanes. He would return at dawn and change the bandages. She was not to worry if the young man became delirious or started to hallucinate. She was to keep him warm and quiet.

After her grandfather had gone, Elisabeth cleaned up and prepared for the long vigil, guarded by the dog at her feet. When her father had died, mangled by a falling tree, she had sat like this, in that very hut, wrapped in blankets, praying and waiting for the end that, mercifully, had come before sunrise. She hoped that this vigil would have a different dénouement.

The hours passed easily enough. At one point, the soldier regained consciousness and whispered something she could not understand. Every hour, she lifted his head and made him drink as she had been told. This simple act seemed to leave him exhausted. He would thrash about with horrible nightmares. After one of the drinks he moaned and screamed. Then he began to shiver furiously. She piled more blankets on top of him, but still he would not stop. Not knowing what else to do she lay beside him, cradling him in her arms and whispering his name and hers over and over again. After a while he lay quiet. Before he fell asleep, he whispered, "E-li-sa-beth."

(This tale I have just told you is not far-fetched. English soldiers were left behind, wounded, after such skirmishes; someone must have looked after them beside the nuns at the Hôpital Général. Other soldiers deserted after meeting a girl along the way. Soon many were involved in various relationships, which the Church had to sanction when it was all over.)

Montcalm's headquarters at Beauport
Later that night

Earlier that evening, Montcalm had tried once again to persuade Vaudreuil to authorize an attack on Pointe-Lévy. For reasons Montcalm could not explain no decision had been taken and, as commander-in-chief, Montcalm had not imposed a solution. Instead he had returned to his manorhouse frustrated and irritable, wondering who, if anyone, was in charge. He had no confidence in Vaudreuil, nor the Governor General in him. And even though Montcalm had the power to overrule Vaudreuil, it never entered his mind to do so.

At his house, he found Lévis' letter insisting that their line of defence should remain as it had been drawn. Since both had to appear to work with one voice, one purpose, Montcalm had to honour Lévis' opinion.

Later, much later after his return, Marcel found Montcalm asleep, his head resting on the top of his work table.

July 5, 1759

(Day Ten)

Carré Saint-Louis, Québec
Early in the morning

The militia stationed in the town of Québec was on strike. They had struck the day before when a few of them had been asked to man a lookout across from the English on the south shore. They had refused, arguing with their captains that unless they were treated like the regular troops and were given the same guns, the same ammunition, supplies, and rations, they would go home and let the French fight it out alone with the English.

Their officers had taken the matter seriously enough to go to Vaudreuil to persuade him to make changes. He had agreed to some, but to be on the safe side, he had asked Montcalm to inspect the militia and knock some sense into them. Consequently a parade had been arranged for the tenth day of the siege.

Since dawn the militia had been drawn up waiting for Montcalm's arrival. The wretched rain had soaked them through and the murmurs of dissension were loud. Lefebvre was one of the militia waiting in the rain. (Mennard was away with the Bishop at Charlesbourg.) When they had both joined the Syntaxe Royale, visions of exciting and brave deeds had danced in their heads. The reality, however, was vastly different. Their days were taken up with drills and exercises, parades and lengthy speeches about loyalty to the King. It was hard work digging trenches, boarding up houses, and building fortifications. Their French officers constantly contradicted each other, and no one appeared to be in command and fully knowledgeable about what had to be done. And they were hungry all the time, the allotted ration barely enough to keep them alive. Lefebvre's mother brought some food when she had any to spare, but more often than not the other soldiers stole it from them.

(The Syntaxe Royale battalion consisted of the students of the Séminaire and of the Collège des Jésuites. The existence of such a unit has provided much merriment to many historians, who have gone out of their way to ridicule the students. They would have had a different reaction had they understood that the students, many of whom were still in their teens, carried guns at vast risk to their vocation for the priesthood. Very few of them returned to their studies after the war. I prefer to see them as young men inspired by a great devotion to their country. They volunteered – and that is the key word – to face temporal and spiritual perils that, at their young age, they could hardly fathom.)

In talking about the war, the students and some of the farmers who served in the militia criticized the apparent standstill of the French war effort. They had joined up in the hope that the English would be stopped where they were and that the whole episode would be over quickly, allowing the students to return to their studies and the farmers to their fields. However, the opposite was happening. The English practically had the run of the country. Every day Lefebvre's mother took up her vigil on one of the quays, watching the English entrenching themselves on the south shore. What she saw – thousands of soldiers and rows upon rows of tents, batteries with huge black guns aimed at Québec, hundreds of ships and barges all waiting for the day of confrontation – terrified her.

It also frightened many of those standing in line with Lefebvre waiting for Montcalm. The passivity of the authorities alarmed them, and they wondered how long it would be before they would see their wives and their children again. They worried about the security of their homes and farms, about the harvest, which had already been seriously endangered, about the winter that would all too soon engulf them, and about Bigot, whose soldiers could force their wives to hand over the food they had carefully hidden.

And so there they were, close to one thousand of them, drawn up, soaked to the skin, and waiting. The students were dressed in a grey uniform with red lapels and cuffs and a black three-cornered hat trimmed in red. A few of the militia had the same uniform, but most of them had come to Québec in their usual clothing: a woollen tuque, which hid their long hair tied in a ponytail, a thick, greenish shirt with a vest of the same material, a pair of thick brown pants tied below the knee, black leggings, and moccasins. On each of their belts hung a cartridge pouch, a tomahawk, and several knives, and they all carried muskets in various states of disrepair. Their officers wore grey breeches, a blue tunic, a gorget (a plaque to protect the neck) made of copper, which denoted their rank. Each officer also carried a sword.

At nine-thirty precisely, Montcalm rode up on his black horse accompanied by Bougainville, his two aides-de-camp, and an escort of cavalry. To the young Lefebvre it looked impressive, and, as if by enchantment, the rain stopped.

Montcalm galloped up and down between the ranks at great speed, frightening the militia half to death. While they remained at attention he had a short talk with their officers, then turning around, he harangued them sternly. There would be no more talk of desertion or sedition, he told them, or he would hang as many as were necessary. He did his best to frighten them, depicting vividly the possible rape of their wives and daughters should the English defeat the French. He reminded them that the enemy was Protestant and that they would certainly go to hell should they assist their religious foes in any way. But then to ease the tension, he announced that their rations would henceforth be the same as those of the regular troops. To deafening shouts of *"Vive le Roi!"*, Montcalm left the square. And the rain started again.

As the militiamen returned to their duties in a better mood, Lefebvre met Father Baudouin on the terrace along the Château Saint-Louis. Across the St. Lawrence, the English were moving more troops to the south shore.

By this time, and in spite of the ceaseless rain, the frightening thunder and lightning, and the paralyzing hail storms that had gone on for days, the English at Pointe-Lévy had done a great deal of work. They had finished setting up and fortifying their camp; the church was transformed into a hospital; redoubts and platforms for the batteries were built; and the installation at Pointe-aux-Pères was progressing rapidly. The food was passable, the officers' baggage had arrived, and life was relatively comfortable in spite of the occasional harassment from a few Canadian and Indian snipers.

Wolfe was by now seriously entertaining the thought of attacking the French, not at Beauport as he had originally planned, but above the town. Admiral Saunders had agreed to a landing, perhaps at Saint-Michel on the north shore, should it be possible for his ships to pass safely the French batteries in the harbour. But before any further preparation could be done, Wolfe had to find if the troops could indeed land at Saint-Michel.

As it was not possible to reconnoitre the north shore directly, Wolfe had sent Brigadier James Murray, his junior brigadier, to Monckton's camp on July 4. From there, Murray was to proceed to the Etchemin River directly opposite Saint-Michel.

A word about James Murray. He was born in Scotland, the fifth son and the fourteenth child of the fourth Baron Elibank, six years before Wolfe. At age fourteen, he became a cadet, entering the permanent army four years later as a second lieutenant. In 1741, he joined the 15th Foot Regiment, with which he served in the West Indies, Cuba, and Flanders, where he was seriously wounded during the siege of Ostend in Belgium in 1745. A year later Murray and Wolfe met, but it does not appear to have been a pleasant experience for either of them. However, by the time they served together in Louisbourg in 1758, they had patched whatever differences there were between them. Murray fought with distinction and valour under Wolfe. In an official dispatch after the battle, Wolfe referred to Murray's "infinite spirit." Wolfe, no doubt, had this quality in mind when he asked Pitt to assign Murray to the Great Enterprise. Wolfe was being generous, for Murray was not a very talented soldier. As an officer, he was hot-headed, impetuous, arrogant, and strict. As a man, he was weak, often silly, and could not forgive himself for not having better connections.

_____

At the head of a column of soldiers from the 43rd Foot, Murray marched in the rain a few miles up the south shore to the Etchemin River. As he went along, he surveyed carefully through his telescope the terrain across the St. Lawrence between the Québec Citadel and Saint-Michel. He made careful notes, particularly of the movement of French troops, about two hundred by his reckoning, in and around Sillery not too far from Saint-Michel. When he was satisfied with his reconnaissance, he returned to Monckton's camp, where he decided to spend the next few days. He sent word to Wolfe that a landing at Saint-Michel was possible and that he was "satisfied with the practicability" of using rafts to carry the troops into shore.

Aboard a French vessel in the St. Lawrence
Noon

The chancellor, as François-Marc-Antoine Le Mercier was called, was somewhat put out to have been summoned yet again. It was raining and not the best of weather for a parley in the middle of the river. But he realized that these flags of truce, arranged by both sides for various reasons, provided opportunities for the enemies to spy on each other. For instance, the English sent engineers disguised as sailors to assess the strength of the French fortifications in and around Québec. The French reciprocated by transforming captains into ordinary seamen in order to observe the size, the extent, and the movements of Saunders' fleet.

François-Marc-Antoine Le Mercier was a thirty-seven-year-old French military officer and trader who had arrived in Canada at the age of eighteen in 1740. Over the years he had become an engineer and an artillery officer – and a very rich man. Montcalm, who considered Le Mercier "ignorant and weak" and occupied more with his finances than his profession, estimated his fortune at about one million French *livres*.

Fortunes were easily made in those days. Le Mercier's came to him through his duties as an artillery officer. He had spent many years in the interior of Canada, where he was able to arrange an effective monopoly on the purchase and sale of furs. Furthermore, in many campaigns he was the officer charged with the distribution of food, supplies, ammunition, and powder to the army. In this capacity, and since he was one of Bigot's associates, he had an opportunity to make a handsome profit, though he was never found guilty of embezzlement.

Money flowed quickly through Le Mercier's hands as he was an habitual gambler, losing vast sums at Bigot's gaming tables. He married well in November 1757 to an heiress, Françoise Boucher de la Bruère. Interestingly, Le Mercier was one of the few Huguenots in New France, a fact that few of his fellow officers knew. He converted to Roman Catholicism and was baptized just three days prior to his marriage. Apparently his religious persuasion did not hinder his career.

Montcalm did not like him in part because he was jealous of Le Mercier's wealth, but also because Le Mercier had been able to bring about the fall of Chouaguen (Oswego) during Montcalm's first campaign in Canada in 1756. Montcalm, with his usual hesitation, had not been able to make up his mind where to place his artillery. Le Mercier had decided it for him. By arranging his nine guns in such a way as to fire over the walls of the Fort, he had brought about the fall of the English stationed there. In spite of this coup, Le Mercier was not a great artillery officer. He was, nevertheless, a conscientious one.

When the English arrived in Québec in June 1759, Le Mercier was placed in charge of the artillery. As such, he was responsible for some three hundred cannon and mortars of different sizes and calibres scattered over twenty miles of territory. By tradition, the commander of the artillery was also the chancellor of the colony, arranging for such matters as flags of truce. This is why on this rainy day Le Mercier found himself in a flotilla of four small boats in the middle of the St. Lawrence River waiting for the return of a group of ladies whom the English had captured on their way up to Québec.

The first time Le Mercier had been called out had been on July 1 when a longboat bearing an English flag of truce had sailed into the basin. The English had wanted to know the health of three young midshipmen whom the Canadians had captured on June 8 riding horses bareback on the Ile-aux-Coudres. One of them was Admiral Durell's nephew. Since then the young men had been confined in Québec in comfortable quarters. Le Mercier had told his counterpart that the midshipmen were well and that they would be sent back to their ships shortly before Admiral Saunders left for England.

The ladies who had been scheduled to be transferred at eleven o'clock, arrived at noon. After the usual formalities, the affable captain of the *Alcide*, Charles Douglas, helped the ladies into the French rowboats and made small talk with Le Mercier. Before returning to his ship, Douglas handed the chancellor two bottles of fine liqueur, a gift from Wolfe to Bigot, and some letters for the Intendant, one of which was from Bigot's sister. After delivering the women to Father Récher, who would make the arrangements for them to travel to Trois-Rivières, Le Mercier sent one of his men to Bigot's headquarters at Beauport with the bottles from Wolfe.

When Le Mercier's envoy arrived at the farmhouse which served Bigot as his headquarters, the Intendant was in a cantankerous mood. He was scared. He was also puzzled at Montcalm's reticence and Vaudreuil's procrastination. Above all, he was not making as much money as he should as there were no parties to be organized, and he missed his mistress.

In cold daylight, François Bigot was an ugly man, small and overweight. He had unruly yellowish hair piled above an unattractive face covered with pimples. Suffering from nasal scabs that gave out an unpleasant odour, he spent vast sums of money on perfumes and fragrant waters to conceal his affliction. One of his many servants was always standing at his side with an armful of handkerchiefs scented with various *eaux de toilette*. The sweet, sticky smell permeated the small room that served him as an office and made Le Mercier's man almost throw up.

As Intendant, Bigot was a career officer in the Department of Marine in the civil administration of ports and colonies. In Canada he was responsible for all internal and external trade, for finances, for industry and agriculture, for prices and taxation, and for police and the administration of justice. Bigot had joined the department at the age of twenty and sixteen years later had been sent to Louisbourg and to Québec in 1740. He was intelligent, well-organized, efficient, and an indefatigable worker. He was also a womanizer, a sybarite, a gambler, and a crook.

His mistress, Angélique-Geneviève Renaud d'Avène des Méloizes Péan, known to her intimate circle as Lélie, was a beautiful, charming, witty, and obliging Canadian woman, who had become Bigot's mistress shortly after his arrival in Canada. She was then twenty-five years old and he twenty years her senior. Eleven years later, he could still find in her the beauty that had enchanted him when he had first met her. Over the years he had come to know her not only as a sensuous woman, but as a formidable one as well. Compared often to Madame de Pompadour, Lélie was strong-willed, determined, diplomatic, and unflinching in the pursuit of her interests, and those of her husband and her relatives. She gave exquisite parties at her house on Rue Saint-Louis, was an amusing conversationalist, and took great risks at the gambling tables. Everyone paid her court and no one dared say anything derogatory against her. What she saw in Bigot, she kept to herself.

Her officer-trader husband was made of different stuff, however. Michel-Jean-Hughes Péan came from an old Canadian military family. His military career had progressed rapidly even though his talents were far from remarkable. What was uncommon about Péan, Bigot had discovered, was his resourcefulness at making important friends and serving them loyally thereafter. When his wife became Bigot's mistress, Péan became Bigot's business partner. He grew immensely rich in the process. He encouraged the relationship between his wife and the Intendant because Bigot made him rich, provided him with social standing in colonial society, and opened doors for him in France.

Bigot was well pleased with the two bottles of liqueur Wolfe had sent and reciprocated by sending Le Mercier back into the St. Lawrence with a couple of baskets of *fines herbes* and an assortment of delicacies for Wolfe. After all, when the war was over, they might meet on the streets of Paris!

La Canardière
Early evening

The pouches from the West the courier had brought the night before lay unopened on Vaudreuil's table. The old man, fearing the worst possible news, had not had the heart to deal with them. The matter could no longer be delayed, however. Before his evening meal, he went through all of them. From Bourlamaque in the Lake Champlain district he found out that an English army of 11,000 men, under Jeffery Amherst, had finally arrived. Bourlamaque had under his command three of the eight regiments of the regular troops stationed in Canada, some colonial troops, a few militia and Indians, in all approximately four thousand men. Far from enough, but Vaudreuil could send him no reinforcements.

Jeffery Amherst was the conqueror of Louisbourg and one of the most overrated men in the annals of warfare and diplomacy. He had an astonishing capacity for fooling people, particularly those in high places, who promoted him accordingly. During the campaigns against the French and Canadians he proved to be relatively incompetent and quite insecure. He was also a domineering racist and a prig.

He became commander-in-chief of the English forces in North America in November 1758. He was forty-two years old and an army veteran of twenty years. While Wolfe went to Québec, Pitt had sent Amherst to put an end to the French empire in Canada "by the Way of Crown Point [Fort Saint-Frédéric] or la Galette [at the head of the St. Lawrence rapids], or both, according as you shall judge practicable and proceed, if practicable, and attack Montreal or Quebec, or both of the said places successively." Amherst was also to rebuild Oswego (Chouaguen) on Lake Ontario, the fort that Montcalm had destroyed in 1756, and to capture Fort Niagara.

Amherst never did anything quickly. He spent some time – not too successfully – seeking the assistance of the American colonies, and then at the beginning of May he went to Albany, New York, where he made his final plans and assembled the large stores he would need for such an undertaking. He had an army of 16,000 regular and provincial troops, 5,000 of which he put under the command of Brigadier-General John Prideaux for the expeditions to Oswego and Niagara. The rest Amherst took to the Lake Champlain wilderness to attack the French positions at Ticonderoga (Carillon) and Crown Point (Saint-Frédéric). He reached the head of Lake George (Lac Saint-Sacrement) on June 21. And there he waited.

In order to send reinforcements to Bourlamaque, Vaudreuil would have had to evacuate Fort Niagara, the most important French fort in the West and the guardian of the French empire in the regions of the Great Lakes. To lose the fort would mean forfeiting the loyalty of the Indians to the English. Without the Indians, the territories could not be held. Without the territories, the lucrative fur trade would fall in hostile hands, brankrupting many in Vaudreuil's entourage.

With Pierre Pouchot, in command at Niagara, relations with the Indians were in good hands. Pouchot, the forty-six-year-old French officer and military engineer, was a most cunning and formidable man. His success with the Indians was legendary. According to Bougainville, "they adored" him and had named him Sategariouan or The Centre of Good Transaction.

Pouchot had obtained his command in Niagara through Lévis' influence. Vaudreuil had had misgivings because Canadians regarded the post as their preserve and they had been successful in forcing the Governor General to recall Pouchot once before in 1757. However, Lévis had persuaded Vaudreuil that the only man who could keep the Indians on the side of France during the coming crisis was Pouchot. Vaudreuil had eventually concurred.

Pouchot had gone to Niagara towards the end of March 1759 but Vaudreuil had not yet heard from him.

Now is the place to tell you how this war, this invasion of Canada on three fronts, came to be. I have delayed this long because I did not want to bother you with a lengthy history lesson. But I can tarry no longer. In a fifteen-year career as a teacher, I never once put one of my students to sleep. I pray I can repeat this feat one more time.

On May 13, 1607, four years after the founding of Acadia by the French, a hundred English settlers established a colony at Jamestown, on the James River, on a tract of land known as Virginia, in North America. A year later, on July 3, 1608, Samuel de Champlain built his house on a point of land jutting into the St. Lawrence River. The Indians called this place The Narrowing of the River: Quebecq.

Several historians claim that with these two foundations, the struggle for North America between France and England, between Canada and the United States of America, began. It is a very seductive claim. The population in the British colonies grew much more rapidly than in Canada – by 1759, there were one and a half million British colonials and only seventy thousand Canadians. According to most historians I have read, it was, therefore, inevitable that war would come and that annexation or some rearrangement of frontiers would follow.

Well I am not going to be seduced by that argument. I am convinced that had there not been circumstances in Europe that made war between France and England desirable, I would be telling you another tale about 1759. I do not believe that the danger to Canada came from the British colonies. If it had, I have no doubt that the Canadians, left to themselves, would have beaten the Americans off, as they were better, more experienced, and more aggressive fighters than their neighbours. After all, the Canadians had spent their existence in North America in almost total warfare: taking possession of the land, assisting the missionaries, dealing with the Indians and learning their ways, mastering the trade routes, and maintaining th ... lines of supply within the interior of their continent. Out of the hundred and fifty or so years that the

French empire lasted in the New World, the Canadians enjoyed a total of only forty-two years of peace.

The first enemies to be conquered or subdued were the native Indians, particularly the five Iroquois nations living around Montréal. When a peace treaty was finally signed with them on August 4, 1701, the violent struggle of the aboriginal and white men had lasted almost a hundred years. The cost in lives had been staggering on both sides, and the final phase of the war, in the 1690s, had practically ruined the economy of New France. But the Iroquois had been neutralized.

In these early days of Canada, the English settlers to the south did not threaten French interests and Canadian settlements. Geography created natural barriers between the colonists: the Green Mountains in Vermont; the White Mountains in New Hampshire and Maine; the Adirondacks in New York; and the Appalachians in the Carolinas, Virginia, Maryland, and Pennsylvania. As well, other factors combined to make the American settlers unwilling to endanger themselves by attacking their neighbours to the north. Despite their differences in religion, language, and government, and despite the natural barriers of the mountains, there was a lucrative illegal trade between them that no one wanted to end. The American colonies lacked cohesiveness, dissension was rife among them, and they resented their British masters far more than their Canadian neighbours. Left to their own devices, both sides might have continued to co-exist. Who knows? The only major hostility between the English and French colonies was on the northeastern seaboard, caused by New England's need to expand northward in order to protect its fishing industry, which was endangered by the strong French presence.

In the eighteenth century, imperial interests determined the fate of North America. Three major European wars between 1702 and 1760 sealed the fate of the Americans and Canadians: the War of the Spanish Succession (1702–1713), the War of the Austrian Succession (1744–1748), and the Seven Years' War (1756–1763). These came here as the Queen Anne's War, the King George's War, and the French and Indian War.

In the Queen Anne's War, the French lost Terre-Neuve (Newfoundland). They also lost all of Acadia except Ile Saint-Jean

(Prince Edward Island) and Ile Royale (Cape Breton) which became the eastern outpost of the French Empire. Its centre was at Louisbourg, founded that same year, which soon became an important base for the fishing industry, a lucrative seaport, and the mightiest fortress in North America. In time, Louisbourg – the symbol of Acadia – threatened New England's prosperity and expansion.

Acadia had originally comprised all of the Maritime provinces, the Gaspé Peninsula and eastern Maine. It had been founded four years before Québec in 1604, and for the next century the life of the small Acadian population had been precarious, as the colony was tossed back and forth between the rival claims of France and England. By the time it became an English possession in 1713, there were two thousand Acadians, mostly French-speaking and Catholic, although there were a few who were Protestant and English-speaking. Buffeted by wars and raids, the Acadians concentrated their energies in establishing themselves firmly in a country they regarded as their homeland. The change of name from Acadia to Nova Scotia in 1713 did not weaken – I am proud to say – their resolve to live on their land. But now let's turn back to the consequences of the Queen Anne's War in the rest of North America.

In that war Canada fared better, for the two expeditions organized to conquer it failed miserably. One expedition was to reach Montréal by land from Lake Champlain. The other, an imposing enterprise of fifteen warships and sixty-nine transports under Sir Hovenden Walker, was to ascend the St. Lawrence and capture Québec. The land expedition was abandoned, and the sea force was wrecked in a thick fog and high winds off Anticosti Island with the loss of many lives.

During the interval between the Queen Anne's and the King George's wars, the French encouraged the Micmac Indians – who hardly needed encouragement – to harass the English in Acadia. They also emboldened the Abenakis to do the same in New England. Meanwhile, the Canadians extended the French Empire beyond Lake Superior. Through the efforts of one of the greatest explorers of America, Pierre Gaultier de Varennes et de la Vérandrye, they reached the foot of the Rockies, eastablishing forts and trading posts and making allies of the Indians as they went along. At the same time the French position in the Ohio Valley was consolidated, to the dismay of American settlers in Virginia.

During King George's War (1744–1748), hostilities were concentrated in and around Nova Scotia. Governor William Shirley of Massachusetts mounted an expedition made up mostly of inexperienced militiamen, who nevertheless managed to conquer Louisbourg in June 1745 after a forty-eight-day siege. The garrison and all the inhabitants of Ile Royale were deported to France. A month later the New Englanders captured Ile Saint-Jean, but they allowed the six hundred Acadians living there to remain in return for their neutrality.

Encouraged by his victories, Shirley attempted to launch a massive attack against Canada. He was not successful, however, since the British colonies could neither muster the manpower nor find the sums necessary for such an enterprise. England, which had promised support, reneged as it was deeply embroiled in the war in Europe.

When peace returned in 1748, Louisbourg was given back to France, but a year later the English founded Halifax, where they built a fortress of their own. By the mid-1750s, Catholic France and Protestant England were harassing each other almost everywhere on earth, making war in Europe inevitable, yet again. Although no official state of war existed between them, they nevertheless pirated each other's ships and caused mischief wherever they could.

In America the colonists, particularly those of Viriginia, turned their attention westward, but everywhere they went a Franco-Canadian settlement, a trading post, a fort, or a missionary station barred the way. Hampered on the Atlantic coast and in the western wilderness, the American colonists were at their wits' end. Consequently, when in 1754, a "volley fired by a young Virginian [George Washington] in the backwoods of America," as Horace Walpole remarked, "set the world on fire," Great Britain acted and began to settle the score in its favour. It agreed to the deportation of the Acadians in 1755, scattering ten thousand of them all over North America. Since the British colonies could not see their way to act in unison despite Benjamin Franklin's efforts at the Albany Congress in 1754, England agreed to intervene directly against the French and the Canadians. And so for the first time it sent regular troops to America.

In the winter of 1755 a British army, under Major-General Edward Braddock, arrived in Virginia, from where he launched a four-pronged attack against the French. One army captured Fort Beausejour in what is now New Brunswick and renamed it Fort Cumberland. Another, made up of three thousand volunteers from New York with elected officers, their own muskets, and no uniforms, under the command of the remarkable William Johnson, was sent to attack Fort Saint-Frédéric at the head of Lake Champlain. There Johnson encountered French regular troops, which had been sent to Canada for the first time since the arrival of the Carignan-Salières regiment in 1665. After some rather strange strategy on the part of the French commander, Jean-Armand, Baron de Dieskau, the confrontation ended in a stalemate. Braddock also sent Shirley to dislodge the French at Niagara. But nothing came of that at all.

Braddock himself marched his mistress and his army of two thousand men through two hundred miles of wilderness to Fort Duquesne, situated at the confluence of the Allegheny and Monongahela rivers (now Pittsburgh, Pennsylvania) where the Americans had begun to build a fort in 1753. Braddock set out in May 1755 and encountered his fate on July 9 on the shores of the Monongahela River. After a battle that lasted five hours, in which he showed extraordinary courage, he was defeated by a force of 892 men, made up mostly of Canadians and Indians under the command of a French officer, Jean-Daniel Dumas. Braddock died four days later of wounds received during the battle: his mistress died fighting at his side.

When war finally and officially came in the shape of the Seven Years' War in May 1756, England was not ready to eliminate France, which was then militarily superior and the dominant European power. William Pitt the Elder, who became head of the government in July 1757 and the architect of the Conquest of Canada, acknowledged this when he told the House of Commons, "In every quarter of the world we are inferior to the French." Lord Chesterfield, the aristocrat famous for his letters to his son, had expressed the same feelings when he wrote, "The

French are masters to do what they please ... We are no longer a nation. I never saw so dreadful a prospect." To counteract this superiority, Pitt set about reforming England's army, limiting her commitments in continental Europe and building the mightiest navy in the world.

In the struggle that ensued, France's possessions in North America – in effect, Canada – became a primary target. A year after he came to power, Pitt made a supreme effort to defeat the French at Fort Carillon (Ticonderoga) between Lake Champlain and Lac Saint-Sacrement (Lake George) in the heart of the colony and at Louisbourg, the mighty fortress of the French on the shores of the Atlantic. Pitt poured 13,000 men into the Carillon expedition and 27,000 at Louisbourg. On July 8, 1758 the French general, the Marquis de Montcalm, with 3,500 troops, defeated Major-General James Abercrombie. A few days later, on July 26, Augustin de Boschenry de Drucour, the French Governor at Louisbourg, surrendered the remainder of his 8,000-man force to Major-General Jeffery Amherst.

Pitt was determined to administer the coup de grâce in 1759. To achieve this, he committed one-quarter of the Royal Navy under Saunders and three fully equipped and well-supplied armies. One army, commanded by Wolfe, was to conquer the town of Québec by way of the St. Lawrence and make its way up to Montréal; the second, with Prideaux at its head, was to march inland to the fort of Niagara, conquer it and then sail down Lake Ontario to Montréal; and the third, led by Amherst, was to reach the same destination through the centre of Canada by means of Lake Champlain.

Now I think you will understand that, by the time of the Conquest, the Canadians were very experienced in warfare. When left to their own devices they had consistently beaten the Americans, and had the English and the French regular troops not come to America in 1755 to "redress the balance of the old world in the new," the Conquest would not have taken place. And Toronto and the West – and probaly large chunks of the United States – today would be French-speaking. History, however, is made up of what did happen, not of what might have happened – or of wishful thinking!

July 9, 1759

(Day Fourteen)

Ile d'Orléans
Around midnight

The plan for a descent above Québec that Wolfe had begun to sketch a week earlier had had time to mature. Saunders was in favour of it, Murray found it practicable, and Wolfe had arranged diversions of various kinds to confuse the French as to his plans. The time had come for him to act.

But then Wolfe changed his mind. There would be no landing above Québec at this time. Instead he put another plan into full operation.

During the eighty-one days the siege of Québec lasted, Wolfe played this game often: He would make a plan only to change it at the first opportunity. Most of the time it is difficult to understand his reasoning.

On July 9, he changed his mind for three reasons. The first one was that Vaudreuil had sent three hundred Canadians to Anse-des-Mères (Murray had seen them) with such a large quantity of tents that Wolfe concluded, as Vaudreuil had intended, that more troops were coming.

The second reason was Wolfe's morbid insecurity. He feared that, once he had established a beachhead at Saint-Michel, he would not be able to reinforce "the body first landed" before it was attacked "by the enemy's whole army." At least that was the reason he gave to Pitt.

And third, Wolfe did not trust the navy to do the right thing and to do it expeditiously. The navy was exasperating him more and more. He complained that the seamen were committing all sorts of irregularities, that they were cowards refusing to engage the French gunboats, which were nothing more than "paltry boats carrying cannon in their prows," and that every day they permitted the enemy "to insult us with cannon fire." His overall conclusion was that there was "an amazing backwardness in these matters on the side of the Fleet." The sailors could not even aim properly. Earlier in the day, their bombardment of the French positions between the St. Charles River and the Montmorency did little damage as the English guns were well out of range. Wolfe had had no satisfaction in watching Montcalm move a few vulnerable troops out of reach of the English ships.

Wolfe's new plan consisted in moving the greatest part of his army (the Grenadiers, six companies of the Light Infantry and two of the Rangers, and the three battalions of the second brigade) to the north shore of the St. Lawrence River, taking position on the Beaupré coast, east of the Montmorency River. When Murray and his brigade arrived a day or so later, Wolfe would establish his camp about three-quarters of a mile east of the river, almost directly across from the French at Beauport. He had already decided to use as his own quarters an ordinary two-storey farm house in the village of Ange-Gardien. It had only one large room, but it would serve his purposes well.

At midnight, he gave the signal, jumped in his boat, and led the first landing.

At first glance, Wolfe's decision may appear to you somewhat erratic and crazy, as it did to me. But think about it. Granted he was dividing his army: half of it on the Beaupré coast and the rest scattered between the Ile d'Orléans and Pointe-Lévy. He was taking an inordinate risk. Or was he?

To answer that question we must bear in mind that if the French attacked him at Pointe-Lévy, he could easily and quickly dispatch troops to Monckton's defence. He knew that the French could not possibly incapacitate the English fleet because their fireships had been destroyed at the end of June. Furthermore, with his army and the navy arranged as they were, Wolfe had a continuous line of communication all the way from the Chaudière River on the south shore to the Montmorency on the north.

On July 9, Wolfe changed his mind to buy himself time to consolidate his plans for attacking Québec. As he had little imagination, I am sure that it never entered his head that the narrow channel between the Ile d'Orléans and the Beaupré coast could become his Rubicon.

A couple of hours after he had received Wolfe's signal to move to Beaupré, Brigadier-General George Townshend, eldest son of the third Viscount Townshend, godson of George I, former aide to the third son of George II, member for Norfolk in the House of Commons, and happy husband of the Lady Charlotte Compton, the only daughter and heiress of the Earl of Northhampton, was not pleased.

Upon landing on the Beaupré coast, Townshend discovered that Wolfe had left neither guides to show the way nor sentries to protect the English flanks. It was dark, and military baggage was strewn everywhere. Townshend ordered it assembled in one place, guarded by an officer and twenty men from each of the regiments of his brigade. He then took the road to the east, which he hoped led to the high ground he was to occupy near the falls.

As he trudged up the steep hill, he had ample time to reflect on the predicament in which he found himself. Here he was in some God-forsaken wilderness serving "under a General who does not consult, is most secretive," and might even be "incompetent." Nor did he relish being commanded by a man from a lower social strata and younger than himself. But then, Townshend had no one to blame but himself. He had used his influence with Pitt to force Wolfe to accept him on this mission.

Townshend's behaviour toward Wolfe during the crossing on Saunders' flagship had not helped to develop an easy relationship between the two men. Townshend had amused himself by drawing many caricatures of Wolfe and had circulated them among the officers in the mess. Only once had Wolfe objected publicly to being portrayed as ugly, foolish, and coarse, when Townshend had passed around a picture of Wolfe reconnoitering a brothel. The general found it most insulting. He crumbled it in his pocket. With fury in his eyes and a dangerous smile on his tight face, he said, "If I live this shall be inquired into; but first we must beat the enemy." Townshend had remained impassive.

After reaching a small farm near the falls, Townshend sent for his guns. With great difficulty, six six-pounders were hauled up the steep hill in three hours, which, given the terrain, constituted record time. At daybreak, as he was giving final orders for the emplacement of the guns, Wolfe arrived with an escort. He was quite curt with Townshend, reproaching the brigadier for being "dilatory." Then not waiting for any explanations, Wolfe marched off to his bed. Disconcerted, Townshend stormed off to his quarters where he entrusted his fury to his journal.

"The man could be so infuriating!" a distinguished and cultured voice tells me out of nowhere. At the time I am in the kitchen cooking for a party of twelve friends who are to visit that night – cooking is one of the main accomplishments of my life. I look around the large and airy kitchen and there, by the door that leads to a sunny deck, is a figure, immaculately dressed in a finely tailored red coat merging elegantly into a pair of elongated pants of the deepest blue I have ever seen. The collar of the person's shirt is of the finest lace, as are the cuffs that peek out of the sleeves of his jacket. His powdered wig is well balanced on an attractive but impish face.

"Who are you?" I ask, as if I do not know.

"Townshend. You need my titles?"

"No, thank you. I have already noted them," I answer as I try to concentrate on the chocolate sauce. In between my stirrings, I ask, "Why are you here?"

"I was a little jealous of my colleague, Monsieur le Comte de Bougainville, who seems to have free access to you. Besides you need a voice from the other side, as it were."

"And you will be my English voice?"

"Yes. Does that please your Canadian soul?"

I do not know what to answer him, but I will not deny him. "Fine. Perhaps I will understand better."

"That's doubtful, but we shall see. As you may have noticed I have decided to address you in an English more familiar to you than the eighteenth-century patois I often affect," he says walking towards the stove, where he plunges his finger into the hot chocolate. He swears and, walking away, adds, "During my mortal existence I did not spend much time in the kitchen. Nor did I, as a gentleman of the realm, indulge in conversations with persons below my status and rank, let alone with peasants."

"Why then are you breaking this splendid record?" I want to know.

He chooses not to answer that question directly, instead he tells me in a voice brimming with sarcasm, "I found your would-be Conqueror a most difficult man, even when he was not trying to be."

"What do you mean by that?"

"Oh, he was more aristocratic than the aristocrat, more loyal than the King, more pompous than anyone I had ever met. Everything about him annoyed me."

"And you could hardly hide it?"

"What was there to hide? I am who I am. I did what I did, and all the time it was in keeping with the code of a gentleman. I bid you good day."

He makes to leave, but adds before he does: "Major-General Wolfe lent himself well to being caricatured. I caught his . . . spirit. You may carry on."

"You are a snob," I yell at him before he disappears from my kitchen. But he does not deign to reply and leaves me to my pots and pans.

Townshend was interrupted in his journal-writing by piercing screeches that shattered the quiet of the early morning. Running out by the side of his house, he saw a company of Rangers, pursued by Indians, headed in his direction. In horror he stood transfixed and watched.

The Indians aimed and fired with great rapidity. Many of the dead and wounded Rangers were immediately pounced upon and had their skulls smashed with rifle butts. As the surviving Rangers returned fire, the Indians threw themselves on the ground and let their tomahawks fly in all directions, finding victims everywhere.

Then the scalping began. Townshend had never witnessed the horror of it. The fallen, whether they were alive or dead – Townshend could not tell – were grabbed by the hair. Scalping knives, penetrating to the skull, cut roughly around the crown of the victims' heads, then with a powerful pull, the scalp was torn off with the hair, the whole process taking no more than a few seconds. As the fighting mass of Indians and Rangers approached his headquarters, Townshend was at once amazed, appalled, and relieved that the Rangers also had bloody scalps hanging from their own belts.

Without waiting for orders, the red-coated Grenadiers came pouring out of a nearby barn, firing at the oncoming horde. Just then, an officer of the Rangers rushed past Townshend, pursued by an Indian. Finally shocked out of his stupor, the brigadier chased after them, but by the time he was within range, the Indian had turned around with the officer's bleeding heart clutched in his hands. Townshend fired, but when the smoke cleared, the crazed figure continued to stagger towards him. Pulling out his sword, Townshend plunged it into the Indian's chest. Townshend was disgusted to see that the man he had killed was not an Indian at all, but a Canadian woodsman disguised in warrior's paints and skins. Enraged by the barbarism, he charged back to his farmhouse, rallied the redcoats and the remaining Rangers, and drove the assailants back into the forest. As they ran away, they killed five of their prisoners.

In the carnage, thirty-six Rangers had been scalped, two had had their hearts cut out, and close to sixty other soldiers had been killed or wounded – the equivalent of an entire company. Their enemy had lost twenty-two men, seven of whom were Canadians.

Way up in the hills, the Montmorency River begins as a trickle. But as it makes its way to the St. Lawrence, it gathers volume and speed. Through a maze of natural steps, it forms rapids and eventually, as if to be done with the journey, it hurls itself over a 252-

foot precipice. As it falls, the river creates a perpetual mist and sends a multi-coloured rainbow arching over the rocks which border it on both sides. These rocks enclose a large basin which can easily be crossed at low tide. A few yards farther on, the Montmorency loses itself in the St. Lawrence.

On June 9, 1759, the two most important powers in the world confronted each other across this awesome creation of nature.

In front of the cathedral
8:00 A.M.

The women waiting for the parish priest to distribute the bread ration of the day talked ceaselessly among themselves. Unlike Madame Lefebvre, they had not been able to send their children above Québec for safekeeping. A few of the youngest ones, undernourished, sickly looking, and listless, found a little energy to play at their mothers' feet.

The women spoke of the miracle that was not forthcoming. They could not understand why God was withholding His favour and punishing them with such ferocity – they knew their sins were not so grave. They prayed, but their prayers seemed useless.

Certainly, they mumbled – not too loud, of course – about the unwillingness of the French authorities to tumble the English into the sea. They could see English batteries being built at Pointe-aux-Pères, the guns aimed at Québec, and they had just been told that the English had landed on the Beaupré coast. When and how would their nightmare end? No one could help them with a satisfactory answer. So they comforted each other, sought news of one another, remembered loved ones wet and cold in the trenches of Beauport, on the palisades of the town, or in the forts out West.

A few minutes after eight Father Récher and Madame Lefebvre arrived with baskets of bread, which they distributed according to Bigot's instructions. The mothers hid the food in the large pockets of their capes. The children wanted more, but Madame Lefebvre had no more to give.

To make conversation and ease their pain and anxiety, the women asked Madame Lefebvre why she had not gone to Sorel with her children. She hesitated, and then replied simply that she was needed in Québec and so had stayed. She did not tell them that her home was in Québec and she was not prepared to abandon it. Her children had been born in her house and a couple had died there in her arms. Her home was full of her life and her memories, and she wanted to protect it even if she was not allowed at this time to return to it.

Before they dispersed for the day, the women saw François Daine, the chief of police, entering the house of Jean-Claude Panet, the notary. Soon other officials joined them. Even Madame Lefebvre did not know what this meeting was all about.

La Canardière
Shortly before noon

The senior officers of the army were cramped in one of the smallest rooms of Vaudreuil's residence at La Carnardière for a council of war. There were chairs only for Vaudreuil, Montcalm, and Bigot. The others found places wherever they could, elbowing each other out of the way. They were there to determine what was to be done with the English across the river from them on the Beaupré coast.

The uppermost question on Bigot's mind was simple enough: How had Wolfe been able to move half his army to the east of them without the French knowing that it was about to happen, let alone that it could happen?

There was no clear answer to that question. The French, like the English, had spies everywhere, and both sides were constantly visited by deserters. The day before Wolfe landed at Beaupré, an English soldier had told a French officer that preparations were being made to move the troops. However, that information could not be verified, and the French by that time were wary of informers bearing gifts. So far they had been told that a French army had recaptured Louisbourg, that Saunders wanted to leave by the end of July, that the King of Prussia had lost twenty thousand men in a single battle in Europe, that the Queen of Hungary had incorporated Silesia into her vast kingdom, that the French had taken Hanover, that most of Wolfe's soldiers wanted to desert, that his army had grown to 12,000 soldiers, 1,200 marines and 1,500 others, and more, and more. Most of the information both sides received was fabricated to please.

Since he could not get a satisfactory answer to his first question, Bigot asked another: What were they to do about the English? Attack or wait?

At the beginning of the meeting, Vaudreuil vacillated between these two possibilities. But as the meeting dragged on and everyone talked out of turn, he tended to favour an immediate attack. Bigot, on the other hand, was definitely for a decisive action. He argued that the English were at a serious disadvantage since the French commanded the forests, mountains, and fords all around the Montmorency River. In Bigot's view the circumstances were "happy" ones for the French: the English were vulnerable, the French stronger – at least they were at Beauport – and the population was united, determined, and ready for action. Seize the opportunity now, was his message. Not to do so would only cause general despair and perhaps even mutiny. He was also quite aware that he had not enough food or ammunition or other supplies for a long siege. They might have to capitulate just to be fed. And he reminded Montcalm that even though there were three hundred cannon at their disposal, the French had little powder for them. But, as Le Mercier said, they did have plenty of mortar, thousands of bullets, and four thousand bombs.

Montcalm disagreed, and as respectfully as he could, he advised caution. He could perhaps defeat Wolfe on the Beaupré coast, he argued, but could he on the Ile d'Orléans or at Pointe-Lévy, or on their ships? He was not so certain. So he preferred the English to stay where they could do him as little harm as possible. "Let them amuse themselves at Beaupré," he told the council. As they played, he told Bigot with a smile, he would order the batteries in the city to fire at the English with moderation, to save the precious powder. He would also take adequate precautions on his side of the Montmorency River.

Montcalm's advice was accepted.

There were three fords on the Montmorency. The first one, known as the Winter Passage, was situated some three miles above the falls, the other two were farther upstream. To protect them, Montcalm ordered bastions erected and entrusted their safekeeping to Louis Legardeur de Repentigny, a Canadian officer in the colonial troops, and a battalion of seven hundred Canadians. Five hundred Indians under the Sieur de Courtemanche could also be moved there quickly if necessary, together with four hundred additional troops. Lévis had also ordered a path opened through the forest for communication purposes.

From Lévis' camp to the Beauport River, that is, in the centre of the line, Montcalm rearranged the regular troops and the one thousand Canadian militia incorporated into them in such a way as to permit them to assist the right or the left flank as circumstances dictated. He assumed personal command of the centre and, for that purpose, he left the de Salaberry manorhouse and erected his tent near the Beauport church.

Montcalm did not worry much about the right flank, the line between the St. Charles River and Beauport, where the colonial troops and the militia of Québec and Trois-Rivières were encamped under Bougainville and Vaudreuil.

Finally he divided his army into detachments of 1,400 men each to relieve one another every twenty-four hours. With nothing else to do, he waited for the English to make the first move.

By the Chaudière River
Later that afternoon

The fifteen-year-old boy fishing quietly on the bank of the river, was suddenly seized from behind by some of Major Scott's Rangers. His hands were tied behind his back and he was led into the woods. The soldiers left him there under guard as they continued their mission.

Shortly afterwards, they came upon a man standing at the river's edge, his two small children playing beside him. The soldiers arrested all three. The children, frightened out of their wits, began wailing and screaming. Then, over the din, the soldiers heard a loud noise in the woods. The officer in charge shook the children violently to keep them quiet, but they yelled all the louder. The father tried to intervene but was severely beaten. In desperation, the officer took the children into the forest, where he shot them, leaving their bodies to rot.

The soldiers then dragged the father, the fifteen-year-old boy, and an old man they found wandering along the way to transports in the St. Lawrence to await the outcome of the war.

(These arrests and murders are recorded in the official documents. What is not written there, however, is that Elisabeth de Melançon witnessed them.)

Shortly before the English arrived, Elisabeth had seen the man and the children. Recognizing them, she had exchanged pleasantries with the father across the water and had continued on her walk. As she picked her way across the stones on the beach, her thoughts turned back to James Montague, who had invaded her life for the better.

In the week that he had been recuperating at the sugar hut, they had talked at length about their families, their hopes, and their dreams. She had found out that he came from a wealthy Virginian family and that he had spent some time in England and in France, where he had learned French. There had been a family crisis, which he would not discuss, which had forced him to join the Rangers.

From Elisabeth he had found out that her people had come to the Chaudière valley a hundred years before. There they had built their homes and planted themselves firmly on the land. Reticent at first, she had nevertheless spoken of her father and of his death and of her mother who had gone to France on family business in the spring of 1758 and had not been able to return. No letters had come either, and Elisabeth missed her terribly.

As she walked and thought of him, she heard the cries of the children. She ran back and, seeing the soldiers, hid in the woods. She saw the officer take the children away and knock down their father. She heard the shots and saw the officer return alone. After the Rangers had gone, she crossed the river and found the bodies, each with a single bullet hole in its small head. Fighting back tears, she went for her grandfather and sent him and two Indians to take the bodies back to their village for a decent burial. She also asked one of the women to go and tell the children's mother. Left alone, she burst into tears and ran to the sugar hut.

When James found her, she was still weeping, her body heaving with deep sobs. She lunged at him with all her strength, hitting him over and over again with her clenched fists, possessed by an uncontrollable rage. "They killed them! They killed them!" she yelled. "*You* killed them!" Then she fell exhausted to the ground.

Gently he carried her inside and laid her on the makeshift bed. Stroking her cheek he waited patiently for her to tell him what had happened. After a while she recounted the story, often looking around in despair, weeping and clinging to him.

James did not know what to do or what to say. He was filled with disgust at his own people, though he tried to tell himself that in a war all sorts of cruelties happened. But instead of making excuses for the outrage, he simply held her. He soon became aware of the pleasure he felt from cradling her in his arms, her tears wetting his cheek, and her body trembling against his. He had a powerful need to cleanse them both of this brutal act. She felt it, too, and returned his caress and his kiss and his love.

Later when she had fallen asleep beside him, he disentangled himself carefully without disturbing her, dressed, and taking up his belongings, he left the hut. When she awakened she would find his note telling her of his love for her and of his promise to return.

July 11, 1759

(Day Sixteen)

Château Saint-Louis
9:00 A.M.

Everyone – priests, merchants, seigneurs, women, officials, clerks, and nuns – was distressed. For almost ten days now the people of Québec had stared across the four thousand feet of water that separated them from the English on the south shore and had watched in anguish as the batteries went up. They knew that sooner or later the English would start bombarding them. Some of the notables were distressed enough that they had dared to be critical of the conduct of the war. They had prepared a petition to be presented to Vaudreuil, and on July 10, the Governor General had come from La Canardière to meet with them.

In their petitition, the merchants and governmental officials or *les notables*, as they were called, had explained that they feared for the safety of their town and therefore were asking Vaudreuil to send a contingent to Pointe-Lévy to attack the English. Vaudreuil had thanked them for their advice but told them he could not accept it. He had implied that he favoured and had encouraged such an expedition, but that the French military authorities were opposed.

The military situation had changed drastically since Montcalm had burst upon Vaudreuil at the end of June insisting that regular troops be sent to Pointe-Lévy. Now Montcalm was faced with a numerous and well-equipped enemy across from him at Beauport, he had no manpower to spare for a sortie at Pointe-Lévy. It was too late.

The petitioners, however, were not to be denied that easily. Leaving Vaudreuil, they had repaired to Panet's house, where they had decided to raise 1,200 to 1,500 volunteers, made up of Indians, the two hundred students enrolled in the Sintaxe

Royale, and themselves. They would equip the volunteers at their own expense and would supply them with boats. They had even managed to convince Jean-Daniel Dumas, the respected hero of Monongahela, to lead them. His second-in-command would be a seasoned soldier, François-Prosper Douglas.

Upon accepting his commission, Dumas had gone back to Vaudreuil. He had found it easy to change Vaudreuil's mind now that the expedition would be Canadian and Indian. Montcalm, who had also changed his mind for reasons he did not divulge, had given his blessing and had even allowed one hundred volunteers from the colonial troops and sixty from the regulars to go with Dumas.

Dumas spent a day or so assembling his soldiers, their number falling quite short of the 1,500 men promised. He was also shocked at their condition. No more than three hundred of them had had any experience of war and two hundred of them were mere boys. He had spent the day of the tenth drilling them, teaching them to walk silently and not to panic at every noise they heard. He and Douglas showed the younger ones how to fire muskets, a difficult task since he did not want the noise to alert the English. Now, on the morning of the eleventh, the time had come to leave. With the townspeople waving them on, Dumas' army marched proudly out of the Porte du Palais onto the road to Sillery, where they were to embark for the south shore. But foul weather that night postponed the whole affair.

The next day, July 12, as he waited for the weather to clear, Dumas continued his attempt to transform the volunteers into soldiers. Father Récher came and blessed them, Mascou took Mennard, who had returned from Charlesbourg, and Lefebvre under his wing, and the petieners sipped wine, waiting for their destiny.

The mention of Mascou reminds me to tell you about the Indians. The French, who regarded them as barbarians and cruel beyond belief, had a tendency to treat them as recalcitrant children. The Canadians, however, found the Indians acceptable companions. They both shared the dangers of a harsh and unpredictable environment. They acknowledged each other as distinct beings with different codes of ethics and chivalry but with a common resistance to authority. They had become dependent upon one another, the Indians for many necessities of their daily lives, and the habitants for survival in the woods and for furs.

This did not mean that the Canadians were not irritated by what they regarded to be the quarrelsome attitude and unreliable ways of the Indians, particularly in war. They were also appalled by the cannibalism of certain tribes and by the Indians' compulsive need to avenge the deaths of their braves. But, even though the Indians often terrorized and tyrannized the habitants, who usually reciprocated in kind, the Canadians could not forget that the Indians had taught them almost everything they knew about tracking, trapping, and surviving in the wilderness.

What the Indians thought of the white man is not recorded.

July 12, 1759

(Day Seventeen)

Pointe-aux-Pères
10:00 P.M.

The time had almost come. The batteries were ready. The men were standing by, and Wolfe had crossed from Beaupré to be with them. The soldiers could clearly see the townspeople walking in the Upper Town and the soldiers manning the batteries by the harbour across the river.

A rocket streaked into the sky from Saunders' ship. It stayed motionless for a second or two then drew a fiery arc in the darkness. A moment later, the officer in charge gave the order to fire the cannon pointed at Québec.

Just before the bombardment began, Father Baudouin, in the absence of Father Récher, who had not yet returned from Sillery, held a short service in the Québec parish church of Sainte-Famille. Coming out of the church, one worshipper saw the rocket and yelled the news to those behind. All rushed to the terrace of the château to see what was happening. They saw the flares lighting the cannon, and heard the catastrophic noise, amplified by the river.

Father Baudouin tried to get his parishioners to go home, but they stayed where they were. When the first projectiles fell into the St. Lawrence, they cheered. A few minutes later, though, a bomb hit the Jesuit church in the Upper Town. The people fell silent. The rain begain to fall. Their long night had started.

The Ursuline nuns were in their cloister praying. The rain that had begun to fall softly a while ago had now turned into a torrent and was battering the windows. Some of the nuns heard a hissing sound, then a large thunder clap, followed by another, and another. One nun rushed out and came back quickly with the news that their convent was seriously damaged, perhaps even uninhabitable.

The nuns did not take refuge in their vaults, as the Bishop had ordered, because there was not enough room for all of them. They stayed at prayer and waited for God in His mercy to calm their terror.

All over the Upper Town women rushed to fetch their children and the elderly to the open squares in front of the public buildings. There they fell on their knees wailing their prayers to God and the Virgin Mary. Since no one else appeared to be in charge, Father Baudouin assumed the responsibility. He directed the people away from the squares and farther up on the ramparts. He prayed with them as they rushed along, helped an old man or an infirm woman here, and cajoled and encouraged the children there. He was thankful that the bombs were not incendiary, but still cringed at the noise they made as they were hurled through the sky.

When a missile hit the Hôtel-Dieu, the priest rushed wheezing down the Côte de la Montagne. There he found the Hospitalières in prayer with their chaplain. He advised them to continue their devotions in the vault and to await the end of the night. On his way back, he met Madame Lefebvre shepherding a group of women and children. Before she disappeared from his view, a bomb hit Notre-Dame-des-Victoires. He saw her make the sign of the cross.

Rapidly – or so it appeared to him – the forty streets of Québec became deserted. Making his way back to the cathedral, he saw that Father Récher's house had been almost totally destroyed. The bursar of the Séminaire approached him as he surveyed the ruins and told him that the cathedral had been hit but that the damage was not too serious. "And the Séminaire?" he asked. Of the vast rambling building, only the large kitchen remained intact.

Thirty houses and almost every public building were seriously damaged, and the houses in the Lower Town were starting to crumble under the intense bombardment. Looting would be inevitable in a day or so.

Baudouin was dreadfully tired and his breathing was laboured, but he ordered himself to go down the Côte de la Montagne again to see after the soldiers and the sailors stationed in the harbour. He found that they were relatively comfortable and had not suffered any direct hit. It did not enter his head to ask their officers why they were not firing back upon the English, if only to confuse them.

The bombs continued to fall, but as his ears adjusted, the noise they made became more bearable. Wearily, he climbed up the Côte again, thankful that no one had reported a death or an injury. It was half an hour past midnight. The eighteenth day of the siege had begun. Baudouin's thoughts turned to his two young friends, Mennard and Lefebvre, on the south shore.

July 13, 1759

(Day Eighteen)

Somewhere on the south shore
Shortly after midnight

Dumas' army had crossed from Sillery to a point near Saint-Nicholas on the south shore at about the same time as the bombardment of Québec had begun. It had taken Dumas and Douglas a great deal of time to organize their troops in some marching order. Finally, around midnight, they were ready and on the move.

First came an advance party of Canadians and Indians, who would scout the terrain. The rest of the troops followed, drawn up in two columns. With Douglas at their head, the professional soldiers were in front, followed by the few members of the militia, then the students, and in the rear, the volunteers. Dumas walked up and down the line, ensuring that everyone moved along smartly.

Some three miles from the English guns, the advance party reached a farmhouse belonging to the Bourassa family. There they waited for Dumas to catch up. When he arrived, he ordered scouts to reconnoitre the English positions. With them he sent Mascou, Mennard, and Lefebvre.

It was dark and the rain was pelting down mercilessly as the Abenakis with his two young companions crept through the trees. Soon they came into full view of the English batteries. The noise was deafening and the dark silhouettes of the cannon loomed ominously in the night. When the soldiers ignited a cannon, a jet of fire briefly lit up their red tunics. Mennard thought that hell would look just like that. Lefebvre prayed silently that none of the bombs would injure his mother or damage his home.

Two hours later, after the scouts had returned, Dumas gave the signal to go forward, but before the march started, lookouts saw lanterns in the distance. Dumas sent yet another party to investigate. It found that the lights belonged to local farmers who had heard of the impending attack and wanted to join in the battle. Upon their return to where they had left Dumas, however, he and his army had disappeared. Dumas, fearing that his soldiers would panic and harm themselves as they waited, had proceeded forward, following the guides.

Fortunately for Dumas' expedition, the farmers knew the countryside intimately. A short search located the missing army and soon all the parties were reunited. They were, however, in some disarray. The regulars and the colonials were still in marching order but were taking a rest; the militia was milling about, some smoking pipes; the students had taken refuge along a fence a few hundred feet from the main body; and the volunteers were agitated and asking endless questions. It appeared to all the amateurs that it was getting darker and that the rain was falling more heavily.

After a brief conference with the habitants of the south shore, Dumas ordered the men to proceed forward again. But no sooner had he done so than he heard a shot coming from the direction of the students. Before he could rush over to calm them, there was another shot, followed by another, and then a whole volley. The students and the citizens, taking each other for Englishmen, had panicked, firing their guns, and had run for the St. Lawrence and the safety of their canoes – all the while shooting at those above them. Two regular soldiers were killed and three wounded.

When Dumas reached the shore, two-thirds of his army were already launched onto the river. However, with the help of the Indians and a few soldiers, he was able to force everybody back to shore. There he harangued them, calling them every name he could think of and threatening them with hanging or with being turned over to the Indians if they did not re-form their ranks and obey his orders. With misgivings and fear they finally agreed to continue on the expedition. Then, abruptly, just as they were about to march up the hill again, Dumas cancelled his orders and sent them back to their canoes and across the St. Lawrence.

When Dumas' army reached Sillery, it was five o'clock in the morning. The English had not heard a thing. But the news of the fiasco had already reached Québec. As the soldiers and the volunteers marched through the Porte du Palais, the people stared at them with sadness and anger.

It is difficult for me, some two hundred and thirty years later, to understand why Dumas gave up. He told Vaudreuil that he was convinced that the English had heard the commotion and were getting ready to attack him. As well, it was obvious that he could not rely on his soldiers, and I found out that the farmers who had volunteered to join him had disappeared, taking the dead with them. Moreover, it was almost daylight by the time the troops had regrouped. I can only assume that to him it seemed appropriate to leave the English to their devices and Québec to its destiny.

In Québec, the rain was still falling, as were the enemy's bombs. The streets of the Upper Town were blocked with vehicles of all sorts loaded with the precious possessions of inhabitants scurrying to leave the town. On the ramparts near the Citadel, women and children were taking turns reciting the rosary. One house after another stood empty, their doors banging in the wind. So numerous were the fugitives from Québec that Ramezay had ordered the two other gates (Porte Saint-Louis and Porte Saint-Jean) to be opened. The people were escaping in all directions, particularly toward the woods in the countryside above Québec and to the Hôpital Général by the St. Charles River, three miles outside the walls of the town, outside the range of the English cannon.

Lefebvre found his mother at Notre-Dame-des-Victoires. With her usual determination, she was sweeping the debris that had fallen into the church through large holes in the roof and walls. He told her what had happened on the south shore and how ashamed he was. Without saying a word, she wiped his tears. And together they swept the church while the bombs flew over their heads.

The Hôpital Général was a pleasant, impressive building with a large dome and two immense wings. Every day since the English had arrived in Beaupré, a half-dozen wounded soldiers had been brought to the hospital. Already the sick bays were filled, and the three men who had just been brought in from the south shore had to be bedded down in one of the large hallways.

The Mother Superior of the hospital was a Canadian from an old family of soldiers and administrators, Marie-Charlotte de Ramezay, known in religious life as Mère Saint-Claude-de-la-Croix. Her father had been governor of Trois-Rivières and of Montréal and her brother was the King's lieutenant for Québec. She was a tall and energetic woman who was determined and devoted. For the moment she was using all of her skills to look after the hundreds of desperate people who were pouring into her hospital.

The civilians who came were mostly relatives of the sisters under her. She lodged them in the sheds. Her employees emptied the barns of cattle and turned them into dormitories for mothers and their young children. They themselves doubled up so that elderly couples could use their quarters. More people were housed in the attics, and Mère Saint-Claude had even had the laundry rooms converted into living accomodations, making it difficult for the nuns to wash the much-needed linens.

Early in the morning, she had gone out to meet more than thirty Ursuline nuns who had had to abandon their convent. She gave them the rooms of her sisters, reserving her own sitting-room for the mother abbess of the Ursulines. Soon afterwards, the nuns of the Hôtel-Dieu arrived. She made them comfortable in the parlour.

To the bursar who wanted to know how she was to feed the six hundred people already in the hospital, she replied that she would see the Intendant, the Governor, and Montcalm to obtain some food. The Ursulines and the nuns of the Hôtel-Dieu had brought provisions with them, which they shared. "Everyone will do without much and we shall have enough," she said. And after a pause she added, "The English cannot stay here forever."

Interrupted in her work by the sister-sacristan, who had to make seating arrangements in the church for everyone, Mère Saint-Claude decided to place the Ursulines on the left of the cloister, the Hospitalières of the Hôtel-Dieu on the right, the general public in the pews outside the grill, and her own sisters would sit wherever they could find a place.

"It shall be quite crowded and noisy," said the sacristan.

As sweetly as she could, the Mother Superior replied: "I am certain, dear Sister, that God will be pleased with the crowd. As for the noise, He shall have to endure it like the rest of us."

Let me tell you about the nuns.

In 1759, there were three religious communities of women in the town of Québec. Marie de l'Incarnation had brought the Ursulines to Canada in 1639. They were a cloistered order of nuns, whose primary function, beside praying and fasting, was the teaching of young girls. They occupied a large and beautiful convent with extensive gardens in Québec.

Also in 1639, three Augustines Hospitalières de l'Hôtel-Dieu under Mère Marie-Guenet de Saint-Ignace had come from Dieppe to establish a hospital. At first they went to Sillery, but in 1644 they founded the Hôtel-Dieu hospital in the Lower Town.

The Hospitalières de l'Hôpital Général de Québec were an offshoot of those of the Hôtel-Dieu. They broke away from the older community at the end of the seventeenth century. Their role was to look after the infirm and to run the Hôpital Général, a hospital founded by the second bishop of Québec, Jean-Baptiste La Croix de Chevrières de Saint-Vallier.

According to all reports the nuns were devoted to their tasks and few scandals marred their contribution to the temporal and spiritual life of Québec. They were also amply provided for by the Crown and by pious citizens.

As the nuns were taking their noon meal, the rain stopped and the English batteries fell silent. In the previous fourteen hours, over three hundred bombs had fallen on Québec. But not a single person had been killed or wounded and not a single fire had broken out. The damage to buildings, however, was considerable.

Montcalm had dispatched Bougainville with three hundred men early in the morning to help with the evacuation of half of the population, inspect the garrison, and move the King's stores from the Lower Town to a warehouse outside the walls. He also sent a message of encouragement to Dumas. The misadventure on the south shore persuaded Montcalm that his original strategy was sound. He would stay in his trenches, he told Marcel, and wait for Wolfe to attack him.

He ate his frugal lunch and allowed himself one glass of wine. He then wrote to Lévis.

"Monsieur le Chevalier!

I am the recipient of a great number of plans for the safe conduct of this war. This morning someone wanted a battery set up nine miles south of here; a few minutes later it had to be nine miles north. Later I was asked to send 600 men to protect La Beauce. Someone else advises me to increase the garrison at Québec, with what and whom only God is aware. News has just come that the eminent brother of our esteemed Governor has set up a camp somewhere without knowing why and how. Every night the commander of the artillery carries out the works he should have done two years ago. We pay for his indolence with our sleep. I am telling you, *mon cher Chevalier,* they are all crazy. I hope it is not catching, but I have my doubts.

Good day, Monsieur le Chevalier."

MIRED IN THE MUD

July 16–August 31, 1759

July 16 to July 20, 1759

(Day Twenty-one to Day Twenty-five)

As the information I have before me is scant, it is hard to know where to begin to relate what occurred on these five days. Few moments are memorable but none are remarkable. There were acts of courage, some of cowardice, and too many of indecision. All I can say for certain is that cruelty prevailed and pain continued to be the normal condition of life.

Here then are some vignettes of those days.

After a hiatus of a few hours on the fourteenth, the bombardment of Québec started in earnest again.

Under a flag of truce, on the fifteenth, Wolfe received Le Mercier and complained to him that the Indians had captured three of his grenadiers and were to burn them alive. Not so, replied Le Mercier, Vaudreuil had ransomed them. After recriminations on both sides, Le Mercier vowed that even if Wolfe demolished Québec, the French would never allow his army to set foot in the town. Wolfe had a vow of his own, "I shall be master of Québec even if I have to stay here until the end of November."

Three days into the bombardment, Bigot, Vaudreuil, the chief of police, and others became alarmed at the extensive looting of the bombed houses and shops. They warned the citizens of dire consequences should they be caught in the act.

By the fifteenth Father Récher, whose house and church were uninhabitable, had moved to the parish of Saint-Jean outside the walls. There he set up a chapel and dispensary in the house of Pierre Flamand. With the help of the militia, he made plans for a temporary cemetery near the walls.

In the orders of the day on July 16, Wolfe allowed the regiments and corps to send to the Ile d'Orléans for one woman per company.

At noon of the same day the alarm sounded. In the Lower Town, an incendiary bomb had set fire to the house of a man by the name of Chevalier. Soon the flames had spread to seven or eight houses in the vicinity. All available men were immediately placed on the bucket brigade, and Montcalm sent a contingent of soldiers from Beauport to assist in controlling the conflagration. At the same time he gave orders to the batteries to shoot at the English at Pointe-aux-Pères. This seemed to have some effect, for soon thereafter – at about four o'clock – the English stopped bombarding the town. The rain continued to pour down, and by seven o'clock the fire was under control.

During these five days both commanders found the weather stifling, unpredictable, and exhausting. One moment they were soaking wet from the rain, the next they were drenched in sweat from the heat of the sun. No sooner had the ground dried than a sudden storm would erupt, flooding the tents and filling the trenches with water. Day and night the sudden clapping of thunder, mixed with the booming of the cannon from the batteries and ships, made rest almost impossible.

Montcalm was overwhelmed by the length of the frontier he had to defend, stretching as it did from the coast of Beauport to Fort Machault on the Ohio River, a distance of over twelve hundred miles. He had neither the munitions nor the manpower to defend one place, let alone all of them at once. He knew that the Indians and the Canadians were exasperated by his strategy. They wanted to attack the English and be done with it. But he would not be swayed. Let Wolfe make the first move, he told everyone who inquired.

Wolfe, for his part, had to make peace with the navy and to devise yet another plan to conquer Québec. After admitting in his journal that he had "to accept certain things more easily," he and Saunders patched their differences over dinner on the sixteenth and both discussed what Wolfe called "The Projected Descent."

This Projected Descent, as he told Saunders, consisted of a two-pronged attack on the French lines at Beauport. Monckton would lead a charge on the right of the line between the St. Charles River and Beauport, thus forcing "the French to move a considerable body of troops in that area." The second assault would occur at what was called the Johnstone Redoubt, a French fortification built on the Beauport shore, near the high-water mark and apparently far from the French trenches. "The Highland Regiment will storm it vigorously and hold it ... This should not be too difficult as it is out of range of the French muskets." With such a plan, Wolfe was certain he could achieve his objective: to bring the French out of their trenches.

To that end he ordered Monckton to send him fifty pieces of artillery, hoping that "we shall create such a tremendous fire, that no human head will venture to peep above the trenches. We shall therefore be safer and fewer of our men will be sacrificed." He also commissioned the construction of flat-bottomed boats, rafts, portable bridges, and floating batteries. And he pressed Saunders to sail his ships above Québec that very night. Saunders initially agreed to risk it. But, later, he sent Wolfe a note saying that the wind had failed and that he would try again the next day.

Wolfe's plan was to attack the French in four days' time. He had completely forgotten the landing at Saint-Michel above Québec he had planned at the beginning of July.

"So Wolfe's relations with Saunders improved," Townshend tells me as we sip tea on the patio.

Since the first time we met in my kitchen, Townshend has visited me three or four times, but he has refused to be drawn into a conversation. So I am rather surprised that on this fine day he is inclined to address me.

"His with me deteriorated," he announces with some flourish.

Not willing to frighten him away, I wait patiently for him to go on. After finishing his tea, he sits beside me and, for the first time, reminisces.

"One day, he arrived in pomp at my headquarters and told me rather regally: 'My dear chap, you have built yourself a fortress which will turn out to be useless to us.' And lo and behold, without my consent or my leave, he ordered my men around and dismantled my defences. Can one of your servants bring us more tea?"

"I do not have servants," I say rather defensively, "but I'll get you some." When I return with a refilled teapot, he says as I pour, "On another day, your would-be Conqueror sent word that two of my cannon were to be moved to his farmhouse. He robbed me of my cannon to ornament his quarters. Do you believe that?"

"Well, he was your commanding officer. Surely if he needed your cannon, he had a right to them."

"If you keep talking like a peasant, I will not address you any longer."

We maintain a brief uneasy truce, then Townshend smiles. "Our commanding officer liked the stately manner when speaking, marching, dining, and everything else for all I know. As you are aware, I hope, I was the second-in-command at our camp at Beaupré. And the General would absent himself often. He would go to the Island of Orleans or to our encampment at Pointe-Lévy or wherever his fancy took him. On one occasion I decided to humble myself. As he was getting ready for one of his excursions, I marched down to the river bank to ask him if he had any orders for me, as I would be most pleased to execute them. Well, he looked down that elongated nose of his at me and with his lips hardly moving he told me in a voice that could be heard for miles around that the Adjutant-General – "

"Isaac Barré," I make bold to say. And as an apology for having interrupted so eminent a person, I add, "My readers need to know his name."

"Was that his name?" he asks, and not waiting for my answer he goes on. "That the Adjutant-General had all the necessary orders and that I would be informed in due course. Imagine that!"

"And you had no other recourse but to rage in your journal?"

He gives me one of those aristocratic glares of his and dismisses me. "You may go back to your readers. I will stay with the cat."

Like a fool I obey him (it is, no doubt, the peasant in me) and turning around before entering the house, I see him petting the cat. We are making progress, I say to myself.

———————

On July 18, around midnight, the fifty-gun HMS *Sutherland*, the frigates *Diana* and *Squirrel*, two armed sloops, and two transports sailed above Québec. Wolfe was watching closely.

The French sentries were not at their posts when the first English ships sailed by. When they returned and realized what had happened, they sounded the alarm, but their officers reacted in disbelief, so certain were they that no English ship would venture to pass above Québec. When they finally admitted what was going on, the French batteries opened fire, but it was too late to stop the ships. However, the *Diana* ran aground at Pointe-Lévy.

As soon as a courier had informed him, Montcalm sent forty men to Anse-des-Mères to help the Indians in case the English attempted a landing. He also ordered the sentries court-martialled.

The next day two scaffolds were erected on a large rock overlooking the St. Lawrence. An escort brought the two sentries forward, followed by the parish priest. The men were hauled to the rock and blindfolded. The ropes were placed around their necks, the priest recited a few prayers, the officer gave the signal, and the soldiers pushed the two men off the edge. They gave choking gasps. Their bones cracked. The priest gave them a final blessing. And the bodies were left there, swinging in the wind.

By July 19, there were over six hundred men under Dumas at Anse-des-Mères. Later in the day additional troops arrived:

three hundred militia from Trois-Rivières, a few Indians, and most of the cavalry.

Vaudreuil and Bigot finally made up their minds. The town criers of Québec and the village around the capital announced Vaudreuil's newest proclamation. Anyone caught looting would be tried, condemned, and executed the same day. The traditional formalities were suspended.

On a hill on the north shore, almost directly opposite the mouth of the Etchemin River on the south shore, with a good view of the river, there was a large house that had once belonged to one of the bishops of Québec. Now Canadians were erecting a battery there. It was known as *la batterie de Samos* and Montcalm attached the greatest importance to it.

Its first victim was the frigate *Squirrel*. The Samos guns caused her so much trouble that she had to leave her anchor and be towed away.

The successful passage of the English ships above Québec sent Wolfe on the move. The north shore once again became the focal point of his thoughts. From the safety of the south shore he examined the terrain across the river as far as Cap Rouge, about twelve miles from Québec. To get a closer look, he had himself rowed in a whaleboat and even sailed on the *Sutherland*. Meanwhile, Major Dalling and his light infantry troops scouted around and suggested two or three places above Québec the army could land and ascend the cliffs without too much difficulty. He even pointed out houses that could serve as caches. To facilitate matters even further, Goreham established a post on the Etchemin River, a few miles west of the Pointe-aux-Pères batteries.

As he paced about on the *Sutherland*, Wolfe came to a conclusion: the Projected Descent at Beauport, which he had been planning with Saunders a few days earlier, would be abandoned. Instead he would now attack the French from above Québec. If he had pursued that course earlier, he wrote in his diary, "I would have probably succeeded by now." So elated was he with what appeared to him as a revelation, that he first wrote the word "infallibly" instead of "probably."

The next day, Wolfe was cheerful and full of purpose. In a letter sent to Monckton on July 20 but dated by error May 20, Wolfe ordered him to embark part of his brigade in flat-bottomed boats and proceed to the *Sutherland*. From there they would be rowed to the north shore, close to Saint-Michel, where they were to secure a landing place, the ground above the hamlet, and the road that led to Québec. "If we can take four or five good Posts; & keep 'em till our friends arrive," he wrote, "it may bring a very desirable affair." The friends he was talking about were the troops in Townshend's brigade, which he had asked to be at the water's edge by midnight in order to be at the Ile d'Orléans before daybreak. In due course they, too, would be taken above Québec.

By early afternoon the troops were ready to march "with two days' provisions, a blanket, thirty-six rounds of ammunition and two spare flints." However, they stayed where they were. At three o'clock, Monckton received another message from Wolfe written two hours earlier: "Particular circumstances make it necessary to delay our attempt for a few days, & to keep it Secret ... You will countermand the embarkation & the march for a day or two."

This was Wolfe's third order of the day. No sooner had one been received that it was contradicted by another one a few hours later. In the space of five hours Wolfe had changed his mind three times. Why?

It appears that Wolfe had come to have grave apprehension about the recommended landing sites above Québec. The terrain rose high above the St. Lawrence and was thickly wooded. High seas broke constantly on the rocks of the shoreline. The few openings he had seen or had been pointed out to him were mostly gullies filled with water cascading to reach the St. Lawrence. He could land, but he doubted that he could hold his position long enough to reinforce it before

Montcalm drove him into the river. Already the French had many troops in the area: Dumas was entrenched at Anse-des-Mères and the Samos battery was being quite effective.

Of course, he already knew most of these problems, but this time he judged them to be of such magnitude that he decided finally "to abandon the proposed attack above Québec." Such a descent above Québec would be hazardous, costly in manpower and "would probably fail."

Many of the officers and men did not relish his on-again, off-again attack. They felt that indecision had characterized his leadership since they had arrived "in this infernal country," as one of them described Canada. Wolfe sensed their resentment. He even tried to placate them. He gave them rum and allowed them to swim in the river morning and evening. He organized "all the diversion" he possibly could; he even sent Carleton to Pointe-aux-Trembles to bring ladies to join the officers at dinner.

July 21, 1759

(Day Twenty-six)

Pointe-aux-Trembles
Early in the morning

It was raining and the little village of Pointe-aux-Trembles, about twenty miles above Québec, was covered in cloud. In the St. Lawrence, a few hundred yards from the shore, four hundred Highlanders and Rangers under Guy Carleton were waiting to disembark. With them, serving as guide, was one of the most astonishing men of the time, Robert Stobo.

Before I tell you about Stobo, I must introduce you to Guy Carleton. He was an Irishman born on September 3, 1724. He joined the army at age seventeen and advanced as his abilities and connections permitted. He knew Wolfe, had been with him at Louisbourg, and was invited to come to Québec as Quartermaster General, but the King refused the appointment. Carleton supposedly had insulted him by criticizing the military capacity of the Hanoverian troops so dear to the royal heart. It took the intervention of Pitt and the commander-in-chief of the army before George II agreed to sign the necessary papers.

Carleton appears to have been a diligent officer and a competent one in 1759. But he certainly was not spectacular. However that is largely the story of his life.

Stobo *was* spectacular. He was a Scottish officer who, at age sixteen, had been sent to Virginia. There he learned fast, became a prosperous merchant and ingratiated himself with the Governor and his circle. In 1754, with ten servants and many caskets of Madeira wine, he had accompanied George Washington on his disastrous expedition against the French on the Ohio River. Washington was defeated and Stobo was brought to Québec as a prisoner of war. There he lived a charmed life, mingling with the best of society and falling in love with Reine-Marie Juchereau-

Duschesnay, one of Vaudreuil's relatives. He was even allowed to carry on business with some of the Canadian merchants. And all the while he spied on his hosts and tried to escape.

In the summer of 1755, he was accused of treason and court-martialled. He pleaded guilty and was sentenced to be beheaded, but the Court at Versailles commuted his sentence to life imprisonment. He continued to live in Québec pursuing his old activities. Two years later, with the help of his mistress, he tried unsuccessfully to escape. Even then no attempt was made to punish him.

He finally succeeded in escaping in May 1759 when, with eight other American prisoners (four men, a woman, and her three children), he rowed down the St. Lawrence in a canoe. It was an incredible thirty-six day journey filled with hardships and hair-raising escapades. He even managed to capture a French schooner and two sea captains.

No sooner had Stobo arrived at Louisbourg than he was sent back up the St. Lawrence to Wolfe's headquarters. He arrived there at the beginning of July. Wolfe used him as a guide.

Eventually he became an alcoholic and killed himself in 1770, a fact discovered only in 1965.

At five o'clock in the morning, Carleton ordered the troops to disembark. On the path to the village they met no one, but near the church the Indians encamped there opened fire, killing three soldiers and wounding several others. Carleton drove them into the woods and, in the process, captured the Reverend Jean-Baptiste de La Brosse, a thirty-five-year-old Jesuit missionary assigned to the Indians. Unbeknownst to Carleton, the Jesuit had sent a messenger to warn Dumas at Anse-des-Mères.

In their search of the village, the English did not find the cache of arms that Wolfe had been told was there. But they did find women: a nun with a group of young girls from Québec, other women and children related to the most important citizens of the town, and two able-bodied men. Some of the women recognized Stobo.

Carleton ordered that the residents of Pointe-aux-Trembles be left alone after their houses had been searched and the refugees from Québec brought to the *Sutherland*. Meanwhile his soldiers rounded up cattle, sheep, and countless chickens which they took to their boats. In a further search of the village, they found a militiaman by the name of Le Sieur La Casse, who had obtained leave because of severe arthritis. When captured, he was in bed with his mistress, both of them unaware of the invasion around them. He, too, was sent to the English ships, but his lady-love was left safe in her house.

At two o'clock in the afternoon, a lookout sighted Dumas and a detachment of troops approaching along the road from Québec. The English rushed to the safety of their boats, but not before a few of their men were wounded and most of the cattle abandoned. By four o'clock Carleton was back on the *Sutherland*.

By then the ladies had gone to confession, heard mass, and had freshened up. Tightening a corset here, lowering a neckline there, adding a ribbon to hastily rearranged hair, borrowing a scarf, a belt, a handkerchief, and placing them strategically, they set out to please the gentlemen-officers who wanted nothing better than the company of gracious, well-shaped, loquacious ladies. When Wolfe was informed of their presence, he invited about twelve of them to dinner. Stobo chose them.

In a low but well-aired cabin, the servants had set up three large tables with eight places laid at each. At the head of the tables would sit Wolfe, Captain John Rous, the master of the *Sutherland*, and Carleton. The officers took special precautions with their toilet and appearance hoping to make a good impression on the women, which could stand them in good stead once they had conquered Québec. As they waited they chatted amicably with Wolfe and each other.

At eight o'clock, Stobo brought in the ladies. Some were young, some older, some matronly, some curvaceous, but all of them of impeccable lineage. Wolfe installed Madame de Charney on his right and Madame Joly on his left. Mademoiselle Couillard sat at Captain Rous' table, and the two attractive daughters of the Joly family were seated next to Captain Smyth, as was the eldest daughter of Madame Mailhot, who had been too ill to attend herself. At Carleton's table were the other ladies of the Charney and Magnan families, Stobo, and, much to her annoyance, Madame Juchereau-Duchesnay, the mother of Stobo's former mistress.

It was a pleasant evening. Soft music could be heard through the open windows, and the service, carried out by the servants of the officers present, was impeccable. The food was good, and the ladies found the wine to their taste. During the dinner, Wolfe made small talk, jesting about Montcalm's reticence in coming out of his trenches. He reminisced about his time in Paris, his presentation at Court, and his audience with Madame de Pompadour.

At Rous' table the talk was just as animated. A young, handsome officer sitting next to Mademoiselle Magnan asked her to write his name and rank in the notebook she carried. He added a personal message of devotion which moved her. Soon they were engrossed in a private conversation in which he begged her to leave Québec as soon as she could upon her return. He could not tell her why, but still persisted. She smiled and bowed her pretty head gently.

Madame Juchereau-Duchesnay was giving Stobo a hard time at Carleton's table for having treated her daughter most cavalierly. He tried to placate her with a declaration of eternal admiration for Reine-Marie, but the old lady was too experienced to accept such nonsense and ended the conversation with a grunt.

At the end of the dinner, the women were told that they would be returned to shore under a flag of truce the next day. Wolfe would take that occasion to send his wounded to the Ile d'Orléans, along with the booty taken at Pointe-aux-Trembles.

Rear-Admiral Holmes, who had arrived on the *Sutherland* earlier to take charge of the naval operations above Québec, did not attend the dinner.

July 23, 1759

(Day Twenty-eight)

Québec
Dawn

The day after the English ships had passed into the upper St. Lawrence, Montcalm appointed new sentries to the harbour. These were men he could trust who reported directly to him. As often as he could after that, he stood by the batteries, unperturbed by the bombs falling about him and watching for more ships sailing upriver, as if his mere presence would deter the English.

On the previous night at nine o'clock, after the ladies had been returned from the *Sutherland*, the bombardment of Québec had begun again with unusual fury. Montcalm, Le Mercier, and Marcel had rushed to the batteries, where they had remained until now. Suddenly out of the darkness a soldier cried out *"Incendie! Incendie!"* Fire had broken out on Rue de la Fabrique in the Upper Town. Montcalm assembled some militia and sailors and ran to the area, leaving Le Mercier in charge of the batteries. When they arrived, they found that the flames, aided by the wind and the wooden roofs of the houses, had already engulfed the street. The English concentrated their bombing in and around the raging inferno, further hindering the firefighters. In all, eighteen houses were burning.

Before long the news arrived that the cathedral was also on fire. There was nothing that could be done. The noble church that had stood proudly over Québec, indeed, over the whole colony for more than a century was a mass of raging flames. The tall belfries that could be seen for miles around collapsed and their three bells melted. The militia and the citizens watched in despair the most important symbol of their faith and existence being destroyed. They did not have much time to pray, however, for both the Séminaire and the Bishop's palace were being threatened by the fire, as well. Then, miraculously, the wind subsided, and the flames spent themselves in the havoc they had already created.

By then it was five o'clock in the morning and Montcalm, who had not slept that night, decided to return to his headquarters at Beauport. As he was readying himself to leave, a sailor ran up with a message from Le Mercier: The English were attempting to sail two more ships above Québec. Montcalm galloped to the batteries, and watched as Le Mercier, directing the guns with great accuracy and efficiency, forced the vessels to retreat to the safety of their fleet.

In the early light of the morning, Montcalm rode through the devastated city. Many of its fine buildings lay in rubble, and in the Lower Town scarcely a house remained standing. The little chapel of Notre-Dame-des-Victoires remained erect, but its walls were breached with gaping holes, and its roof was half gone. In the Upper Town, the cathedral was in ruins. At the Séminaire only the kitchen remained serviceable. The Bishop's palace would have to be completely rebuilt. Montcalm's own house on Rue des Ramparts was uninhabitable. The convent of the Ursulines was a complete disaster. A bomb had hit the roof of the chapel and had gouged a large hole by the main altar. Other bombs had destroyed the choir stalls and the grill behind which the nuns used to pray.

At the Porte du Palais, Montcalm saw Father Baudouin, Father Récher, and Madame Lefebvre setting up a temporary infirmary to take care of the wounded, the sick, and the homeless. Even in the worst days of the colony there had never been so many in such desperate need. When he lifted his eyes from the misery before him, in the distance, Montcalm could see the Ile d'Orléans, surrounded by a threatening forest of masts.

Aboard the HMS *Stirling Castle*
Later that afternoon

Wolfe was desperate. He had been at Québec almost a month but had little to show for it. He had first wanted to land at

Beauport, but the French were already there, forcing him to plan a landing above Québec. He had changed his mind about that plan in favour of the "Projected Descent" at Beauport. Then he had abandoned the landing at Beauport in favour of one at Saint-Michel. Then he had countermanded that order as well. He had six more weeks at most before the fleet had to leave for England or be caught in the ice. He had to act.

To help devise yet another plan to deliver the crushing blow to his enemies, Wolfe summoned Saunders and his three brigadiers – Monckton, Townshend, and Murray – to a conference. There were four possibilities before them, Wolfe told them. The English could attack Montcalm above Québec, or between the St. Charles River and the Beauport tidal flats, or by the Montmorency where Lévis was encamped or, alternatively, Wolfe could storm the Lower Town from the harbour.

No records of this most important council of war have survived and Townshend is not here to help me out. However, it would be no surprise to hear that neither Townshend nor Murray favoured a direct attack on the French right or left flank at Beauport since the navy could not provide adequate cover. Until they all knew more about the terrain above Québec, and the location of the landing had been chosen with great care, I suspect that the brigadiers, like Wolfe, felt that this plan was premature. As for storming the harbour, it was never seriously considered as far as I know.

They talked for hours and, after their departure, Wolfe noted in his journal that there had been a "resolution to attack the French Army" but no final agreement, only a heated "debate about the method."

It was therefore up to Wolfe. He set to work to prepare a new plan of attack. This time he would see what could be done along the Montmorency.

By this time Wolfe's patience with the Canadians living in the territory occupied by his troops was at an end. Not a day went by without Canadian partisans shooting at troops, wounding and killing many soldiers. Information was passed constantly to Vaudreuil's headquarters at La Carnardière and the habitants often used their barns, their houses, and even their churches as ammunition and arm depots. So exasperated was he that on July 25, Wolfe issued a new proclamation in which he accused them of abusing "his kindness, his magnanimity, and his sentiments of humanity." Considering the people he hoped to conquer unworthy of his good faith, he ordered his commanders to lay waste to the countryside on both banks of the St. Lawrence, to take as many prisoners and hostages as they could, and to seize whatever private property they deemed appropriate. However, to demonstrate his humanity, he would wait until August 10 to put his threat into action.

Major Dalling of the Light Infantry took the proclamation to Saint-Henri on the south shore and posted it on the door of the church. While there, he captured 250 men and women, including the parish priest of Pointe-Lévy and forty men who could bear arms. Among the booty he brought back with him, were "almost an equal number [forty] of black cattle, seventy sheep and lambs and a few horses," or so Knox recorded in his diary. Dalling had not waited for August 10.

The object of the Great Enterprise: Québec, as seen from the south shore. During the siege, the English destroyed the majority of the town's buildings.
[Archives nationales du Québec à Québec (ANQ-Québec) GH470-136]

Louis-Antoine de Bougainville, devoted aide to Montcalm, looking much older in this portrait than he did in 1759. (ANQ-Québec E67-10934)

Le Marquis de Montcalm, the commander of the French regular troops in Canada. He was indecisive, morose, and pessimistic, but a hero to Bougainville. (ANQ-Québec GH571-5)

James Wolfe, the general sent to conquer Québec. He was devoted to his men, arrogant with his officers, loyal to his King, and sadistic towards the Canadians. He was an ugly man, but a fine dancer.
(ANQ-Québec E67 43-10929)

Le Marquis de Vaudreuil, Governor General of Canada – and the first Canadian to fill this position. A difficult person to get along with, he and Montcalm fought over strategy throughout the long siege.
(ANQ-Québec N775-12)

Notre-Dame-des-Victoires, the small church in the Lower Town named in thanks to the Virgin Mary for having previously saved Québec twice from the English. The miracle was not repeated in 1759. (ANQ-Québec 597-600)

The Montmorency Falls, as seen from the Beaupré coast. The English ships can be seen in action during the battle of July 31, in which Wolfe demonstrated the immense limitations of his generalship.
(ANQ-Québec GH470-134)

Monseigneur de Pontbriand, Bishop of Québec. His first and last concern was the survival of the Roman Catholic Church in Canada.
(ANQ-Québec N474-20)

Jeffery Amherst, commander-in-chief of the English forces in North America and Wolfe's superior officer. (ANQ-Québec GH1072-2)

Charles Saunders, the admiral who sailed one-third of the entire English navy up the St. Lawrence River to conquer Québec. A pirate by inclination, he rose to prominence by manipulating the levers of power. (ANQ-Québec N474-45)

Montcalm waited all summer long for Wolfe to make the first move encamped in this charming manor-house at Beauport, near the Montmorency Falls. (ANQ-Québec GH272-58)

Robert Monckton, senior brigadier and English second-in-command.
Wounded during the battle on September 13, he was shunted aside by
Townshend and played no role in the capitulation of Québec.
(ANQ-Québec N479-49)

Le Chevalier de Lévis, the most senior French officer after Montcalm. Had he been present at the battle of the Plains of Abraham, history might have recorded a very different outcome. (ANQ-Québec GH1172-35)

James Murray, brigadier and fourth-in-command of the English troops.
After the fall of Québec, he was made its first English governor.
(ANQ-Québec GH770-35)

François Bigot, the Intendant and the second
most important French official in Québec after
Vaudreuil. He was a repulsive creature both
physically and morally. (ANQ-Québec N574-23)

*Michel-Jean-Hughes Péan, a Canadian merchant and crony of Bigot's.
Both Péan and Bigot profited from the misery of the Canadians during
the long siege.* (ANQ-Québec N177-107)

Angélique-Geneviève Renaud d'Avène des Méloizes Péan, known as "Lélie." She was a charming and intelligent woman – the Pompadour of Canada. At age twenty-five, she became Bigot's mistress, with the approval of her husband. (ANQ-Québec GH770-163)

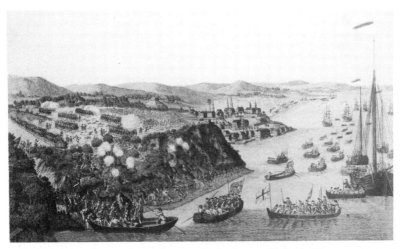

A view of the Plains of Abraham, which shows all the military action of September 13 taking place at once: the English ships in the St. Lawrence; the troops disembarking at the Anse-au-Foulon and scrambling up to the plains; the tight formations of the British troops; and the mass of French troops, Canadians, and Indians. (ANQ-Québec GH970-159)

George Townshend, one of Wolfe's brigadiers and his third-in-command. He caricatured the general mercilessly.
(ANQ-Québec PN-T/2)

The Death of Wolfe, as painted by Benjamin West. About twenty minutes into the battle on September 13, a Canadian marksman shot Wolfe in the chest. He died shortly afterwards. His final order to cut off the French retreat to the St. Charles River was not obeyed.
(National Gallery of Canada, Ottawa, #8007)

Montcalm blessé. During the French retreat, Montcalm was mortally wounded. However, this picture of him on the field of battle is inaccurate. Montcalm remained on his horse after being shot, and died in Québec the following day. (ANQ-Québec GH1070-144)

July 26, 1759

(Day Thirty-one)

Montmorency River
3:00 A.M.

Followed by a battalion from the 35th Regiment and a detachment of Rangers under Murray, a company of light infantry, and two field-pieces, Wolfe was on his way to the first ford on the Montmorency River situated about three miles above his camp. Every step of the way Major Moncrief urged on the soldiers pulling with slow progress the field-pieces up the steep and uneven trail. The last thing the major wanted to do was to annoy the general. But Wolfe became exasperated with the field-guns before he reached the ford and had them sent back to camp. The path they were following had narrowed abruptly as it passed through a ravine some three hundred yards long with steep banks about twenty feet high on each side.

As he emerged from the ravine, Wolfe could see the elaborate French defences on their side of the river. Knowing that the French were certainly spying on him, he had his men take cover near an abandoned house in a nearby clearing. He also sent the Rangers and a Canadian informer to the second ford about one mile farther upstream.

By nine o'clock Wolfe was inspecting the first ford. It was about a hundred and fifty yards long and four feet deep, and the water flowed over it in a gentle current. On the opposite bank the French had built strong fortifications augmented by the steep, woody bank. He was so impressed that he decided, as he wrote in his journal that night, that "it was to no purpose to attempt a passage there." After his tour of inspection, he and his party rejoined the troops to rest and wait for the Rangers. As he walked away from the ford he could sense the presence of his enemies hidden in the woods across from him.

His intuition was right. Nine hundred restless Indians and a few Canadians had been there since dawn, waiting silently, crouched behind trees and large boulders. They had wanted to attack before Wolfe reached the ford, but their captain, Charles-Michel Mouet de Langlade, had persuaded them to wait a little longer while he conferred with Lévis. By one o'clock he had not yet returned, as Lévis kept him waiting while he dispatched a message to Montcalm. Lévis realized he needed Montcalm's and Vaudreuil's consent before ordering an attack that could bring about the total engagement of both armies. But Montcalm's answer came too late.

At the ford the Indians and the Canadians finally lost patience. With a terrifying war cry, they were up and across the Montmorency attacking the English with fury. Almost naked, covered with paint, with tomahawks, knives, and scalps hanging from their belts, and carrying their muskets, the Indians ran through the ranks of the English soldiers, shooting and scalping as they went. The Canadians, most of them disguised as Indians, followed with the same speed, just as ready for the carnage. The English were horrified. Wolfe, thinking that the whole French army would engage him in battle, rushed to his main camp to order Townshend to turn out the troops.

The battle of the first ford, however, did not last long. At the beginning of the attack the English troops had scattered. But Murray, whom Wolfe had left in charge, was able to rally them. Under his encouragement, the troops managed to drive their attackers back across the Montmorency. They did not pursue the Indians and the Canadians beyond the river, as Murray had no orders to do so. Instead he buried his dead and sent the wounded soldiers back to camp with a message to Wolfe that it was all over. The English had lost forty-five men. The French did not keep a record of their losses on that day. But Murray's short battle with the Indians had been costly. They became so badly dispirited that they were practically useless for the rest of the campaign.

Wolfe's visit to the first ford had, as Murray said, "turned out to be little short of a disaster."

It is seven o'clock in the evening. The chapel of the Charlesbourg parish church in which the ecclesiastic, wearing a white surplice and a violet stole, was praying at an ornate *prie-dieu* was dedicated to the Virgin Mary. Mary was his favourite saint. He came to her often, especially in times of trouble, and he was by now most troubled and in need of comfort. The Bishop of Québec, his Excellency Henri-Marie Dubreil de Pontbriand, was a tall, ascetic man of frail constitution. In fact he was quite ill, but from what, I do not know. In 1759 he was fifty-one years old and he had arrived at Québec in the late summer of 1741. I will let him tell you about himself in his own words.

"I am the sixth Bishop of Québec. When I came here in 1741, my large diocese had been in existence for more than half a century. François de Laval, whom the Church will certainly declare to be a saint some day, founded it and nurtured it during the difficult early days of the colony. It is he who established most of the ecclesiastical institutions we are blessed with and who made the Church of our Lord an integral part of everyday life in our vast empire in America.

"His successor, also a holy man, Jean-Baptiste La Croix de Chevrières de Saint-Vallier, consolidated his work. Some found Monseigneur de Saint-Vallier too authoritarian and reformist, others complained that he meddled extensively in matters that were not of his authority, and a few recalcitrant souls accused him of being too prone to bring down God's wrath upon them. Be that as it may. For forty-two years he ruled the Church in Canada, until his death on December 26, 1727, at the age of seventy-four. God has already judged him; the verdict of history is of little value.

"Monseigneur de Saint-Vallier's coadjutor, the Capuchin monk Louis-François Duplessis de Mornay, should have succeeded him, but he never set foot in Canada. His successor was Pierre-Herman Dosquet, who spent about two years here, went back to France and resigned his see. My immediate predecessor, François-Louis de Pourroy de Lauberivière (what a beautiful name!) died almost immediately upon his arrival.

"So for fourteen years, between the death of Monseigneur de Saint-Vallier and my appointment, the Church in Canada was more or less leaderless. I had to rebuild almost from the bottom, creating new parishes, founding missions, ordaining priests, and preaching.

"Monsieur LaPierre, who is somewhat anti-clerical, will tell you that I also firmly positioned the Church among the privileged few who ruled over Canada. No doubt he finds fault with me because I attended dinners at the Governor's residence, soirées at the Intendant's, and because I entertained, as well. Again I refer to the judgement of God. All I did, I did to ensure the preservation of the Church."

As he takes a short walk around the chapel, shuffling some papers, I stand to ask him a question. But he glares at me and stares me back into my pew.

"A good illustration of my concern for the Church is my orders to the priests of my diocese should the English invade their parish. I told them they had to cooperate, to take the oath of allegiance to the English king if that was demanded of them, to lend their parish church to Protestants if it were necessary for their worship, and never to do or say anything that would harm the interests of the invader.

"My young friend Mennard said to me that I was exhorting my priests to be traitors. And then he added: 'Are we not to defend our homeland?' I had to help him understand that the priest serves God, not temporal princes. And furthermore, that I was not instructing my clergy to help the enemy. I was only asking them not to obstruct them and risk the destruction of our Church. It is not the same thing. But Mennard's anxiety about the defence of his homeland remains to this day.

"The Governor General uses my priests as spies. He is even encouraging them to harass the English. And some are listening to him, like the *curé* of Pointe-Lévy, Charles-Marie-Madeleine d'Youville, who has been arrested and sent to the English transports down the St. Lawrence. He is said to have led the resistance at Saint-Henri and to have exhorted his parishioners to annoy the enemy. Is this in the service of God or King?"

He is interrupted by the parish priest of Charlesbourg, who hands him what appears to be a letter. Pontbriand reads it quickly, becomes agitated, and kneels to pray as we in the congregation wait in silence. A few moments later, he stands and, turning around, he says sadly: "I have just been informed that the parish priest of Baie-Saint-Paul on the north shore, Louis Chaumont, constantly informs Monsieur de Vaudreuil about the movements of the English fleet. His colleagues, Pierre Chaufour of the parish of Saint-Michel de Bellechasse and Louis Saurault of Saint-Charles de Bellechasse, are more or less in charge of the militia in their parishes. The Abbé René Portneuf of Saint-Joachim on the Beaupré coast leads his people in opposing the English. And to top it all, Jean-Basile Parent, who is in charge of the parish in which General Wolfe has his residence, Ange-Gardien, often accompanies his parishioners in their sorties, the latest being on July 26. While His Excellency was inspecting the first ford on the Montmorency, the habitants of Ange-Gardien, accompanied by Monsieur Parent, killed two soldiers and wounded six. The abbé is also one of Monsieur de Vaudreuil's spies. In fact I have before me a letter, which Brigadier Townshend has found and sent to me, in which the Governor General invites Monsieur Parent to La Canardière on July 28 to obtain more information.

"And the *séminaristes* are following this poor example. Some have joined the Syntaxe Royale battalion and others have enlisted in the militia. The twenty-one-year-old son of Joseph Couillard des Ecores, the seigneur of La Rivière-du-Sud, is practically the captain of the militia of his village, and he is an ecclesiastic in minor orders. In a skirmish above Québec he was wounded and taken to the Hôpital Général. There he received a note from the Governor General expressing his vice-regal hope that the young man would recover soon. In his reply, Couillard informed Monsieur le Marquis de Vaudreuil that he was leaving the hospital as he had no time to be sick; he only had time to fight the English.

"I am at a loss to know what to do. I understand that they are Canadians, that this is their land, their country. They find it hard to be neutral when their people are attacked, wounded, killed, or made prisoner. I understand all that, just like I understand that it is heartbreaking for my priests to see their parishioners' homes destroyed, their property confiscated, and their future reduced to ashes. I understand. And believe me, I sympathize. But their first loyalty should not be to Canada. They are priests of the Church! And the work of God comes first. We must ensure that the Church survives."

By this time his eyes are full of tears. He wipes them off with a fine lace handkerchief and he walks slowly towards me. Towering above me, he says, "I pray for them as I pray for you. But, per-haps, as they have done, you will ask, What does he know, this bishop from France?"

He stops speaking for a moment. Then, with his eyes boring into mine, he whispers, "I have no answer for that, except, Go now in peace!"

He throws me a blessing and returns to his *prie-dieu*.

July 28, 1759

(Day Thirty-three)

Ange-Gardien
Throughout the day

When the first grey light of day awoke Wolfe, he also awoke from his torpor. He wrote to Monckton that his mind was made up. And this from a man who had hatched four plans only to reject them one after the other.

Wolfe decided that he would attack the French at the Johnstone Redoubt, situated on the Beauport tidal flats with no tree or even a shrub in sight, a fortification just west of the Montmorency River. It was not to be a decisive blow, only a minor operation, using four companies and one ship – too minor for him to command it himself. Nevertheless, he ordered the expedition equipped with 200 spades, 200 shovels, 50 pick-axes, 20 felling-axes and 100 hatchets, and to be on the safe side, he placed his grenadiers on alert.

James Cook, who was outfitting the ship to be used to reach the redoubt, had assured Wolfe that one of his "cats" (armed transports) would be able to come within a hundred feet of it. The whole affair should not take too long, according to Wolfe. The major problem he saw would be to keep the redoubt once it had been captured.

The same morning, Vaudreuil was also making decisions. He decided to attempt once again the destruction of the English fleet, despite the botched attempt of June 28. Bougainville was sent to Anse-des-Mères with a company of grenadiers to launch the new fireships. The wind was fair, although the night was not as dark as Bougainville had hoped. At nine o'clock the flotilla was towed down the St. Lawrence, arriving at the foot of Québec around midnight undetected by the English ships now above the town.

These fireships were very different from those used in June. This time sixty vessels – skiffs, barges, schooners, and shallops – were linked together by massive chains to form a 600-foot line across the St. Lawrence. At each end of the line small manned ships were stationed to prevent it from drifting. This naval contraption was filled with various flammable materials, with bombs and grenades, and with old cannon and pistols, their barrels loaded up to the muzzle with grape shot.

As this infernal device was launched, the French batteries increased their fire against the English positions at Pointe-aux-Pères to provide cover, but the gunboats, which were to lend their support to the expedition, were nowhere to be seen. Nevertheless, the fireships were allowed to drift towards the advance guard of the English fleet. Not a moment too soon, their fuses were lit, and the flames spread swiftly from one craft to the next until the whole line was ablaze.

This time the English did not panic. The lookout on the *Stirling Castle* was the first to raise the alarm. In no time, the sailors, most of whom had been resting in their hammocks, jumped into their boats and rowed towards the floating inferno. With a reckless courage that amazed their officers, they wrenched apart the chains, slashed the ropes, and towed section after section of the roaring fire to shore. They had taken "hell in tow!" And, their deed done, they were rewarded with half a pint of brandy each for their good work.

Vaudreuil showed no emotion upon being told of the second failure of his fireships. When informed, he shrugged his shoulders and sent word to Montcalm, who accepted the news with nonchalance. As for the Canadians in Québec and the troops at Beauport, by then they were accustomed to reverses and hardly paid attention to this latest. Wolfe was incensed, though, at the French temerity. The next day he arranged for a flag of truce and sent Vaudreuil a letter in which he stated categorically: "If the enemy presumes to send down any more fireships, they will be fastened to the transport ships housing the French and Canadian prisoners."

July 29, 1759

(Day Thirty-four)

Beaupré Coast
Throughout the day

The second failure of the French to destroy the English fleet buoyed Wolfe's spirits and made him start to think more boldly. He arose the next day determined to transform the minor operation of seizing the Johnstone Redoubt into a major one, to take place the following day, July 30. Saunders, who had already hoisted his flag on the *Centurion*, was to take charge of the participating flotilla, which included two other vessels, the *Three Sisters*, under James Cook, and the *Russell*.

By five o'clock in the afternoon most of Wolfe's troops on the Beaupré coast were standing at the ready, Monckton's brigade was holding itself in readiness to march at a moment's warning, and the flat-bottomed boats were all gathered at their designated areas.

So certain was Wolfe that July 30 would be a day of great portent in his life that he altered his last will and testament and entrusted it with his notebooks and the miniature of his fiancée to a former classmate and friend, John Jervis, master of the *Porcupine*. Wolfe then waited for the next day.

July 30, 1759

(Day Thirty-five)

The day dawned hot and still. There was no wind and there would be none, of that Saunders was certain. Wolfe had no choice but to cancel the operation, ordering that "the troops are to hold themselves in readiness tomorrow, to execute the orders of yesterday."

As the day dragged on Wolfe revised his plans and consulted with his brigadiers, none of whom, as Wolfe later remarked in his journal, approved of his plan. However, they proposed "nothing better."

While Wolfe was listening to his brigadiers' criticisms, Montcalm arrived in Québec with Bougainville and other senior officers to inspect the batteries. An English deserter had informed him that Wolfe intended to send more frigates above the city for a possible landing near Sillery.

He found the soldiers and sailors manning the batteries at Québec alert and confident. To send a message to the English across the St. Lawrence, Montcalm ordered them to fire in unison. The noise was impressive, if nothing else.

Sastisfied with his tour of inspection, he stopped at the Hôpital Général on his way back to Beauport for a piece of cake and a glass of wine with the Mother Superior and the nuns. He assured them that, once the English attacked, he would defeat them and Québec would be safe again. He also visited the sick and wounded lying on makeshift pallets scattered around the large building. Taking some money out of his purse, he gave it to Mère de Saint-Claude-de-la-Croix to provide a glass of wine in his name to each wounded soldier.

While in Québec, Montcalm did not see the two gallows that had been erected in haste. Nor did he see the two bodies dangling from them. Two soldiers, one twenty and the other sixteen, had been hanged that morning for stealing a barrel of whisky. They had been caught at about six o'clock, and by ten they had been tried and condemned. Their accomplice, known as la Charlan, had been declared insane and confined for life in the Hôpital Général.

For many days the bodies of the two young men remained rocking from the gallows' ropes over the St. Lawrence.

July 31, 1759

(Day Thirty-six)

Beaupré coast
5:00 A.M.

The day was clear. Wolfe realized that by noon it would become extremely hot, but there was already a strong breeze from the southwest to cool the air and blow Saunders' ships across to the Johnstone Redoubt. An hour earlier, Saunders had sent word to Wolfe that, under these fair conditions, the navy could take part in the operation. Now, from the windows of his farmhouse, Wolfe could see the sails being raised on many of the ships. He had already sent Colonel Howe and his troops on a march to the first ford to trick the French into thinking that an attack would come from there. Monckton's grenadiers had arrived earlier on the Ile d'Orléans, and flat-bottomed boats were transporting the rest of his brigade to the appointed rendezvous. Major Dalling and a few hundred men guarded the batteries on Pointe-aux-Pères, with orders to bombard the town with as much fire as possible when Wolfe gave the signal.

Wolfe saw no need to delay any longer, and he ordered the operation to commence. Then he was rowed to the *Russell* from where he would orchestrate the capture of the Johnstone Redoubt. Four companies of grenadiers were already aboard the *Russell* and the *Three Sisters*.

At nine o'clock, Saunders ordered the three ships participating in the attack to proceed to the redoubt about a quarter of a mile west of the Montmorency Falls. Two hours later, Wolfe had reason to be bitterly disappointed.

Captain Cook had miscalculated. His cats had gone aground much further away from the redoubt than the hundred feet he had estimated. Then they discovered there were two redoubts, not one as expected: the Johnstone, the bigger of the two, and a smaller one hidden from view behind it. Both were too far away for the guns of the *Centurion* to provide the necessary cover for a direct attack, and both were far closer to the French trenches than Wolfe had foreseen. In these circumstances, no assault against either of the fortifications was possible.

It was noon by then and Wolfe was faced with the options of cancelling the attack, and appearing to be just as indecisive as before, or of ordering a full bombardment, no matter what. He decided not to back down. He gave the signal for the sixty-four guns of the *Centurion*, the combined twenty-eight guns of the *Three Sisters* and of the *Russell*, the forty guns located on the Montmorency, and the twenty-nine guns at Pointe-aux-Pères to open fire all at the same time.

There were by now close to three hundred flat-bottomed boats in the channel between the Beauport coast and Ile d'Orléans. They carried Monckton's brigage, a large contingent of marines and sailors, and most of the soldiers who had been stationed on the island. The boats lay motionless in the intense heat, awaiting Wolfe's orders. Many of the men on board were already heat-struck. Now they also had to endure the terrible din of 161 guns bombarding all French positions in and around Québec.

The French troops were faring better. As soon as Lévis had been informed of Howe's march to the first ford, he had dispatched five hundred Canadians from the Montréal brigade and as many Indians as were available with instructions to keep Howe on his side of the river. He had also ordered the soldiers under his command to their trenches and had extended his line closer to the isolated redoubts, which he judged accurately to be Wolfe's goal. When the cannonade started at noon, Lévis sent instructions to the men in the redoubts to fire all their ammunition and then retreat to the trenches.

From a grassy hill some two hundred feet above the beach, Vaudreuil, Montcalm, and Bougainville had watched for some time the English ships and boats. They were at a loss to figure out Wolfe's tactics. When the bombardment had begun, Montcalm had replied as best he could with his twenty small-calibre cannon and had ordered all the troops to their posts. He sent the Royal-Roussillon and the Guyenne regiments closer to Lévis' camp with instructions to Lévis to make full use of the troops should he be attacked. Vaudreuil had seen enough, and returned to La Canardière, but Montcalm and Bougainville remained on the hill.

With thousands of bombs flying at them from every conceivable direction, the defenders of the French redoubts stayed where they were, firing mercilessly on the *Russell* and the *Three Sisters*. To save lives, Wolfe ordered most of the grenadiers off the transports to the shore. He himself remained where he was, walking about the deck of the *Russell* in full view of the enemy and unperturbed by the cannonballs falling around him. The ship had already been struck three times, and his stick had been knocked out of his hand by the force of one impact.

By two o'clock in the afternoon, Wolfe was feeling utterly frustrated. He did not know what to do. He had assembled a huge force, half of which was waiting on the Beaupré side of the Montmorency, the other half bobbing in the St. Lawrence. All his soldiers were in full battle array, suffering for hours in the sweltering heat, unfed, with no latrines, and at the mercy of enemy fire. And to add to his frustration, the naval guns were hardly accurate at all. In fact he thought the navy had been most incompetent. It had not been able to sail close to his objective and, so, could not knock out the guns that were decimating his grenadiers.

But there was no way he could abandon the operation. His soldiers would never forgive him should he do so. For over five weeks they had waited patiently for a chance to do what he had trained them for – to fight. If he cancelled now, their morale would be so low as to render them utterly useless. His officers – particularly the brigadiers – would make him the butt of their jokes. In time, they might demand a parliamentary inquiry. Wolfe had no way out. He had to see it through.

As he was deliberating what to do next, Wolfe noticed that

the enemy troops on the high land above the redoubts appeared to be moving confusedly. Judging that he should seize this opportunity, he sent an aide to tell Monckton in the channel between Beauport and the Ile d'Orléans to "prepare for action" and to tell Townshend and Murray to ford the Montmorency as per his orders of July 29. The time had come to fight the French.

What Wolfe had taken to be confusion was merely Montcalm on his way to Lévis' camp with an escort. Together Montcalm and Lévis inspected the men in the trenches. At every turn they were greeted enthusiasticlly. In their discussion, Montcalm and Lévis came to the conclusion that Wolfe's objective was the left of the French line. Montcalm therefore ordered reinforcements to the left flank. When word came that Howe was returning to the main English camp, the Chevalier de Johnstone, Lévis' aide-de-camp, was dispatched to bring back most of the Canadians and Indians guarding the ford. When they returned they were stationed between the threatened redoubts and the entrenchments on the high land behind.

After Montcalm's departure, Lévis went back to the trenches, where his soldiers were suffering considerably from the oppressive heat and the din of the cannon. Over and over again he refused the advice of his senior officers to take cover. He was cool and self-possessed under fire, and he knew his example would be a great encouragement to his troops. He watched the English flat-bottomed boats bobbing near the shore and realized that Wolfe would have to make a move: the tide had turned and was beginning to flood the flats.

Townshend and Murray welcomed the news that they could cross the Montmorency as they had been in full readiness since seven o'clock that morning. When Howe arrived from the ford, he and his men joined Townshend's brigade. In the distance, the men could see Monckton's boats moving towards the shore.

At Townshend's command the troops began to march towards the Montmorency. They had almost reached the riverbank, when one of Wolfe's aides came galloping in their tracks with an order for them to halt. The unexpected had happened. The barges leading Monckton's convoy had hit an unseen barrier as they approached the shore and had run aground. Upon inspection, the sailors had discovered an underwater ledge of rock that ran for a considerable distance. Access to the shore was impossible.

Monckton had sent an officer to row back to inform Wolfe of this setback and had ordered the grounded boats to be dragged back to safety in the channel. The French troops, witnessing this confusion, had burst into roars of laughter and fired a number of shots that did considerable damage.

Admiral Saunders on the *Centurion* and Wolfe on the *Russell* were told about the ledge at about half past three. Saunders, some five hundred yards from the *Russell*, sent word to Wolfe to take a barge and go out himself to look for a suitable landing place. Before too long, Wolfe and Captain James Chads were underway.

For the next hour or so they tried to locate an opening in the shoal, all the while dodging enemy fire. Finally a narrow passage was found. The signal went up for Monckton to begin the landing again.

This time they were successful. A beachhead was secured on the west side of the Montomorency. The troops were ordered ashore to wait there for Townshend's forces. For a while Wolfe remained with Captain Chads in the channel watching the disembarkation amid powerful enemy fire. Near them, two barges were sunk with the loss of many lives.

Tired of their cramped quarters, many of the soldiers did not wait for their boats to reach the shore but jumped out and waded to the beach. The Louisbourg Grenadiers were in front, the Royal American Regiment was next, and the others behind. As the last men were scrambling ashore, a naval officer arrived from Saunders to inform Wolfe that the French had abandoned the redoubts and had gone to their trenches. It was by then five-thirty in the afternoon.

Like stallions let out of their stables, the Louisbourg Grenadiers paced on the shore forgetful of the order to form ranks and be silent. To quiet them, one of their sergeants, Ned

Botwood, began to sing a song he had composed, which most of the soldiers now knew by heart. With great zest, they took up the last refrain: "So at you, ye bitches, here's give you Hot Stuff."

Unfortunately the song did not have the desired calming effect. It actually made the Grenadiers more restless and foolhardy. Suddenly all hell broke loose. The Grenadiers charged up to the abandoned redoubt closest to them. Finding it empty, they stormed up the hill toward the French trenches. As they neared the crest, the French fired with great fervour. One line of Grenadiers after another fell back, covering the steep slope with dead and wounded redcoats. Botwood and the officers tried valiantly to restore order out of the chaos, but to no avail. And the rain which had been threatening all day chose this very moment to come down in torrents, shrouding the area in darkness. Thunder and lightning competed with the roar of the cannon. The entire battlefield became a sea of mud. The surviving Grenadiers on the grade began to slide back, losing their balance and tumbling over their dead and wounded comrades. Those who could retreat rushed to relative safety behind the abandoned redoubts, where their officers tried once again to create some order in the ranks. Sergeant Botwood was not there. A musket ball had smashed his skull.

Wolfe stood on the shore, immobile with anger as he watched his enterprise being washed away by the folly of men and the fury of nature. He did not even bother to order back the two companies of the Royal American who were behaving as foolishly as the Louisbourg Grenadiers. Nor did he make any move to order the rest of Monckton's brigade into battle. He just stood there, impassive on the outside, raging on the inside.

But, when Townshend and Murray tried to attack the second redoubt, Wolfe ordered them back. The rising tide would soon cut them off and prevent their escape to the Beaupré coast. He sounded the retreat. Monckton was sent back to Pointe-Lévy, Saunders burned the two beached transports, abandoning their combined twenty-eight guns for Montcalm to do with as he pleased, and Wolfe began to supervise the withdrawal of his army.

On the battlefield Captain David Ochterloney of the Royal American lay dying, a bullet through his lungs. Lying beside him was his friend and companion, Ensign Peyton, whose left leg had been shattered. Despite the drenching rain and the cries of the wounded, they lay quietly, conversing peacefully and waiting. When the retreat was sounded, some soldiers came to carry them away, but Ochterloney refused to be moved and Peyton would not abandon his friend.

An hour or so later, Indians and Canadians came on the field to loot and scalp the fallen. Ochterloney and Peyton were robbed in spite of Ochterloney yelling in French that he and Peyton were surrendering. They stole Ochterloney's money and whatever else they could find in his pockets. One of the Indians then stabbed him in the groin. As another was about to finish Ochterloney off, a shot rang out, killing the Indian.

Unnoticed, Peyton had succeeded in crawling to where a double musket lay close at hand. He was about to fire a second shot when the other Indian sprang upon him and wounded him in the shoulder. They grappled fiercely but Peyton had the upper hand, and soon the Indian lay dead upon him. Exhausted, he rolled over and crawled behind a rock, believing that Ochterloney was dead. He was about to pass out when some Highlanders came by. They gave Peyton a drink of rum, and one of them slung him over his shoulder and carried him to safety. A half-hour later, a French officer, surveying the battlefield, came upon Ochterloney. Seeing that the captain was still alive, he commandeered a cart and supervised his removal to the Hôpital Général.

To Wolfe's amazement the English retreat was being carried out "in good order," and the French were helping him by not firing at the retreating soldiers. However, the Highlanders refused to cross the Montmorency until they were certain that their regiment (the 78th) was all assembled. The exasperated general and his brigadiers threatened and swore, but the Scots would not move. With great dignity and patience they explained that they could not, and would not, abandon their clansmen. Only when they were finally persuaded that all "had re-embarked" did they follow Wolfe. By that time the water was so high that the regiment could barely make it to the opposite bank.

Shortly after nine o'clock in the evening, Wolfe was back at his house at Ange-Gardien. Before he took a short rest, he visited the wounded and later had dinner with his officers. Montcalm stayed in his trenches.

There you have it, the story of the Battle of Montmorency, the first major encounter of the Great Enterprise. The English lost 443 men; dead, wounded, missing. Among them were one colonel, two captains, twenty-one lieutenants, and three ensigns. The French casualties were sixty dead or wounded.

Lévis was quite satisfied with himself. For over twelve hours he had been on his feet, most of that time under relentless enemy fire. And he was pleased with the efforts of the Canadians who had been stationed closest to the attacking English. In his report of the battle, he praised their courage and good will.

All day Vaudreuil had felt left out. Not once had Montcalm consulted him or even gone through the motions that Vaudreuil's advice had been needed. Now it was all over, Vaudreuil gave his praise to Lévis, whose effective planning, he wrote, had brought about the "happy event" of the English retreat. "Be careful of yourself, I pray you, for we need you."

To Bourlamaque in the West, Vaudreuil sent a message of hope. The old man no longer had any doubt about being able to safeguard Québec.

Montcalm was wiser. To the same Bourlamaque, he wrote: "You see, Monsieur, the affair of today is but a small prelude to something more important, for which we are now waiting."

No doubt it was a splendid day for the French and the Canadians, but I can not help wondering why Montcalm did not pursue the English. Why did he allow them to cross the Montmorency into safety? When I put the question to Bougainville, he replies, "We ran out of ammunition, and the rain had soaked the powder."

"There's another reason, surely?" I insist.

He looks at me as if he does not want to be bothered any longer, but after a while he says, "Le Marquis de Montcalm was in his trenches and there he would stay. The English general was not about to lure him out."

"But your general could have destroyed the English army?"

"Only a part of it. We had no idea of how many troops were on the Ile d'Orléans or at Pointe-Lévy. And then there was the fleet. So it was thought better that we stayed where we were and wait for another day."

"I'm not persuaded."

"You need not be," Bougainville replies, smiling. "You weren't there." And he leaves.

Wolfe must have been in despair. After weeks of indecision, he had nothing to show for the decision he had made but a startling defeat. He had to assume the total responsibility for it even though most of the mistakes made were not his. He could reproach himself, however, for having put too many men in too many boats at the same time. Later he would say that "It is unfortunate that a man sees his error often too late to remedy it," and he would explain that he undertook the operation at Montmorency to carry out the orders of the King, persuaded as he was "that a victorious army finds no difficulties."

As for the soldiers, Wolfe rebuked the Grenadiers mildly for supposing that, all by themselves, they could beat the French army. He controlled his anger at them because he did not want any of them to be discouraged. The English defeat at Montmorency on July 31 was, in his word, "inconsiderable" and could be "easily repaired when a favourable opportunity" presented itself.

That opportunity, obviously, had yet to come.

August 2-8, 1759

(Day Thirty-eight to Forty-four)

The week following the Battle of Montmorency saw only limited action on both sides, frustrating everyone concerned.

On August 2, the English asked for a four-hour truce to allow them to send Ochterloney his personal effects and a letter Wolfe had written him. Ochterloney had asked for his servant, but Vaudreuil would not permit it. In his short note, Wolfe made a pledge to the nuns of the Hôpital Général that, should he be victorious, he would protect them and their hospital.

During the truce, the soldiers and sailors at Québec started to clear the streets of rubble and repair their batteries. The people retrieved what they could find of their possessions. At six o'clock in the evening the truce came to an end and the bombardment of the town began again. Four days later it was still going on.

Meanwhile, Vaudreuil received an imposing delegation of Indians who presented him with a necklace, thus ransoming a Canadian who was to be executed that day for theft.

On August 8, Murray was cold and wet. It was a good thing he had brought his hat.

Wolfe had sent Murray with 1,200 men to the upper St. Lawrence to burn the four or five frigates which the French were said to have at Trois-Rivières, to destroy a munitions depot rumoured to be at Deschambault, less than thirty miles west of Québec, and to open direct communications with Amherst who was not giving any signs of life.

Murray made two plans. One was to land a force at Saint-Michel and walk to Deschambault; the second was go there by water. But he was not able to carry out either plan. A landing at Saint-Michel would be suicidal given the large French presence above Québec, and Mother Nature would not provide the winds necessary for him to sail to Deschambault. Unwilling to remain idle with his large force at the ready, Murray decided to attack Pointe-aux-Trembles, where Carleton had found dinner partners in July. Murray assumed that, since the French had erected powerful batteries on the heights around there, he had to silence them before they did serious damage to the English ships above Québec. On August 8, a rainy day, he was in the St. Lawrence, glad to be wearing a hat.

In front of Pointe-aux-Trembles, Murray surveyed the shore one more time and then he waved his hat. At this signal, his lead boat rowed forward, followed by the rest – all of them running aground on an underwater ledge, similar to the one that had thwarted Wolfe on July 31. Murray lost precious moments searching for an opening and, once he had found one, his advance party proceeded to the shore only to come under intense fire from French guns. Instead of charging up the hill to the church as Murray had ordered, the soldiers took cover, infuriating their commanding officer, who had himself rowed to shore in order to take personal command of the operation, still wearing his hat.

Sixteen minutes had passed since Murray had launched the encounter that would save the English expedition above Québec. He waved his hat again, this time to order the retreat. The tide was rising; the fire of the French guns was relentless. The advance party scurried back to the shore and jumped into the drifting boats. Three feet of water had defeated Murray.

After his troops were out of range of the French guns, he sent his wounded to the *Sutherland* and left the dead to drift down the St. Lawrence. Some distance from the shore, he portioned what was left of the dry ammunition. Then, huddled against the rain, he and his men waited until the tide reached its highest point.

This happy event occurred at two o'clock in the afternoon. Murray waved his hat and the flotilla was again in motion. Only the muffled creaking of the oars was heard as the boats glided to shore. The French were nowhere to be seen.

The first English boat grated on the rocks and its soldiers jumped out and walked up onto the beach. They were joined quickly by the rest of the army and by Murray. Not one shot greeted them.

Murray smiled, but a thundering yell, shattering the quiet of the day, wiped all his satisfaction away. Hundreds of men – French, Canadian, and Indian – rushed out of the church, the windmill, the adjoining houses, the woods, from everywhere. On the height of land a French officer, resplendent in his uniform, sat erect on a fine horse, his sword in hand. He raised his sword in salute, and hundreds of muskets fired.

The English sailors standing by their oars were mowed down. Their boats floated aimlessly among dead and wounded bodies. The soldiers on the beach turned tail and scrambled to retrieve the crafts. When they found one they threw themselves aboard and rowed furiously out into the St. Lawrence beyond range. One soldier stopped, aimed carefully, and shot the French officer's beautiful horse. It was Murray's only consolation of the day.

The memory of this rout of the English brings a smile to Bougainville's lips.

"Not bad for a first independent command?" he laughs. Before I have the time to reply, he has launched into a declamation about this, the most glorious day of his career. He will never forget it, he promises me.

"How did you get to Pointe-aux-Trembles?"

He laughs again, "I rode." But then he gets serious, "Monsieur le Marquis de Montcalm was perturbed by the number of English ships above Québec and feared for the safety of his supplies, which he had ordered taken to Batiscan, some fifty miles above Québec. So he sent me with a thousand men to stop the English from landing. I used about six hundred of them, the best of our army, fine Grenadiers, good riders in the cavalry, superb Canadian sharpshooters, and reliable Indians. Your friend Mascou was there with the young Mennard."

"What about Lefebvre?" I ask.

"He would not leave his mother. But let me tell you, that day I tasted the sweet savour of *la gloire* for the first time. It was a great day!"

Safely aboard the *Sutherland* Murray assessed his losses: 140 soldiers and thirty sailors dead, wounded, or missing. He and Admiral Holmes discussed how to continue their mission. They abandoned Wolfe's idea of destroying the French frigates at Trois-Rivières, for, as Murray later wrote Wolfe, "we want water to carry us much higher." They agreed that the soldiers would now be taken by boat to Deschambault the night before the planned attack and that the navy would arrive there the following day, catching the French by surprise – or so they hoped. However, the landing at Deschambault could not take place until Holmes had taken additional soundings and the tide was just right. In the meantime, the soldiers would disembark at Saint-Antoine on the south shore, almost directly across from the *Sutherland*. If the Canadians resisted, their village would be burned to the ground.

In his report to Wolfe, Murray added a note of bravado: "I have attacked them [the French] three times with various success. Hitherto they may sing Te Deum, but the tune will certainly be mine in a few days." Murray had an astounding capacity to delude himself.

Father Récher did not fool himself. He never ceased to work, managing to be everywhere he was needed. While Murray and Bougainville were playing their games at Pointe-aux-Trembles, he had gone to the Hôpital Général to meet with the Bishop, who was there on his daily rounds. He had found his ecclesiastical superior looking aged and frail, his eyes sunken in his face and the rings around them blacker than ever. Pontbriand was sitting in the alcove with Captain Ochterloney who, despite the kind ministrations of the sisters, was not recovering. A day or so before, Wolfe had sent money as a reward for the officer who had saved Ochterloney's life, but Vaudreuil had returned it, explaining that the officer had only done his duty. After a brief conversation with Pontbriand regarding dispensation and other ecclesiastical matters, Récher returned to the town to look after the sick and the poor.

Jean-Felix Récher had come from France in the summer of 1747, and two years later, barely twenty-five years old, he became the parish priest of Québec. For most of his ministry he had been caught in the usual wrangling between the various ecclesiastical authorities over his powers and prerogatives. A Norman, Récher stood his ground, and the matter of jurisdiction was not settled until after his death in 1768.

Récher played a minor role in the affairs I am relating to you, but an invaluable one for me. He left a diary, an extensive one, of the events between 1759 and 1760. In his writing, he is not too concerned with the events of the war as they unfolded, contenting himself to repeat only what he heard. What is important about his diary is that it is the only document I have read that chronicles the hardships of the people. For me, then, he is a major figure.

Récher returned to Québec after curfew but was able to enter the town as the Porte du Palais had been left open. Shortly after Récher arrived, four or five soldiers on horseback came through the same gate. More soldiers followed on foot, then came a hundred women, children, and old men. All were in rags and hardly able to walk. Their bodies were a mass of sores and bites from thousands of mosquitoes and black flies. Their eyes told a horrifying story of cruelty, deprivation, and exhaustion.

Unable to bring down supplies by the river because of the English presence above Québec, Cadet had force-marched these half-starved people fifty miles to pick up provisions from his stockpile in Bastican. In Batiscan he gave them 271 carts but neither horses nor oxen to pull them. And so they had dragged the carts through almost impassable terrain, on a path hardly wide enough for two people, by hand, back to

Québec. They travelled day and night with nothing more to eat than their normal meagre rations, and when they fell down from exhaustion, the soldiers beat them.

They returned to Québec with 700 barrels of pork and flour.

———————

In my meanderings through the past, I meet Father Baudouin on the esplanade. He has just witnessed the delivery of the carts. His eyes are full of tears. Through the din of the bombs we can just hear each other.

"A little girl died. She was raped, I think. An old man could not make it back alive and a small boy was crushed by a cart. Monsieur LaPierre, there is no relief in sight."

"You find Montcalm too cautious?"

"He seems unwilling to seize the initiative, contenting himself with waiting for the one glorious battle that will end our nightmare –"

"Or he is waiting for the English to go home," I yell above the noise, interrupting him as I often do when I am interviewing someone.

"Perhaps, but he should encourage them to do it quickly. He gets enough advice. But most of it, I suppose, is of little value."

His wheezing forces him to halt in mid-outburst, and I jump in, mentioning that I have heard that some in Montcalm's entourage want him to abandon Québec and make his stand at Montréal, where Amherst is bound to arrive sometime this century. The harvest is pretty good west of Québec, he should have plenty to eat, I add.

Baudouin smiles and admonishes me: "Do not be uncharitable. Le Général Amherst is like Caesar. An emperor always moves slowly. I had not heard about the possible move to Montréal. I suppose your informants tell you that even if it were the right thing to do, it still would not happen. Le Marquis de Vaudreuil will oppose it because it was not his idea. His Excellency is always blamed for Montcalm's dilatoriness."

He catches his breath again and adds, "Did you know that today or yesterday Montcalm received a delegation of Indians stationed at the first ford on the Montmorency and of militiamen from Montréal? They all proposed to him the same idea: that he should attack the English *dans les bois* from the Beaupré camp, using the first ford as a passage. Did you know that?"

"No."

"He did not even bother to reply, except to say, 'Let the English make the first move.'"

"He is repeating that *ad nauseum*," I say maliciously. We stand quietly for a minute or so listening to the bombs attacking like mosquitoes.

"I suppose that the Indians and the Canadians are restless?" I ask.

"Yes, they both are. The Indians are not used to long sieges and the Canadians just want to get back to their homes. Already two thousand are said to have done just that. To stop the hemorrhage, Montcalm has threatened to turn any who leave over to the Indians, but this hardly frightens the militia. He has whipped some almost to death, but still they leave."

"Bougainville tells me that they are deserters, traitors. What do you think of that?"

"With all due respect, what does he know of it, Monsieur le Colonel de Bougainville?"

His eyes fill with tears again. "I see young men like Lefebvre hardly out of their childhood and old men barely able to lift an axe or a shovel. They are doing their part. I see frightened children and desperate women alone on their farms, many of which are in the front lines of the English destruction. And they, too, harass the enemy. I see all that and I get angry that the French do not fully understand. Winter is coming and there will be, obviously, no further help from France. The people have to harvest their crops. Their going home has little to do with treason or with cowardice. They have to survive. They have given much in this campaign, and they have received little in return."

He wipes his tears and catches his breath before going on with a smile. "A man from Saint-Antoine by the name of Houle sent a floating battery downstream with the hope of destroying the English ships. His fireship had four stories, two filled with grenades and the others with gun barrels. There was a mechanism to ignite the whole contraption but it did not work. No attempt to burn the English fleet has worked. I can only think, Monsieur LaPierre, that God does not want us to burn the English fleet."

We both laugh, then Baudouin gets to his feet and looks over the city, at the bombs falling. Before he leaves, he says, "We are alone. When the French have had their fill of *la gloire*, they will go home. But we shall still be here – with nothing."

August 9, 1759

(Day Forty-five)

Since it had begun in the middle of July, the bombardment of Québec had hardly stopped. Close to nine thousand bombs and ten thousand cannonballs had fallen on the capital. Panet, who as a notary knew these matters, estimated the value of the losses at over ten million *livres*.

Around supper time on August 8, the English had increased their fire upon the town. There had been no let-up since then. By two o'clock the next morning, the entire Lower Town was on fire. The northeast wind fanned the flames into an immense conflagration and carried it to the Upper Town. Over a hundred and sixty houses were burning; twenty-two casks of brandy blew up, adding to the blaze. Soon the Canadians' symbol of hope, Notre-Dame-des-Victoires, was engulfed.

Beyond manning the interminable and exhausting bucket lines, there was nothing to be done except to wait until the English became exhausted, or the wind died down, or the fire, having nothing else to burn, extinguished itself, or God had spent His wrath.

By mid-afternoon He had not done so. The town was almost pitch black. A thick cloud, which could be seen all the way to Beauport, filled the sky and burned the eyes of those unfortunate enough to be there. The heat was intense. Street after street was engulfed, and left empty and smouldering. The walls of what had been elegant houses stood like ghosts. There were hardly thirty houses still standing and most of them were uninhabitable. In his walk through the rubble looking for victims, Baudouin found a crucifix. He took it to the Séminaire as a talisman.

Only a smoking shell remained of the church Madame Lefebvre loved so much. As long as Notre-Dame-des-Victoires had stood, she had hope. Now she had none. Her son held her trembling in his arms. Suddenly she had become an old and weak woman. After a while, she slowly disengaged herself and walked into the ruins of the church. Wiping his tears, Jean-François-Xavier followed her. A few moments later she was on her knees in front of the remains of the altar, cradling the blackened head of the statue of the Virgin. She gazed at it for a long time, then she began to rub away the soot. He watched her for a minute or two, then he helped her.

While Québec was burning, Captain Joseph Goreham of the Rangers was in the countryside carrying out Wolfe's orders to burn every house, every barn, every building. Only churches would be spared, unless they were being used for military purposes. Goreham's first target was Baie-Saint-Paul, a small village about fifty miles east of Québec on the north shore. The inhabitants, mostly women, children, and old men, had been firing on the English ships. When Goreham arrived to punish them, they had the temerity to shoot at his party, killing one Ranger and wounding eight others. Then they took to the woods.

Unable to round up any human captives, Goreham had to be satisfied with twenty head of black cattle, forty sheep and hogs, a great quantity of poultry, and an impressive load of food, books, apparel, and household belongings. In the house of the parish priest, Louis Chaumont, a Canadian and a fierce militant, Goreham also found incriminating letters from Vaudreuil.

His plundering over, Goreham ordered every building burned except the church. There he posted the proclamation Wolfe had prepared at the end of July. In thick smoke and raging flames, the Rangers left for La Malbaie, downriver, where they destroyed the entire village. Then they crossed to Sainte-Anne-de-la-Pocatière on the south shore, where fifty farms were soon aflame.

The terror had begun. In Saint-Antoine, not too far from the Etchemin River, Murray was landing his troops. As the soldiers disembarked, the Canadians fired upon them, killing a captain and four men. Incensed, Murray had Major Dalling burn down the whole village, except for the church. For the rest of the day and well into the night, smoke from the burning villages, farms, and the town of Québec rose steadily into the sky.

At La Canardière, Vaudreuil was holding a council of war. News had come from the West.

Amherst had arrived in the Lake Champlain district at the end of June, and by the end of July he was at Carillon. At seven o'clock on the night of July 26, he was about to storm the fort, but it literally blew up in his face. Bourlamaque, following his orders, had evacuated it, leaving a slow fuse in the powder magazine. The English walked in and renamed what was left of the fort, Ticonderoga.

While his engineers were redesigning and rebuilding the fort, Amherst set out for Saint-Frédéric, dragging his boats to Lake Champlain. There, again, he found that Bourlamaque had already blown up the fort and had sailed north to the Ile-aux-Noix at the entrance of the Richelieu River. Amherst proceeded to rename Saint-Frédéric, Crown Point and to build an imposing, but useless, fortress on its ruins.

"Like a Roman Emperor, Monsieur Amherst travels in style," Bougainville tells me. "He erects forts he has no use for, builds navies to take him nowhere, and probably will not get to his destination, Montréal, in this campaign."

"What about his other generals?"

"There was only one," he replies, abandoning the conceit of the present tense. "John Prideaux was his name. I am not even too sure if he was a general. He first went to our Chouaguen, their Oswego, and then went on to lay siege to Niagara. What do you know about Niagara?"

I think for a moment or two, then scurry to find a book.

"Niagara means Thunder of the Water, and it says here in this book that, once upon a time, a God by the name of Hinv lived in the falls. The local Indians held him responsible for their being sick and dying and also for their continuing bad crops. To placate him they sacrificed the chief's beautiful daughter by sending her cascading down the smaller portion of the falls in her canoe. There she was caught by one of Hinv's sons who took her for his wife. When she complained to her new husband about the misery of her people, he told her that it was the fault of a serpent that lived in the larger falls. In a dream she told her people to kill the serpent, which they did. To honour her beauty and courage, Hinv took the body of the serpent and arranged it in the form of a horseshoe over the escarpment."

"Interesting and amusing," Bougainville says in a petulant voice. "But you should tell your readers that if we lose Niagara, it is the end. We will no longer have control of the region from the Ohio to the Mississippi, Prideaux will come down Lake Ontario to meet Amherst around the rapids of the St. Lawrence, and both armies will march in triumph to Montréal."

Bougainville adds that Vaudreuil announced to his officers at the council of war that at five o'clock in the afternoon of July 25, after a three-week siege, the commander of the fort at Niagara, Pierre Pouchot, had surrendered with his 607 men.

"I was not present when he made this announcement," says Bougainville, "I was with my army above Québec. But Monsieur le Marquis de Montcalm told me all about it. We had made many mistakes in the West. Pouchot had been too optimistic or reckless. For instance, he had sent the greatest part of his force, 2,500 men with much needed supplies and arms, to what the English call Pittsburg or our own Fort Duquesne. When the English were upon him, Pouchot called them back. But on July 24, and in sight of the defendants of the fort, they were butchered. After that, Pouchot could barely keep his men at their posts, so he had to surrender. By the way, the English general was not able to enjoy the fruit of his labour, as it were. Five days before the capture of the fort, one of his own soldiers shot him accidentally. Pouchot had to surrender to William Johnson – that creature who stole the Indians from us."

"Bourlamaque made no mistakes," I said to calm him. "He was resourceful, ingenious, and full of energy in spite of an old wound that caused him much pain and robbed him of his much-needed sleep."

"But most of his men were of little use," Bougainville retorts angrily. "He had about three thousand of them –"

I interrupt him again, even though I know this annoys him. "He had exactly 3,040 men, 178 sailors, 173 officers, and 131 servants. I cannot recall the number of clerks and labourers assigned to him."

As if he had not heard me, Bougainville repeats the three thousand figure and goes on, " – including twelve hundred militia, but many of them were young boys or old men. More than two hundred of his soldiers were in the hospital, and not a day went by that others did not declare themselves incapacitated. The majority of the rest were undisciplined, drunk half the time, unwilling to work or discouraged, and too many deserted."

"Your general should have sent him reinforcements!"

"Do not be more of a fool than you need to be. We had none to spare . . . although, I must say, the arguments of le Chevalier de Bourlamaque were very solid. He asked Monsieur de Montcalm, 'What is the use of guarding the main door if we allow the enemy to enter through those on the sides or in the back?'

"With the fall of Niagara, *Mon Général* came to the conclusion that only a miracle would prevent the colony from falling into English hands by the end of the campaign. Even he, surrounded as he was by charlatans and felons, could not save it. He could not stop the gangrene that infected the whole body and which was about to reach the heart."

With Niagara in English hands, the front line for the defence of Montréal moved to the head of the rapids on the St. Lawrence. There the French had 1,100 men under le Chevalier de la Corne. To make the best of a poor situation, the council decided to send Lévis to assume command of the French forces on what was left of the western front. He was to leave that night by post-chaise, be in Montréal by August 12, arrange for supplies to be sent to Québec, and then proceed to the rapids, where he was to arrive on August 14 and start building a fort. Eight hundred troops, one hundred of whom were regulars and the rest militia, were to follow him over the next two days.

"Tell them," Bougainville, who is reading over my shoulder, insists, "that Jean-Guillaume Plantavit de LaPause de Margon, an army officer close to Monsieur le Chevalier de Lévis and the author of a fine diary of these sad days, went with him. Your readers may also want to know that our artillery commander and chancellor, François-Marc-Antoine Le Mercier, asked to go as well. *Mon Général* agreed but could not help himself being caustic about it. 'By being everywhere, you shall be nowhere!' he said with much ceremony in his voice. A friend of mine, Fiacre-François Potot de Montbeillard succeeded Monsieur Le Mercier in his functions."

Vaudreuil was quite upset at Lévis' new orders. "I have no need to tell you," he wrote, "of the sorrow and the anxiety I feel at your departure. Only the most critical situation would permit me to be separated from you. I have full confidence in you, as does our King. Your presence will encourage our soldiers, temper the Indians, and frighten the enemy. The only consolation I have at your leaving is that Madame de Vaudreuil will be happy to see you in Montréal. I pray that God will be with you in your mission and that glory will crown it."

Montcalm was disturbed as well. "The colony is lost," he wrote Bourlamaque in a letter dated the same day. "Le Chevalier de Lévis leaves at midnight and brings 800 men with him; it is a great sacrifice from a little army, obliged to keep watch from Jacques-Cartier to the Montmorency Falls." He added that he did not know which of the three of them would be the first one to be defeated.

Lévis' departure left Vaudreuil and Montcalm without an intermediary to calm their rivalry. Montcalm, particularly, missed the sound counsel of a friend and colleague in whom he had complete confidence. It is no coincidence that his natural tendency to pessimism increased after Lévis departed.

August 10-17, 1759

(Day Forty-six to Day Fifty-three)

After the capture of Niagara, nothing much of great importance on the English side happened until Murray waved his hat again. But to keep the record straight: Forty new cannon were installed on the batteries bombarding Québec. This led some of Wolfe's officers to believe that he was about to storm Québec from the harbour, but others argued that it was only "to do the town all possible damage." By this time, after fifty days of siege, a consensus had emerged among the officers' corps: Québec could not be taken "as there was little or no appearance of making good a landing upon a coast naturally strong" and so well defended.

Captain Ochterloney died on August 14 with Mère de Saint-Claude-de-la-Croix at his bedside. The day before, sensing his approaching death, she had sent for Panet so that Ochterloney could make his last will and testament. He left all his earthly possessions to the French officer who had saved him from the wrath of the Indians and Canadians. For unknown reasons, Vaudreuil waited ten days to write to Wolfe with news of Ochterloney's death.

Bougainville informs me that on August 15 he received a letter from one of his English friends, James Abercrombie, who was an aide to Amherst. "*Mon cher confrère*," Abercrombie called him. He congratulated Bougainville for being awarded the Croix de Saint-Louis. All those whom Bougainville knew in Amherst's army sent their greetings and hopes that, when they had conquered Canada, Bougainville would introduce them to some young, beautiful, Canadian brunettes. The two young men had a bet of several bottles of champagne about the outcome of the war, but Abercrombie, ever the gentlemen, would wait until he was in Montréal to collect.

Bougainville, who has come for a drink, reads these lines and is annoyed.

"The trouble with you peasants is that you do not understand the protocol of war. Gentlemen do not condemn each other for fighting on opposite sides," he tells me in his most didactic voice.

I ask him why he did not follow Murray to Saint-Antoine after his much appreciated victory at Pointe-aux-Trembles.

"The tide was against us and the opportunity was lost."

"The opportunity? What are you talking about?"

"*Mon Général* believed that war was a series of opportunities. You gained some; you lost some. You just had to be prepared for the right one. Without a favourable tide, I could not follow Brigadier Murray. After that, I had to wait for new orders.

I do not know what to say to that, so I ask him belligerently, "Why do you call Montcalm *Mon Général?*"

"In New France, tradition had it that only the Governor General was called *Général*. With all due respect, le Marquis de Montcalm was *my Général*. Monsieur de Lévis also referred to him as such."

No doubt to get even with me for some injury I may have caused to his self-respect, he tells me out of nowhere, "I recommended that our frigates be used to destroy the English ships in the upper St. Lawrence. But *your* Canadian Governor would not allow it."

And he leaves me, but not before I tell him that the last entry in Wolfe's journal is August 16.

"What happened to the rest of it?" he wants to know.

"Wolfe destroyed it."

"Well that should make your life difficult!" And he goes away laughing.

August 18, 1759

(Day Fifty-four)

Deschambault
4:00 A.M.

A favourable tide the previous night had brought Murray to the Baie de Portneuf, a short distance from Deschambault. Again he waved his hat and his troops were rowed ashore. No one stood in their way, so Murray led his troops toward the parish church. On the way they frightened a group of about fifteen injured soldiers who had been sent to Deschambault to recuperate in a large house at the entrance to the village. The French soldiers fled into the woods, leaving their hostess, an aristocratic-looking woman, sitting calmly in her night clothes. She was "l'Amazone," Cadet's sister and known to the world as Madame Joseph Rouffio. A woman of legendary beauty, she had defied the Church and her parents in the name of love for a suitor unacceptable to her family. Murray kissed her hand, placed her under guard, and moved on.

A little way from the church, Murray's troops met a company of sixty French regulars who, seeing themselves outnumbered, retreated to the nearby woods without firing a shot. Murray then went into the church while the soldiers searched the village. They did not find the munitions depot that Wolfe had been led to believe was there, but they got their hands on many of the precious household effects belonging to Montcalm, Lévis, and other officers and civil officials. Instead of having been sent to Trois-Rivières for safekeeping, as had been intended, their silverware, china, and court uniforms had been hidden at Deschambault. Murray ordered the lot burned.

While he waited for the afternoon tide to carry the troops back to the ships, Murray allowed the soldiers to round up over one hundred head of cattle, many sheep and pigs, and countless hens, all of which were duly herded to the square in front of the church to be loaded onto the boats to feed the army. From time to time the French soldiers fired from the woods, but did little damage. Murray left them alone, preferring to spend time entertaining "l'Amazone."

By half past three the escapade was over, and by half past eight that night, Murray, his men, and their loot were safely aboard the English ships.

"You arrived too late to be of much use," I remark to Bougainville, who this time has come for dinner.

"I was at Cap Rouge, about twenty-one miles away from Deschambault. I gathered the foot soldiers, sent a note to *Mon Général*, and dispatched the cavalry. I know that I did not cause much harm that time to Brigadier-General Murray and his troops. I regret that now."

"You only captured three prisoners," I point out. "Hardly anything to write home about. But you made Montcalm turn out. He was so afraid that his precious supplies would be destroyed that he covered the thirty or so miles from his camp to Pointe-aux-Trembles in record time. Of course, when he got there he was too late. The English had already re-embarked."

Bougainville sips the Canadian wine I have served him and sighs. "He was tired when he returned. The only consolation he had after this long and – I can hear you say – useless journey, was a note from *your* Governor General criticizing him for his absence and his hysteria. It was indeed a strange war."

August 19, 1759

(Day Fifty-five)

Ange-Gardien
During the day

Wolfe had been suffering from a high fever for several days and now he hardly had the strength to move about. He tried to work and give orders, but he found it too taxing. When his servant came to prepare him for bed, he found Wolfe collapsed on the floor. He and an aide laid the general gently on his cot. The doctor confirmed that Wolfe was gravely ill. He even had doubts whether Wolfe would last the night.

It had been a rough two weeks since the setback at Montmorency. Every time he looked into the eyes of his subordinates, Wolfe saw disappointment and resentment. The feeling that he had failed them almost drove him mad. He had quarrelled with his friend Carleton about nothing in particular. He had had to apologize to Monckton for losing his temper over a trivial incident. Townshend was becoming more insolent, or so Wolfe felt, and Murray had disappeared with all the boats, sending back what Wolfe thought were supercilious reports. Then there was Amherst, the elusive Amherst who, Wolfe felt, should have met him in Québec by then.

To keep his sanity, he ordered new training and facilities, made plans for the conquest of Québec but kept them to himself, and nourished the thought of terrorizing the Canadians.

He was determined to continue bombarding Québec even though it would make the town uninhabitable should he conquer it. He was somewhat comforted by the thick black pall of smoke rising over both shores of the St. Lawrence, the result of Goreham's handiwork. Now, he decided, it would be the turn of all the farms between the Etchemin River and La

Chaudière, those around him on the Beaupré coast and on the Ile d'Orléans. In a few days Major Scott would leave with a company of Rangers to destroy everything between Kamouraska and Pointe-Lévy, a distance of over fifty miles. Even if he had to return to England without conquering Québec, he would make the Canadians feel the sword of the King of England.

He drilled his soldiers mercilessly, but he had great worries about their adequacy. His hospitals were filled with sick men as well as with the wounded. They suffered from scurvy as a result of an inadequate diet and improper sanitation. Insubordination had become rampant, and the officers were becoming more and more paranoid. Every day they ordered an increasing number of men to be stripped to the waist and tied to wooden crossbars while regimental drummers took turns whipping them with a cat-o'-nine-tails. The drummers often administered hundreds of blows which left the victim a mess of torn and bloody flesh. Some of them died; others spent an average of three weeks recuperating in hospital. A few committed suicide to escape the lash.

Desertion, the curse of any army in the eighteenth century, was a daily occurrence in Wolfe's. Many deserters, depressed and distressed, sought refuge in the welcoming arms of a good Catholic Canadian girl. Even the possibility of being court-martialled and executed did not deter them.

Wolfe sensed panic around him. His soldiers, although professional and well-seasoned, were accustomed to fight battles in daylight, at a chosen location, and with a respected and welcomed opponent. But on the banks of the St. Lawrence, the battles were often fought in darkness; the enemy was rarely seen and often resorted to a level of cruelty that even the soldiers found hard to stomach. No wonder many of his regulars shrieked at every noise they heard. Parading the cowards with a woman's cap on their heads did not prevent the others from panicking.

Drunkenness and gambling were his soldiers' only forms of relaxation and recreation. Many were often so intoxicated that they could not perform their regular duties. Lives were endangered by drunken sentries, and soldiers were sometimes poisoned by the alcohol they brewed in secret. Drunken brawls were commonplace. In their gambling sessions, which Wolfe could not stop, men lost their clothes or were forced to share their women with other men. Some took to looting to pay their gambling debts.

One of the few satisfactions Wolfe still had was to review the men on parade. Dressed in white waistcoats, breeches, gaiters, and magnificent red coats trimmed with multi-coloured cuffs, they looked splendid. Their cocked hats gave them an air of purpose and gallantry, and the kilts of the Highlanders brought a note of gaiety to the whole parade. They were all so magnificent, Wolfe thought.

Other pleasing moments came when he heard the soldiers singing softly around their campfires, songs about the girls they had left behind. His favourite was:

Why should we be melancholy, boys?
Whose business 'tis to die!
What, sighing? Fie!
Damn fear! Drink on, be jolly, boys.

He even secretly enjoyed the vulgar songs like:

And when we have done with the mortars and guns,
If you please, Madame Abbess, a word with your nuns.
Each soldier shall enter the convent in buff,
And then never fear, we will give them Hot Stuff!

Sex! It seemed to be as thick and pervasive as the clouds of flies and mosquitoes which harassed them all at every turn. Wolfe did not spend much time meditating on his own sexual needs, but he was experienced enough to know that men slept with men in times like these. At Louisbourg he had dealt harshly with such incidents.

It was not, however, for lack of women that a few of his men sought sex with each other. There were plenty of women from the colonies who had followed his army to Québec. They were everywhere, dirty, full of lice, and reckless. Many of them were prostitutes, such as those who had come from a New York brothel called the Holy Ground because it had operated there on church property. Others were the sad daughters of indigent families or of mothers who themselves were camp-followers. A few were children who were easily exploited. Some of his officers had appropriated the most interesting women for themselves and lived openly with them. Pregnant women wandered about looking for some way of getting rid of their unwanted burdens.

Wolfe found this aspect of army life most distasteful. War was indeed hell. But, for Wolfe, the war was temporarily halted. He was seriously ill.

August 20-31, 1759

(Days Fifty-six to Sixty-seven)

On August 22, Father Récher heard rumours that the English were planning to leave Québec. He recorded in his diary, "They are beginning to burn the houses on the Beaupré coast."

The next day, Captain Alexander Montgomery rode to Saint-Joachim, a small parish a few miles east of Québec on the north shore, near where the English were encamped. Montgomery had already been to Saint-François and Sainte-Famille on the Ile d'Orléans and had burned their farms. At the same time his colleague, Major Dalling, had been on the south shore torching the parishes of Saint-Michel and Sainte-Croix.

Before his illness, Wolfe had sent Montgomery to destroy Saint-Joachim because its parishioners, under the leadership of their priest, René de Portneuf, a fifty-two-year-old Canadian, had harassed the English and had spied for Vaudreuil.

The raid began early in the morning without incident when two farmhouses and their outbuildings were set on fire. At the church, however, one soldier was wounded by Canadians who then ran to the woods. Montgomery and his squad hid just outside the village and waited for them to come back. Eventually about thirty Canadians returned to the village, thinking Montgomery had left. Among them was Portneuf. The English opened fire, scattering the Canadians again into the woods but not before nine of them had been captured, including the priest. Unable to obtain any information from any of them, Montgomery ordered them executed and scalped and their bodies left in the square before the church. Then he set flame to the church, the priest's house, and the rest of the village. After he and his men had marched off to destroy the two adjacent villages of Château-Richer and Sainte-Anne de Beaupré, the villagers took the bodies of their priest and neighbours to be buried in consecrated grounds.

It was not until August 24 that the English soldiers were informed of Wolfe's grave illness. "The soldiers lament him exceedingly," Knox wrote in his diary. That same day, the new batteries at Pointe-aux-Pères were completed and mounted with nineteen guns. Montgomery continued relentlessly with his mission, burning all the Canadian farms between Saint-Joachim and the Montmorency Falls.

Meanwhile, officers of the militia came to Vaudreuil to ask him to allow the Canadians to return to their farms above Québec on a rotating basis to gather the harvest. Vaudreuil refused, promising to make good their losses after the victory. The Canadians, not trusting him, left for their farms just the same. Someone estimated that, every night, two hundred Canadians escaped, some with land below Québec and on the south shore where the English were in command. Montcalm was worried lest Wolfe conclude that he was being abandoned. He pleaded with Vaudreuil to put an end to such desertions, but the Governor General would not comply.

Vaudreuil would not listen to Montcalm, but he did heed Bougainville's advice. He gave orders on August 25 for six hundred sailors to proceed to board the frigates near Trois-Rivières and, coming down the river, to destroy the English fleet in the Upper St. Lawrence. At the same time he gave Bougainville orders to be ready to cross the St. Lawrence and attack the English at Saint-Antoine. Since the sailors were needed to man the batteries at Québec and help protect the town, Montcalm was furious; Vaudreuil adamant.

That night, Murray finally returned to Pointe-Lévy with the news that the English had taken Ticonderoga, Crown Point, and Niagara. It was the first news Wolfe had of it. What Wolfe did not know was that the French had captured Amherst's couriers and their four Indian guides at Yamaska. From them the French had found out that Amherst would not move from Saint-Frédéric (Crown Point) until Wolfe had conquered Québec. In a letter to Montcalm written towards the end of August, Bourlamaque stated categorically that Amherst would not undertake any other engagement in the 1759 campaign as it was now much too late.

By August 27, Wolfe was feeling better but not well enough to leave his room. He dictated a letter to his brigadiers asking them to meet to "consider of the best method of attacking the Enemy" at their Beauport encampments. The brigadiers, who had opposed an attack on Beauport all along, were determined that there would be no repeat of the fiasco of July 31. They met together first, and then later with Admiral Saunders, to prepare their answer. They were kind enough not to reply that Wolfe was out of his mind.

The night the brigadiers deliberated, the English passed five more ships above Québec, making them masters of the upper St. Lawrence. Both Vaudreuil and Montcalm were disturbed, but they were still confident that the English could not attack from above Québec. Not once did they doubt that Wolfe would come for them at Beauport, if he came at all.

Bougainville was warned of the ships passing above Québec and told to be most vigilant. Vaudreuil, who had hoped that Bougainville would attack the English at Saint-Antoine on the south shore, abandoned the idea. The army on the left of the line at Beauport was placed on alert and officers were dispatched to the frigates to countermand Vaudreuil's previous orders. The sailors were to march back to Québec as quickly as possible.

Whenever anyone asked Montcalm what the English were doing above Québec, he always replied that they were there to cut the French off from their supplies. Nothing more.

· · ·

Two days before the end of August, Bigot cut the rations by a quarter. It was his hope that by September 15 the Montréal harvest would supply all of his needs. In the meantime he offered additional alcohol instead of bread.

On the last day of the month the sun shone warmly in a bright sky, and for the first time in two weeks Wolfe felt well enough to leave his room. His loss of weight, his paleness and general frailty shocked many, but his recovery brought "inconceivable joy to the whole army," Knox reported in his diary. In the afternoon, Wolfe met with the brigadiers and Admiral Saunders to discuss the answer they had written him a day earlier in response to his request of August 27.

With great courtesy, they had rejected his proposal for an attack at Beauport. In their view it was dangerous and un-workable. Montcalm could retreat behind the walls of Québec, or anywhere above the town for that matter, leaving the English army exposed and vulnerable when it crossed the St. Charles River on its way to the town.

Instead, they proposed to abandon the camp by the Mont-morency, bring all the troops to Pointe-Lévy, and from there "direct the Operations above the Town." Their plan, they argued, would allow Wolfe to fight the French on his terms, standing between Montcalm and the French army opposing General Amherst in the West. Should the English defeat Montcalm above the capital, they said, "Québec and probably all of Canada will be ours."

The brigadiers described to Wolfe a "Plan of Operations in consequence of the preceding Answer." Within three days the camp at Montmorency was to be evacuated, 600 soldiers were to be left to guard the hospitals and stores on the Ile d'Orléans, another 600 at Pointe-Lévy, and 1,000 at Pointe-aux-Pères. The remainder of the army would march to a camp on the west bank of the Etchemin River, and from there the troops would be transported by ships and flat-bottomed boats to a landing place. The brigadiers did not spec-ify where that landing place should be.

Wolfe concurred with them. He wrote to Saunders, "The generals seem to think alike as to the operations; I, therefore, join with them, and perhaps we may find some opportunity to strike a blow." He gave immediate orders for all the artillery and stores to be moved that night from Montmorency to Pointe-Lévy. Wolfe left it to the next day to order Townshend "to form a disposition of a retreat from Montmorency."

But Wolfe could not totally give up his obsession with Beauport. He allowed himself one more attempt to lure Montcalm out of his trenches. During the last day of the evacuataion, five battalions were to remain hidden, in complete silence. Should Montcalm take the bait and attack the departing army, Wolfe would be waiting for him. If, on the other hand, Montcalm remained true to his defensive strategy, Wolfe would inflict him a mortal blow from above Québec. Exactly where, Wolfe did not know.

His letter to Saunders completed, Wolfe next wrote to his mother:

"Dear Madam,
My writing to you will convince you that no personal toils, (worse than defeats and disappointments) have fallen upon me. The enemy puts nothing to risk, and I can't in conscience put the whole army to risk. My antagonist has wisely shut himself up in inaccessible entrenchments, so that I can't get at him without spilling a torrent of blood, and that perhaps to little purpose. The Marquis de Montcalm is at the head of a great number of bad soldiers. And I am at the head of a small number of good ones, that wish for nothing so much as to fight him – but the wary old fellow avoids an action, doubtful of the behaviour of his army. People must be of the profession to understand the disadvantages and difficulties we labour under arising from the uncommon natural strength of the country. I approve entirely of my Father's disposition of his affairs, tho perhaps it may interfere a little with my plan of quitting the service, which I am determined to do the first opportunity; I mean so as not to be absolutely

distressed in circumstance nor burdensome to you or to any-
body else. I wish you much health, and am, Dear Madam,
your obedient and affectionate son,
Jam. Wolfe."

As he went to bed, he was informed that five more ships
had passed above Québec.

There was now a formidable fleet in the upper St. Lawrence
to assist Wolfe in carrying out his brigadiers' plan.

The moment was at hand.

ON THE MOVE AGAIN

The first twelve days of September 1759

September 2, 1759

(Day Sixty-nine)

Beauport
At night

Montcalm's pessimism was at its height. In a sombre mood, he sat down and wrote to Bourlamaque. "The night is dark, and it is raining; our troops are afoot and dressed in their tents ... I am booted, and my horse is saddled, which is, in truth, my ordinary manner at night ... I wish you were here ... I have not been undressed since June 23."

Across the river from Montcalm in Ange-Gardien, Wolfe was also anxious. Even though he had agreed to evacuate his Montmorency camp, he nevertheless felt apprehensive about doing so. He had not been able to hide his anxiety from his mother nor was he able to avoid it in the letter he was now dictating to Pitt. He had wanted his report, he wrote, to be "a more favourable account of the progress of His Majesty's arms" but it could not be so for many reasons.

He was facing a recalcitrant enemy, he told Pitt, and every day his men encountered bloody and deadly skirmishes with the Indians and the Canadians. The toll of disability in his army, particularly among the officers, was heavy, limiting his resources and movements. The inclement weather and the nature of the St. Lawrence and of the terrain had often left him unable to carry out his planned operations, and his own illness had paralyzed the troops for some considerable time. So affected was he by all these conditions that he was "at a loss how to determine."

But in the long run, Wolfe was certain, he would do honour to the King's arms in the "small part of the campaign which remains." And he was in the process of beginning an operation that might do just that: "We are preparing to put [the brigadiers' plan] into execution."

September 3, 1759

(Day Seventy)

Beaupré
Dawn

The early morning found Wolfe in a flat-bottomed boat in the middle of the channel between the Ile d'Orléans and the Beaupré coast. Since midnight no one had stirred on the English side of the Montmorency. All the artillery had been removed and the fires had been extinguished. But thick clouds of smoke still hung over Ange-Gardien and Château-Richer, which Townshend's troops had set ablaze upon leaving. Shortly before Wolfe had vacated his house at dawn, over a hundred canoes and barges had left Pointe-Lévy carrying most of Monckton's brigade, fully armed. The canoes were now lying among the ships of the fleet. Wolfe would use them either to confuse the French or to attack them should they cause any trouble during the evacuation. The companies that Wolfe wanted to use as a decoy were hidden in complete silence as Wolfe had ordered. Everything he had planned was in readiness; his staff had done a remarkable job arranging the logistics of this massive move. Even the weather was cooperating. It was a fine morning with a breeze from the northeast.

As Wolfe waited in his boat, he saw Townshend give the pre-arranged signal of burning the barn in front of his house. His brigade proceeded to the water's edge, where the embarkation was carried out slowly and deliberately, as if to present Montcalm with an irresistible target. By ten o'clock, it was evident that the Marquis would not be teased out of his trenches. So Wolfe summoned his decoy party and at noon he landed at the Ile d'Orléans.

Montcalm, who had been kept informed of every movement in the Montmorency camp since September 1, observed the English evacuation. He was standing on the same hill from which he had seen them preparing to attack him on July 31. At first he believed that they were coming for him again. He sounded the general alarm and waited. From all parts of his army messengers came, imploring him to allow the soldiers to leave their trenches and attack the English. But he delayed his answer, only allowing his soldiers to fire at the departing redcoats.

Around eight o'clock he galloped up and down his line seeing for himself the activities on the opposite bank of the Montmorency. Finally, some time after nine, Montcalm made his decision. He would refuse Wolfe's challenge. He went back to his headquarters, leaving his army in their trenches and Wolfe in the channel to do as he pleased.

Montcalm's generosity at this critical juncture appealed to Townshend, who wrote about it in his journal. He concluded from Montcalm's behaviour that the French general "will make no other use of the Canadians." Even so, Townshend was sure that Montcalm had to be "concerned to see Montmorency abandoned, it not being safe for him to depend on part of his troops to give the least annoyance; likewise permitting us to detach what numbers we please, to lay waste their country, and still remain in his entrenched camp at Beauport."

If I had Montcalm in front of me, I would pelt him with questions. "What happened to you, Monsieur le Marquis? Why did you miss the one opportunity Wolfe gave you to destroy most of his army? No, don't tell me stories about what Monckton could have done, or Saunders, or those left on the Ile d'Orléans or at Pointe-Lévy. Even the English were convinced that you could have attacked them 'with great advantage' either as they marched slowly down to the St. Lawrence or as they waited three hours – three hours, Monsieur le Marquis – in the channel for the tide to take them away."

If I had him in front of me, I would not give him a moment's rest. "Was it your misplaced sense of honour that would not allow you to take advantage of a worthy opponent in such a vulnerable situation? After all, you gentlemen don't have the same reactions that we habitants have. But let me tell you, Monsieur le Marquis, Wolfe may have been a gentleman in your eyes, but he was allowing his troops to destroy the land, the homes, and the villages of practically your entire militia. I can see no honour in your position!"

I am furious with Montcalm, but then, I hear a polite cough behind me and the clinking of glasses. Bougainville gives me a glass of wine. He bows to me and solemnly declares, "Monsieur le Marquis de Montcalm has ordered me to inform you that there are two ways to view his decision. You can choose which you prefer. In our camps at night we used to play a sort of dice game we called Toque and Tinque in which the players must not be caught but leave their opponents constantly guessing as to their next move. Monsieur le Marquis would like you to consider le Général Wolfe as such a player, and a very good one, who could play to the left, to the right, then to the middle, but never fix on one course. *Mon Général* was not about to be taken in. He, too, could play well."

He sips his wine and then adds, "Monsieur le Marquis would like you also to consider another possibility. What if he saw in Brigadier-General Townshend's camp what no one else saw: a movement, a reflection in the sun, a shadow? Perhaps something that gave him good reason to let the English leave. Beyond that he has nothing more that he wishes me to convey to you."

"Then I will never know what really happened."

"No, you will not."

And as quietly as he had arrived, Bougainville leaves.

Beauport
In the afternoon and evening

Throughout the day Montcalm found himself constantly being asked to second-guess Wolfe, a pastime for which he had no talent. To some he gave the opinion that Wolfe was moving to the upper St. Lawrence to mark time until he had to return to England. He told others that Wolfe wanted to land around Cap Rouge in order to cut off the French from their supplies but not to attack them. The crops were good in Montréal, and Lévis had employed every able-bodied person from cleric and official to nun, woman, and child to bring in the harvest. Some of it had reached Québec on August 23 and 24, and Montcalm was certain that deserters had told Wolfe who now meant to stop any further shipments.

To a young officer, who argued that Wolfe could land at Anse-au-Foulon and march to Québec, Montcalm retorted that a hundred good professional soldiers posted at the Foulon could tie up the English until daylight, when he could march from Beauport to keep them in the river. The idea of an attack above Québec amused him. "It is not to be supposed," he added rather pompously, "that the enemies have wings so that in one night they can cross the river, disembark, climb the obstructed acclivity, and scale the walls, for which last operation they would have to carry ladders."

He was adamant that Wolfe would attack only at Beauport, and so he reorganized his line of defence there, reinforcing the right with two thousand men and moving additional troops to the left which, since Lévis' departure, was under Lieutenant-Colonel Poulhariez, the commander of the Royal-Roussillon Regiment. He also proposed to station the Guyenne Regiment near the Plains of Abraham to serve as a mobile force for either Bougainville above Québec or himself below it.

He visited Wolfe's camp on the other side of the Montmorency and found it well-kept with extensive fortifications. But he also discovered that their overall position was not as defensible as he had thought. He was also surprised that Wolfe's house had not been burned like the others in the village. His inspection done, he returned to his manor-house to await Bougainville who was coming to dinner.

In the light of the early evening, Bougainville rode into Québec, which he had not visited for close to a month.

"It was all in ruins!" he says with sadness. "The whole town and all its imposing buildings and fine houses. As I rode through the destruction I kept thinking of the pleasure, the camaraderie, the flirting we had known in better days. No more! Just devastation. For a while I stood by the charred cathedral and I wondered about God's mysterious ways. Unable to bear it any longer, I rode quickly to the Porte du Palais where I met Montbeillard and we both galloped to Beauport, he to his duties and I to visit *Mon Général*."

Montcalm had missed Bougainville, and the two men quickly recaptured the close intimacy and affection that bound them. They talked of the siege and Montcalm shared his views and anxieties. He had by now divided his forces considerably. Close to five thousand men under Lévis and Bourlamaque were west of Montréal; three thousand with Bougainville above Québec; two thousand in Québec itself; and six thousand at Beauport.

By this time, Bougainville had become, in Montcalm's words, "the key to our safety." As the guardian of a fifty-mile-long front, Bougainville was the watchman. With a great number of vessels above Québec, the English could go wherever they pleased. Bougainville's mission was always to be above the fleet, never below it; in that way, according to Montcalm, he would be in a good position to prevent them from landing.

"Should Montcalm have entrusted, you, a novice, an apprentice in war, with such a responsibility?" I ask Bougainville.

"Why not? Oh, I know that many of the senior officers around *Mon Général* thought I was either incompetent or inexperienced. But I knew what I was doing. And you must remember that after Lévis and Bourlamaque, I was the senior officer."

I laugh.

"Why are you laughing?" he asks, somewhat hurt.

"I'm sorry. I am not insulting you. I just had the image of you watching over a fleet and a large movement of troops. The only information you could trust was the one your eyes gave you. Yet you did not even own a spy glas and the only one you could have borrowed had been stolen. Please forgive me, but it is a humorous situation."

"I am glad you think so," he says peevishly. He walks around for a moment or two, then he adds, "*Mon Général* was glad to see me. And so was I to see him. I worried about him. He was quite alone. His health, I think, had gone to pieces. He was much thinner than the last time I had seen him, and his eyes were so sad. But still they teased. He had complete confidence in me. I was not going to let him down. When I left him, he had tears in his eyes and I in mine. We did not know if we would ever see each other again."

After Bougainville's departure, Montcalm was left alone with his worries. Insubordination and desertion in his army had become greater threats than the presence of the English. He had increased the canings and the floggings and even the hangings, but to little avail.

It seemed to Montcalm that the Canadians were acting more and more treasonably. The resistance to the English in the parishes was dying down, particularly in those places where the English were well entrenched. He sent parties of Indians to frighten the habitants and stop them from selling provisions to the enemy, hiding deserters with whom their daughters were involved, and assisting the enemy in many other ways. Many in the militia just got up and left. The merchants of Québec wanted to surrender arguing – irrationally – that, once defeated, the Indians would sell their children to the English.

Montcalm failed to understand the impossible situation in which the Canadians found themselve. Bound by their oath of fealty to the King of France, they were obliged to harass the English at every opportunity – and the record shows that they did. But then Wolfe, in retaliation, burned their villages and Montcalm took no action to protect them. Instead, if there were any signs of what he considered to be collaboration, he dispatched Indians to mistreat the population. Whatever they did, the habitants were severely punished. I leave it to you to judge them, your ancestors.

September 4, 1759

(Day Seventy-one)

Point-Lévy
Around noon

Early in the afternoon, two officers and four privates arrived from Crown Point with a letter from Amherst. Their six-hundred-mile journey had taken them twenty-seven days. They had travelled first to Boston, then through the wilderness of Massachusetts to the Kennebec River in Maine. They then followed the river to a large lake and thence down the Chaudière to within fifteen miles of Québec on the south shore.

Amherst's letter, dated August 7, related the surrender of Niagara, the death of Prideaux, and the general behaviour of the troops. Amherst wrote that he was rebuilding Ticonderoga and Crown Point and making them more impregnable. He ended with: "I want to hear from you ... You may depend upon my doing all I can for effectually reducing Canada. Now is the time."

By the time Wolfe received that letter, the "time" had already passed. Amherst was not coming and Wolfe was alone.

That night, Wolfe was terribly sick. Although he was somewhat better by mid-morning the next day, the army remained apprehensive in case his health should prevent his commanding "this great enterprise in person," as Knox wrote in his journal.

September 6, 1759

(Day Seventy-three)

Point-Lévy
Mid-afternoon

By mid-afternoon most of Wolfe's army was on the south shore. Troops under Murray were already aboard the transports in the upper St. Lawrence, as were the supplies and other light baggage. Admiral Saunders remained with the bulk of the fleet in the lower St. Lawrence, and Carleton guarded the installations on the Ile d'Orléans. Burton was in command at Pointe-Lévy and Pointe-aux-Pères, and Major Scott and Goreham, with sixteen hundred soldiers, were on their way to burn the villages along the south shore. Monkton, Townshend, and the rest of the soldiers who were to execute the brigadiers' plan were beginning to cross the Etchemin River to board the vessels.

Townshend has returned from some long journey, the purpose of which he keeps to himself.

"Where are you in your writing?" he asks me, perhaps less authoritatively than before.

"At the beginning of September. You're on your way to board the ships anchored in the upper St. Lawrence."

He comes close to my computer and reads about the seventy-third day of the siege. With some emotion, he says, "I remember this day well. As I waited to march my troops, I had the time to write to my dear Charlotte. God, how I missed her and the children. You have difficulty believing that, don't you? You with your stereotype of us Englishmen: emotionless, incapable of affection, especially the cold, calculating aristocracy."

I choose not to reply. In the silence that follows he fidgets around, and I see tears in his eyes. "Did you know that my brother, who was in Amherst's army, had been killed? I was fond of him."

Again there is another silence, but eventually he bangs his fist on the table, frightening the cat half to death, and almost yells, "Wolfe made us English soldiers fight a war of the worst shape. LaPierre, that war was nothing more than a scene of skirmishing, cruelty, and devastation."

He stops to control his temper and when he has done so, he adds, "I was not suited for this kind of war, or for the blind ambition that propelled most of my colleagues, or for the confusion engendered by our commanding officer, or for the misery of the people – misery inflicted on them in a most unnecessary way and made more poignant by the wailing of the captive women and children which filled our camps and transports."

His look is faraway. I find a photocopy of the letter he wrote to his wife and in which he expressed the same thoughts. I read to him from it: "Our campaign is about just over. I shall come back in Admiral Saunders' ship and in two months shall again belong to those I never ought to have left – " Recalling it, he finishes the letter for me: "*Adieu*, Your most affectionate husband and faithful friend."

He bows and leaves. I have the feeling that he will not visit again.

The English had kept Bougainville busy all day, watching them and firing upon them, at times with some success. He was also kept on his toes by the barrage of conflicting instructions, orders, and remonstrances he was receiving from Vaudreuil, Montcalm, and their assorted aides. In one letter, he was informed that the Guyenne Regiment was assigned to him and that it would camp overnight in the vicinity of the Plains of Abraham, close to Anse-au-Foulon. A few hours later, the Guyenne was ordered to take position on the road behind Sillery and to make itself available either to Bougainville or Montcalm as circumstances dictated. In response to Bougainville's request that the Guyenne move its tents to the Anse-des-Mères, Vaudreuil replied around five o'clock in the afternoon refusing permission because, he wrote, the terrain did not lend itself to a regiment of regular troops and furthermore there was not enough firewood at Anse-des-Mères to keep the regulars warm. Later the regiment returned to its camp east of the St. Charles River.

"The confusion over the Guyenne," Bougainville admits, "was not the only moment of confusion I had to bear. But before I say more, you must understand that the strategy was to use the Guyenne as a flying force and also keep it close to the Plains of Abraham in case General Wolfe would venture to Québec."

"Are you saying that where the regiment was at any given time is a key factor for me?"

"Yes, a key factor. As I said, there was much confusion over what the English were doing in such large numbers in the upper St. Lawrence. At four o'clock in the afternoon of September 4, *Mon Général* sent me an urgent message that the English were boarding their ships in order to turn around and come either to Québec or back to Beauport. An hour later, an aide to your Governor General arrived bearing a complimentary letter in which he wrote, 'I have no need to tell you that the salvation of the colony rests in your hands,' and that all the enemy wanted to do was 'to separate us from our supplies.'"

"Would it have made it easier for you, Monsieur de Bougainville, had both my Governor, as you call him, and your General talked to each other?"

He smiles and replies, "I would not have survived on earth for eighty-two years if I had judged the decisions of my superiors."

In Montréal Lévis had just returned from his tour of inspection at Ile-aux-Noix and at the head of the rapids, where, on the island that bore his name he had supervised the construction of Fort Lévis. The engineers had assured him that the fort would be completed by the end of September. The lateness of the season convinced him that Amherst would wait for the campaign of 1760 to besiege Montréal, if peace had not returned to Europe before that time. He also believed, as he wrote to Montcalm from Montréal, that Wolfe "would not be long in leaving." But before he did, Lévis was certain that Wolfe would attempt an operation that would justify his coming to Québec in the first place. Consequently, Montcalm in Beauport was to be on his guard, and above all he was not to divide his army. *"Je désire bien ardemment de pouvoir vous rejoindre,"* he wrote, but neither Vaudreuil nor Montcalm ordered him back.

At eight o'clock in the evening Wolfe, accompanied by Admiral Holmes, came on board the *Sutherland*. From there Wolfe began to prepare for the landing of his army somewhere on the north shore.

September 7-8, 1759

(Days Seventy-four and Seventy-five)

The strategy was clear: Admiral Saunders was to keep Montcalm on his toes at Beauport; Admiral Holmes' squadron in the upper St. Lawrence was to exhaust Bougainville; Colonel Burton at Pointe-aux-Pères was to bombard Québec; Major Scott was to burn the south shore; and Wolfe and the brigadiers were to plan the landing of the army on the north shore above Québec.

To that end Wolfe held a council of war on September 7 aboard the *Sutherland*. The army was redivided into three groups and then reorganized into two lines of battle. Monckton and Murray were to command the first line and Townshend the second. "When the coast has been examined, and the best landing-places pitched upon," Wolfe's orders went on to say, "the troops will be ordered to disembark, perhaps this night's tide." Mackellar estimated full tide to be at about three o'clock in the morning.

In order to find "the best landing places," Wolfe sent the brigadiers to reconnoitre the north shore as far west as Pointe-aux-Trembles while he went in the same direction in the schooner *Terror of France*. He returned to the *Sutherland* earlier than the brigadiers, who had encountered a low tide that kept them stranded in the St. Lawrence until two in the morning.

By dawn on the eighth, the rain was coming down in torrents. Bougainville, who had followed the movements of first the brigadiers, then Wolfe, up and down the coast the previous day, received a fresh message from Vaudreuil. The movement of the English troops had only two objectives the Governor General wrote, "either to divert us or to establish themselves above Québec. For myself, I believe it is the former; they will not succeed in the latter if you are vigilant."

Bougainville spent another anxious day keeping track of the barges containing the brigadiers and Wolfe and the whaleboats and the smaller vessels ferrying the soldiers up and down the river. By nightfall he was back at Pointe-aux-Trembles.

By noon Wolfe had returned to the *Sutherland* with a satisfied grin on his face. Speculation in the army had it that he had found a suitable landing place between Saint-Augustin, twelve miles west of Québec, and Pointe-aux-Trembles, eight miles farther on. If he had discovered such a place, Wolfe told no one.

September 9, 1759

(Day Seventy-six)

HMS *Sutherland*
1:30 A.M.

The weather was so bad with heavy rain and gale-force winds, it was decided early in the day that no military operations could take place. Since the men could not possibly spend another moment in their cramped quarters on the ships without many of them becoming sick, Wolfe sent them back to the south shore for air and exercise. Wolfe himself went off again to search the north shore. When he returned several hours later, the operation above Québec changed direction.

Wolfe and his brigadiers were in agreement about landing above Québec. But the place of the landing had not been decided, except, possibly, that it would be west of Sillery. Following Murray's lead, the brigadiers were keen on going ashore between Deschambault and Pointe-aux-Trembles, where they felt the terrain would be more suitable. Once the troops had disembarked, a beachhead could be maintained relatively easily and the soldiers marched to Québec on the Chemin Royal road. A descent that far above Québec would not leave them vulnerable to an attack should Montcalm use secondary roads behind the Chemin Royal to reach them. On the Chemin Royal the English could maintain their ground and protect their rear.

When Wolfe returned from his reconnaissance in the afternoon, he was convinced that he had to land elsewhere than in the vicinity of Pointe-aux-Trembles. He needed to take the French totally by surprise. During his cruising up and down the north shore in the torrential rain, he had found "a place more to his mind," as Mackellar noted in his journal.

Wolfe cancelled the brigadiers' operation and devised a new one. But he did not tell them.

Beauport
Early evening

The French camp was completely flooded. The bridges had washed away, and the incessant rain had turned the soil into a quagmire that made the carts useless. During the day the Guyenne had been moved again from Cap Rouge, where it had spent the previous night, to its camp east of the St. Charles River. By this time Montcalm estimated that there were twenty-five English ships and fifty to sixty barges of various types opposite Sillery and Cap Rouge.

Despite his sense of gloom, Montcalm was sure enough of himself to make plans and arrangements for the quartering of the troops during the forthcoming winter. Québec would be uninhabitable, but Montréal should be pleasant. His natural pessimism, however, surfaced openly in a letter he wrote to Lévis that evening. "In truth," he said, "there is nothing to fear in your part of the colony." But at Québec "*tout n'est pas encore dit.*" Something was coming; he did not know what it was, but he feared it. He wished Lévis were with him: "*J'avoue, mon cher Chevalier, que je vous désirerois bien pour celle-ci.*" However, Montcalm did not order him back.

On board the *Sutherland*
Later that night

Wolfe was also writing a letter. In spite of his "discovery" during the morning cruise and his new determination, he was still in a despondent mood as he wrote his official report to the Earl of Holderness, one of the secretaries of state in Pitt's ministry. He related at length all his reverses since the beginning of the campaign. He attributed his failure to capture Québec to the "strongest country perhaps in the world to rest the defence of the town and the colony upon"; to the French disposition of their army and armaments; to Montcalm's strategy, which he called "circumspect ... and entirely defensive"; to the continuous skirmishings of "old people seventy years of age, and boys of fifteen" who fired upon detachments, and killed or wounded his men from the edges of the woods; and to the uselessness of the navy which "can give no manner of assistance in an attack upon the Canadian army." Then there were Amherst's ponderous march to Mont-réal, the "most violent ebb tide," the rocky riverbed and the swift currents, the lack of equipment, the extreme heat, the inopportune rain, and so on, and so on. The only accomplishments he could brag about were that "the town is totally demolished and the country in a great measure ruined, particularly the Lower Canada."

He was not at all confident about a landing above Québec. He gave the Earl a long litany of what he was up against: the distance from the ships to the landing place, the temperamental nature of the tide, the darkness of the night, the possibility of the boats drifting too far, the difficulties of the terrain, the quick action necessary, and more. All these left much of the expedition in the hands of chance. Still, he *had* agreed to a landing above Québec, as the brigadiers had suggested, and so "we are now here, with about 3,600 men, waiting an opportunity to attack them when and wherever they can best be got at."

As for his health, Wolfe stated: "I am so far recovered as to do business, but my constitution is entirely ruined, without the consolation of having done any considerable service to the State, or without any prospect of it."

Here was a general about to send 3,600 men to their possible death and he had no faith in either himself or his enterprise! History has judged Wolfe too kindly.

At midnight the rain stopped.

September 10, 1759

(Day Seventy-seven)

In Québec, a French gunner and a young sailor, who was said to be no more than seventeen, were hanged for robbing a merchant's house near the Bishop's palace. The wind was to the southwest and the sun shone radiantly.

At half past one in the afternoon, Wolfe, Admiral Holmes, Monckton, Townshend, Mackellar, and Captain Chads, all disguised in the greatcoats of the Grenadiers, were rowed in three barges to Goreham's post on the Etchemin River. They were spotted by the sharp lookout at the batteries in Sillery, who reported to Bougainville that they were officers. In their vanity, Wolfe and the others had left the markings of their ranks clearly visible.

They spent most of the afternoon at Major Dalling's house, situated on a high plateau, inspecting the north shore (the vigilant officer at Sillery noticed them waving in his direction) and driving stakes in the ground. Wolfe hoped that the French would conclude that he was devising a new camp. They did.

While at Dalling's house Wolfe reaffirmed in his mind his decision to abandon his brigadiers' plan and the location of the landing of his army. He neither consulted nor confided in Monckton or Townshend, who were with him, or with Murray, who had been left in charge of the troops at Saint-Nicholas.

At six o'clock in the evening, Wolfe was seen returning to the *Sutherland*, where he arrived an hour and a half later. After a sparse supper he wrote a note to Burton at Pointe-Lévy: "Tomorrow the troops re-embark, the fleet sails up the river a little higher, as if intending to land above upon the north shore, keeping a convenient distance for the boats and armed vessels to fall down to the FOULON and we count (if no accident of weather or other prevents) to make a powerful effort at that spot about FOUR in the morning of the 13th."

There has been much speculation why he picked the Foulon. Some historians have claimed that Stobo put it into his head; but Stobo was not at Québec at this time. A few days after receiving Amherst's letter, Wolfe had sent him with Ensign Hutchins and the soldiers back to Amherst's camp. He chose the Foulon, we are generally told, because it best served his essential objective of totally suprising the French. Montcalm would not expect him to land there, even though it was only two and a half miles above Québec and less than three thousand yards from where Wolfe had spent the afternoon. Its steep and wooded escarpment rising 175 feet above the St. Lawrence made an ascent there most unlikely. The narrow path which ran up the ravine from the shore, the Saint-Denis brook, was blocked with trees and rocks. However, Wolfe had noticed what perhaps no one else had: about two hundred yards to the right of the brook there was a slope, a declivity, which Wolfe thought might "answer the purpose," that is, to permit an easier climb.

Yet when you are judging Wolfe's generalship at Québec, bear in mind the following. His days of reconnoitering must have told him that a small force of about one hundred men guarded the Foulon, and that Bougainville, with an army as large as his own, was camped seven miles west of the Foulon at Cap Rouge. There is no record anywhere that Wolfe ever considered the fact that there was a large plateau almost adjacent to the Foulon, known as the Plains of Abraham to which the French had easy access. Nor did he understand at all what the brigadiers had grasped: Montcalm could use the back roads to get to his enemies.

Despite what historians tell you – particularly those who want you to believe that the English conquest of Québec was a salutary act for mankind – strategy, tactics, and surprise had little to do with Wolfe's decision. He chose the Foulon because he refused to be beholden to the brigadiers. This was his enterprise, not theirs. He refused to tell them where the landing-place would be because he knew his brigadiers would not approve of the Foulon. And he certainly was not about to arrange his affairs in such a way as to make it necessary for him to thank Townshend.

There you have it. I have resolved one of the great riddles of Canadian history. And if I am wrong, then Wolfe must have been utterly insane and should have been removed from his command.

September 11, 1759

(Day Seventy-eight)

HMS *Sutherland*
Morning

In the forenoon, Wolfe issued the orders for the landing. The embarkation was to begin at nine o'clock the following day – September 12. As his men would be confined to the boats for a long time, he authorized their officers to give them extra rum to mix with their water. He appointed Captain James Chads, the master of the *Vesuvius*, to be in complete command of the landing. No officer was to attempt to make "the least alteration, or interfere" with him. Still he chose not to inform Monckton, his second-in-command, or Townshend, or Murray about the exact location of the landing.

South shore, Kamouraska and Rivière-Ouelle
In the course of the day

The old people were desperate and the children stared vacantly. The soldiers had already burned one house of their village and they were now herding the inhabitants into the square in front of the church. There the people fell on their knees and recited the rosary. When the commanding officer of the Rangers, Major Scott, was satisfied that he would meet no resistance, he began by confiscating the cattle, fruit and vegetables, household effects, and other goods, which he ordered sent to his barges in the St. Lawrence. Then he burned the rest of the buildings in and around the village and the crops in the fields. Whenever anyone interfered, he had the person shot. His work done, he proceeded to the next village, leaving the inhabitants of the last to provide for themselves as best they could. But unbeknownst to him a boy stole away from the crowd to his horse and galloped to the next village to warn of the coming of *"les Anglais."*

Scott had been engaged in this exercise since nine o'clock in the morning of September 7. He had under his general command some sixteen hundred Rangers, half of whom were with Goreham farther up the St. Lawrence.

In and around Kamouraska, Scott burned 225 houses and buildings of various kinds – a large number considering that no more than 135 families were registered as living there.

In my mind I am again walking through the devastated town of Québec, where I meet Father Baudouin. He is thinner than the last time I saw him and his wheezing has worsened. Yet, he goes on.

"I can't imagine where they find all these bombs. Maybe they manufacture them in one of their ships," he says as the bombs fly over and around us.

"They have a great number. You are not to get relief for some time."

"I know. And there is hardly any food left. The soldiers receive three-quarters of a pound of bread a day; we, the rest of the people, get one-quarter pound. Not much. I fear for the children. The harvest from Trois-Rivières up is pretty good I hear, but whether some of it can reach us before it is too late is another matter."

"Is there now hunger everywhere?"

"It varies from place to place. The habitants where the English are prefer to sell their wheat to the English than have it confiscated. In Québec, it is hunger for most of us, but I suspect that some wealthy merchants and high officials have more to eat than the rest of us. The prerogatives of office, I suppose."

"Major Scott has been destroying as much of the south shore as he can for five full days."

"I have heard," he tells me, then he adds "And le Marquis de Montcalm stays in his trenches."

We walk in silence for a while, shuffling through the rubble. In what was the beautiful church of the Récollet friars, Father Baudouin sits on a large piece of masonry and says, trying to control his emotion, "Monsieur LaPierre, we are a people accustomed to despotism, which is often benevolent. We have been taught not to question authority; it comes from God. *Quand même*, we are also a rebellious people. Do the people think God has abandoned them? Are they angry at Him? Do they doubt the value of their prayers? Do they lose hope? Or do they remain steadfast, finding whatever comfort and guidance they can in their ancient rituals?"

Without waiting for my answer, he continues, "I do not know. Their pain and misery are so great that perhaps they think of nothing else but surviving the next minute, the next *torche*, or the next bomb. I do not know."

He gets up and walks around, surveying the wrecked remains of the church. Moving a piece of plaster out of his way with his foot, he adds stiffly, as if addressing Vaudreuil, "Confronted by the confusion and indecision of the French authorities, their long refusal to take adequate precautions, and their present wait-and-see attitude, the people are criticizing their temporal masters very harshly. In the secrecy of their hearts, they are concluding that they are governed by incompetents and cretins. Maybe they are beginning to think that it does not really matter which foreign power rules over them, as long as their few cherished spiritual and temporal possessions are safeguarded. It is astonishing how short their list is. I have no doubt that the thought germinating today will become a conviction tomorrow."

Baudouin stops. He takes one long, last look at the devastated church, then leaves with a curt "Bonsoir Monsieur."

September 12, 1759

(Day Seventy-nine)

The army of General Wolfe waited in the twenty-odd vessels lying in the St. Lawrence between Cap Rouge and Pointe-aux-Trembles and at Goreham's post on the south shore. To those who were to carry out his planned "vigorous blow" at his enemies, Wolfe's orders were explicit: avoid the repetition of the events at Montmorency at the end of July. He ordered the soldiers to form "with expedition, and be ready to charge whatever presents itself." They were at all times to be "attentive and obedient to their Officers, and resolute in the execution of their duty." They were also to "remember what their country expects from them, and what a determined body of soldiers, inured to war, is capable of doing, against five weak French battalions, mingled with a disorderly peasantry."

Throughout the day, Bougainville was kept busy as usual, watching and following the English. For days now, in the most inclement weather, he had managed to stay above them as he had been ordered, but it had not been easy. The movements of the ships were unpredictable and the number of boats and barges differed greatly in number from one excursion to the next. His marches were sudden and long and all on difficult terrain. He and his men were often hungry, dirty, tired, and frustrated. To move as rapidly as was necessary, he had to keep five to six hundred soldiers on constant alert, the rest following as quickly as possible.

Earlier in the day, Admiral Holmes had moved some barges and two boats in the direction of Pointe-aux-Trembles. Bougainville followed, thinking the English would make a landing, only to return to Cap Rouge later, empty-handed. There he found a letter from Cadet asking him to facilitate the passage of a convoy of boats loaded with supplies and provisions which had arrived at Pointe-aux-Trembles from Montréal two or three days previously. The convoy was to go down the river that night. Bougainville issued the necessary orders to his posts but later he learned from them that none of his lookouts had seen any sign of Cadet's boats. Neither Vaudreuil nor Cadet had sent word that the operation had been cancelled. In some agitation, Bougainville spent the night at Cap Rouge.

The Guyenne Regiment was still in its original camp. There was some talk during the day of moving it farther west, to the Plains of Abraham, near the Foulon, but neither Vaudreuil nor Montcalm ordered the move.

At four o'clock in the afternoon, the brigadiers met aboard the *Sutherland*. They did not relish being kept ignorant of the location of the landing and wrote to Wolfe accordingly: "We must beg leave to request from you as distinct orders as the nature of the thing will admit of, particularly to the place or places we are to attack."

When Wolfe received their note at eight-thirty, he was furious at their audacity. He wrote Monckton a nasty letter in which he informed him that the ascent would be at the Foulon. At the same time he remonstrated with him. "It is not a usual thing," he wrote to his second-in-command and the one person who would have to carry out the operation should Wolfe become incapacitated, "to point out in the publick orders the direct spot of an attack, nor for any inferior Officer not charg'd with a particular duty to ask instructions upon that point."

This correspondence is unbelievable and no attempt at historical posturing – as some historians have tried – will salvage it. Monckton was no "inferior Officer not charg'd with a particular duty." He was the second most important person in the English army at Québec, and he was the commander of the first line of attack.

_____

Monckton passed Wolfe's information to Townshend but not to Murray, who, no doubt, found out from Townshend. And with that little contretemps out of the way, an aide informed Wolfe at nine o'clock that the troops were beginning to embark in the longboats.

At Beauport Montcalm was anxious, nervous, and worried, particularly about the supplies that had to get through. There was food for only a couple more days. Unable to contain his restlessness, he took Monsieur Marcel for a walk shortly after nine o'clock in the evening. Montbeillard soon joined them. They walked along the beach, looking up at the entrenchments above them. They could see the soldiers' evening fires illuminating the closing darkness. From Québec they could hear the sound of the English cannon bombarding the town, with perhaps greater intensity than usual. In the distance, Montcalm could just make out the English ships in the lower St. Lawrence preparing to set sail. On the Ile d'Orléans soldiers were embarking in barges. Montcalm walked on. By eleven o'clock it was obvious to him that the barges were coming towards his camp.

An hour earlier in the upper St. Lawrence, Colonel Howe, who was to lead the advance, called together the soldiers who had volunteered to "scramble up the rock." Eight men were willing to "put in execution his agreeable order ... with the greatest activity, care, and vigour." He allowed them to take sixteen more men for a total of twenty-four under Captain William Delaune. Should they survive, he told them, they would be "recommended to the General."

In fine weather, on a calm night, and in silence, the volunteers embarked in the lead boat.

• • •

At about the same time, a lookout in the *Hunter*, off Sillery, three miles west of Québec, spotted a canoe gliding from the shore with two French soldiers from the Royal-Roussillon Regiment in it. They were deserting from Bougainville's patrol. On board the *Hunter*, they told Captain Smith that provision barges were to come down the river that night. It was too late to inform Wolfe, but the captain ordered all aboard to keep a sharp eye.

Wolfe knew that if he miscalculated, he, and he alone, would be answerable to the King and the public. But he had fixed on the Foulon, and there he would play his hand.

He had under his command for the landing at the Foulon a little over forty-five hundred men, all professionals, well trained and most from established regiments that had served in many theatres of war: the 15th (Amherst's Battalion), the 28th (Bragg's), the 35th (Ottaway's) the 43rd (Kennedy's), the 47th (Lacelle's), the 48th (Webb's), and the 58th (Anstruther's). In addition there was the Light Infantry, made up of good marksmen and proficient soldiers, two battalions from the Royal American Regiment (mostly German mercenaries and hardly any Americans), the "*sans-culottes*" – men of the 78th Highland Regiment, known as Fraser's Highlanders – and the Louisbourg Grenadiers.

He was ready for his moment of destiny. The weather was cooperating and every thing appeared to be going well.

"The boast of heraldy, the pomp of power,
And all that beauty, all that wealth e'er gave,
Await alike the inevitable hour,
The paths of glory lead but to the grave."

Wolfe said many times that he would sooner have written these words from Thomas Gray's *Elegy in a Country Churchyard* than take Québec. However, it is highly improbable that, as folklore would have it, he recited these lines as he was being rowed to the Foulon.

Montcalm had about six thousand men at Beauport, of these less than two thousand belonged to the regiments of regular troops (the Languedoc, the Béarn, the Guyenne, the Royal-Roussillon, and La Sarre). Many were hired mercenaries who could fight well when they so wished, but they tended to be unreliable. There was also the colonial troops, the *compagnies franches de la marine*, under Canadian officers. They were competent fighters, especially in the bush. However, they, too, lacked discipline and tended to dress as they wished, which distressed Montcalm no end. They also prefered the Canadian way of warfare to the discipline of the French one. He knew the Canadians were good marksmen, indefatigable when aroused, and often fearless, but they were largely untrained for European warfare. And he had incorporated about one thousand of them into the ranks of the regular troops.

As for the Indians, he expected nothing from them and hoped for the best.

Part Two

THE BATTLE
September 13–18, 1759

ON THE PLAINS OF ABRAHAM

September 13, 1759

Please note that most of the battle of September 13, 1759, did not take place where the Plains of Abraham or the national park in Québec City which commemorates it are situated today. It took place a little farther to the east. Nor did the plateau, known as Les Hauteurs d'Abraham, ever belong to a man by the name of Abraham Martin. His property was much closer to the city. However, I have bowed to the harmless convention of calling the battle site the Plains of Abraham. Tradition and truth often have different stories to tell.

September 13, 1759

(Day Eighty)

By Cap Rouge
1:00 A.M.

The moon, in its twentieth day, lit the sky and cast shadows over the thirty flat-bottomed boats, three longboats, the boats of two smaller ships, and the schooner *Terror of France* waiting by the *Sutherland*. In them were Monckton and Murray and the 1,700 soldiers under their command: Howe's volunteers, the men of the 28th, 43rd, 47th, and 58th Regiments, and a party of Highlanders and of Royal Americans. The tide had begun to ebb and the weather was fine, with the wind from the southwest.

On the gangway of the *Sutherland* a young drummer in a bright uniform walked toward one of the crafts, followed by a small group of darkened figures – the adjutant-general, a couple of servants and aides, and a few soldiers. Behind them came a tall figure wrapped in a huge black cloak to ward off the cold night air. Wolfe carried a stick and his hat was askew on his head. Without a word he got into his boat and waited for the signal to begin the operation that could bring about the conquest of Québec.

At Beauport, Montbeillard, for some unknown reason, was suddenly impressed by the French entrenchments. "The more I looked at them," he wrote, "the more I was persuaded that the enemy would not attempt to attack them." But an hour after midnight, a courier arrived with news that "a great noise of boats" on the right of the line had forced the troops into their trenches. Montbeillard immediately mounted up and rode along the line ordering the batteries to get ready.

Montcalm dispatched a canoe to reconnoitre the English movements, then resumed his lonely vigil at Beauport waiting for the enemy to attack.

By the HMS *Sutherland*
2:00 A.M.

Captain Chads saw the two lights, one above the other, shining from the topmast shrouds of the *Sutherland*. He gave the order, and his oarsmen began to row his boat silently into the ebbing tide, followed by the other crafts. The tide was running at six knots – the St. Lawrence was heavy with the torrential rain that had fallen over the last few days – and he had a distance of slightly less than ten miles to cover. Chads reckoned that it would take him roughly two hours to reach the beach of the Foulon. But first he made for the the *Hunter*, which had been designated as his "point de repère" or reference mark.

Forty-five minutes later, the armed sloops and transports carrying the ammunition and ordinance stores joined Chads' procession.

At Beauport
3:00 A.M.

The reconnaissance canoe Montcalm had sent a couple of hours earlier returned with word that the English were approaching La Canardière. Montbeillard galloped there to move a small cannon on the bank and to order the Québec militia to advance on the beach. Montcalm, to be doubly sure, sent another canoe to investigate and dispatched Marcel to Vaudreuil's headquarters at La Canardière. Marcel was to keep Montcalm continually informed of goings-on there. And then Montcalm waited.

In the upper St. Lawrence the second wave of English forces, 1,900 men under Townshend from the 15th and 35th regiments, the Light Infantry battalions, and the rest of the Royal Americans, left for the Foulon in the *Lowestoft* with Admiral Holmes on board, the *Squirrel*, the *Seahorse*, and other transports. The *Sutherland* remained anchored at Cap Rouge, keeping an eye on Bougainville.

At Beauport
3:30 A.M.

The *Hunter* had dropped anchor about two thousand yards from the Foulon, and Captain Smith waited for the French provision boats to come downriver.

The lookout heard the sound of muffled oars and alerted the officer of the watch, who summoned the captain. Peering into the night, Smith saw a boat emerge out of the darkness some fifty feet away. He ordered his sailors and marines to be ready to fire, but an officer in the approaching craft identified himself quickly as Captain Fraser of the 78th Highlanders. Relieved, Smith told him about the French supply ships. Fraser made a mental note of Smith's information.

At Beauport
4:50 A.M.

The second canoe returned to Montcalm without having seen anything at La Canardière. However, in the distance, Montcalm could make out in the moonlight the dark shapes of Saunders' barges and boats turning around to rejoin the ships lying at anchor in the basin.

The alert over, Montcalm ordered the troops back to their tents. He returned to his manor-house, where he drank innumerable cups of tea and talked with Johnstone, who had become one of his aides since Lévis' departure for the West on August 9. Over and over again, Montcalm worried aloud about the provision and supply boats, repeating how vital it was that they get through the English blockade safely.

Near the Foulon
4:00 A.M.

The moon was now hidden, making it difficult for Chads and his men to see. As well, the current was faster than anticipated. When Chads approached the beach, a sentry called out,"*Qui vive? Qui vive?*"

Without hesitation, Captain Fraser replied, *"La France et vive le Roi!"*

The sentry, believing Chads to be a French officer with the expected supply boats, accepted the answer, and rushed down the shore, telling his companions, *"Ce sont nos gens avec les provisions. Laissez-les passer."*

Without further difficulty Chads and a few other boats landed on the beach, where the soldiers quickly disposed of the sentries. However, the tide carried many of the other boats downstream. They landed about four hundred yards east of the ravine and the path which was to take them to the top of the cliff 175 feet above them. One of these boats carried Howe and the volunteers. About this time, a light rain began to fall.

While Delaune and a squad cleared the path up the Saint-Denis ravine of the abatis the French had built, Howe, with Captain Donald McDonald of the Highlanders, the twenty-four volunteers, and some Light Infantry troops, decided unilaterally to climb to the top. With their guns strapped to their backs, they inched upwards grabbing hold of branches, bushes, and small trees. They were walking slowly west along the ridge when a soldier accosted them. McDonald, who had learned French in one of England's many European campaigns, represented himself as a French officer sent by Montcalm to help guard the Foulon. He ordered the soldier back to his post to inform his commanding officer, a man by the name of Vergor. The guard went off in the direction of the tents, which could now be seen in the early light of dawn.

For some reason known only to himself, the militiaman fired his gun on his way there, alerting Vergor and the thirty or so soldiers left in the camp – the others having been permitted to return to their farms to take in the harvest. Upon seeing the English, many of Vergor's men ran off toward Québec, but Vergor himself led a stiff resistance. He was wounded and surrendered, but not before he had sent a messenger to Vaudreuil. Shortly afterwards Delaune arrived.

At Sillery
4:45 A.M.

The fifty soldiers guarding the four-gun Samos battery at Sillery heard the commotion to the east of them. By this time it was light enough to let them see the ships and boats in the river below them. Their officer, le Chevalier de Douglas, opened fire, killing and wounding many men trapped in the transports and causing some damage to the ships.

At Beauport Montcalm heard the booming of the cannon of Samos. He thought them to be English guns attacking the supply boats. Pessimistically he remarked to Johnstone that it was the end. He decided to wait until Vaudreuil had confirmed the "catastrophe," before taking action. He continued to drink his tea.

At the Foulon
5:00 A.M.

Wolfe was by now on the beach of the Foulon supervising the disembarkation of the first landing division. He marched in front of the troops, urging them on, as the guns of the Samos battery continued their deadly task.

Cap Rouge
5:15 A.M.

A soldier at Bougainville's camp at Cap Rouge, hearing the commotion a few miles away, awoke Bougainville. The young French colonel made no attempt to find out what it was all about.

At the Foulon
5:20 A.M.

When Wolfe received the all-clear signal from above, he personally led his army up the ravine path to the consternation of his aides. As Wolfe began his ascent, Chads was rowed back to the *Lowestoft* and the other transports to bring Townshend's second division to the landing place.

At Beauport
5:30 A.M.

While Montcalm was still waiting for word from Vaudreuil, an officer rushed in to announce that the "red flag" was flying over the Citadel. It was the signal agreed upon to warn the troops at Beauport that an English landing had taken place above Québec. Montcalm finished his tea, changed into a clean uniform, had his horse saddled, and left for Vaudreuil's headquarters about two miles away.

The French adjutant-general, Pierre-André Gohin, Comte de Montreuil, had also not slept all night, frustrated by Saunders' phantom invasion. He was on the last leg of an inspection of the troops around Vaudreuil's headquarters when Vergor's messenger arrived to tell the Governor General that the English were at the Foulon. The soldier was exhausted and frightened, and many, like Montreuil, who talked with him thought he was incoherent. However, the adjutant-general took no chances and ordered the Guyenne Regiment immediately to the Plains of Abraham. He calculated that it would take them an hour to an hour and a half to get organized and cover the two-mile distance. Then he went to inform Vaudreuil.

At Québec
5:45 A.M.

Le Chevalier de Bernetz, second-in-command of the Québec garrison, had just heard from another of Vergor's men about Wolfe's landing. Thinking that Vaudreuil had not been informed, he immediately dispatched a courier to the old man at La Canardière. His message, however, was rather confused. He told Vaudreuil the English had disembarked, but since he could no longer hear the noise of the muskets firing, he believed that Wolfe had re-embarked. Even so, he told Vaudreuil that the Gueyenne "cannot make too much haste."

Meanwhile, invigorated but out of breath, Wolfe arrived at the top of the cliff to find that Vergor's detachment had already been taken captive and English sentries posted along the cliff edge. He sent Murray and Howe to silence the Samos battery, then he took a short rest. As his troops arrived from the beach, they were, according to Knox, lined up "facing the road in front and the river to our back." Their right flank extended towards Québec and their left to Sillery. There they halted for what Knox described as "a few minutes," but what was in fact, almost an hour.

So far all had gone as planned, but Wolfe remained fearful that he would be attacked before he had had a chance of establishing himself. The French prisoners had told him that, aside from Vergor's detail, there were no other French troops in the immediate vicinity. But Wolfe knew that Bougainville was behind him at Cap Rouge and Montcalm in front of him at Beauport. Fearing for the safety of his men and unsure about what he had just accomplished, he summoned his adjutant-general, Isaac Barré, and sent him back down the path to delay the landing of further troops until he had had time to survey the terrain and see for himself where the French were positioned. When Barré reached the beach, however, Chads' boats had already begun to disembark Townshend's division. Instead of delaying their landing, Barré ordered it speeded up, then he returned to Wolfe, whom he found watching some of Townshend's men making their way up the path in the rain which had been falling since about four-thirty. Both Barré and Wolfe congratulated each other that Wolfe had been able to install himself more quickly than he had anticipated. He could not, however, leave the troops against the edge of the cliff. Taking an escort, Wolfe went reconnoitering. It was then six-thirty.

From a hill not too far away, he saw a plateau or an "even piece of ground," as Knox described it, about a mile from the Citadel. Less than a mile wide, the Plains of Abraham were guarded to the south by the steep cliffs of the St. Lawrence, and by the Côte Sainte-Geneviève and the St. Charles River to the north. Crossing through the fields of wheat and pasture were two roads running parallel to each other: the Chemin Saint-Louis, stretching roughly southwest from the Porte Saint-Louis to Sillery, and the Chemin Sainte-Foy, running northwest from the Porte Saint-Jean to Sainte-Foy. On the edge of the plateau, facing the walls of Québec, Wolfe noticed a shallow ravine rising to an uneven ridge, known as the Buttes-à-Neveu, which extended to the walls. The terrain was dotted with clumps of trees and shrubbery. After considering his options, Wolfe decided to line up his troops on the back incline of the ravine, some six hundred paces from the crest of the Buttes-à-Neveu.

It was still raining lightly as the English troops marched slowly to their new position, stopping frequently when they were fired upon by the advance party of the Guyenne, which had arrived on the Plains. The Guyenne were followed by a contingent of soldiers sent by Bernetz from the garrison at Québec. These skirmishes forced Wolfe to recall both Murray and Howe. Murray returned at once, but Howe took the time to capture the Samos battery.

The first Canadian to see the English on the Plains was a young nun at the Hôpital Général on the banks of the St. Charles River. Making her rounds, she glanced out of the window in the large ward and saw redcoats walking slowly and deliberately near the hospital. She cried out a prayer and all the soldiers who were able rushed to every window on that side of the hospital. The nun, having regained her composure, ran to find her Mother Superior.

Mère Saint-Claude-de-la-Croix was in conversation with her brother Ramezay, the commander of the Québec garrison, who had been ill at the hospital for a few days. As soon as the young nun reported the presence of the English, Ramezay dressed quickly and left for Québec. On his way he met with le Chevalier de Boishébert and a few other soldiers who had left the hospital to rejoin Montcalm's army.

At La Carnardière
6:20 A.M.

When Montcalm reached Vaudreuil's headquarters, the old man showed him Bernetz's letter, which he had just received. Vaudreuil was agitated, exasperated, and almost incoherent. The English might or might not have landed, they might or might not have re-embarked, he was not certain, even though gunshots could clearly be heard. Alarmed, Montcalm decided to go and see for himself. Before he left, he reinforced the Guyenne with a detachment from each of the regular regiments to be sent to the Plains as quickly as possible, along with six hundred Canadians from the militia of Montréal, all those from Trois-Rivières, and one hundred from Québec.

After Montcalm's departure, Vaudreuil sat alone, not knowing if he had enough information to warrant issuing marching orders to all the troops at Beauport. As he waited for confirmation, he wrote to Bougainville.

After dealing with a couple of insignificant matters, he wrote: "It seems quite certain that the enemy has made a landing at the Anse-au-Foulon. We have put a great number of people in motion. We hear some insignificant firing (*petites fusillades*) ... As soon as I know positively what is going on, I shall inform you." Out of habit he noted the time: "At a quarter to seven." He then added a note, saying, "Your messenger will see M. de Montcalm on his way to you and will be able to give you news of him." He signed the letter, then felt compelled to add: "The enemy's forces seem considerable. I do not doubt that you will be attentive to his movements and follow them. I rely on you for this."

The courier took a shortcut to Cap Rouge and never saw Montcalm.

At the Foulon
7:00 A.M.

With great difficulty, the British sailors were hauling two cannon up the Foulon path. By this time all of Townshend's division had reached the heights, and Chads had left for the south shore to ferry over Carleton's and Burton's men.

On the Beauport-Québec road
7:20 A.M.

Montcalm rode to the Plains in silence with an aide, the Comte de Malartic, at his side and with Johnstone, Marcel, Joseph Barbeau, his coachman with the horses, his valet, and a few soldiers following behind.

His journey took him across the bridge on the St. Charles River and up the winding and curbing road to the Porte du Palais, through which he entered the town. The only time he spoke was when he ran into le Chevalier de Boishébert, who confirmed that thousands of redcoats were on the Plains and more were continuing to arrive. This English operation clearly had nothing to do with the French supply ships.

Montcalm came onto the Plains through the Porte Saint-Jean close to eight o'clock in the morning. As he rode quickly towards the Buttes-à-Neveu, he could see some of his soldiers firing upon the English as they advanced towards the ravine. On the height of the Buttes, dominating Wolfe's chosen battlefield, he saw for himself what Boishébert had told him. *"Ils sont là où ils ne devraient pas être!* [There they are where they ought not to be]," he whispered to himself.

Realizing for the first time the magnitude of the force about to meet him in battle, Montcalm sent Johnstone and Marcel back to Beauport with orders to Poulhariez to dispatch to the Plains all soldiers except two hundred men who were to remain by the Montmorency. At the same time, Marcel was to hurry the Béarn Regiment along.

Everywhere he looked, Montcalm saw the English: the multi-coloured uniforms of the Highlanders and the royal livery of the drummers and fifers contrasting sharply with the redcoats of the other English soldiers in the battle lines. The beating of drums, the blaring of trumpets, and the playing of the fifes created an unnerving sound. But the bagpipes were quiet.

When Montbeillard arrived with his five guns, he stationed two on Montcalm's left, one in the centre of the field, and the remaining two on the Chemin Sainte-Foy off to Montcalm's right. Realizing that the Canadian and Indian harassment of the English was reaping benefits, Montcalm sent more of them under Dumas to do the same. Then he waited for the rest of his army to arrive. But Johnstone was encountering difficulties at Beauport. Poulhariez and other senior officers would not dispatch the troops as ordered without Vaudreuil's authorization.

By this time, Vaudreuil had finally concluded that instead of an insignificant skirmish, he was confronted with the probability of a full-scale battle. Tired beyond belief, he barely summoned the energy necessary to correct his miscalculation. He gave orders for the soldiers remaining at Beauport – except for 1,500 men under Poulhariez – to leave for the Plains immediately.

It is said that he also wrote to Montcalm: "The success which the English have already gained in forcing our posts should be the ultimate source of their defeat; but it is to our interest not to be overly hasty. It is my view that we should attack the English only when all of our troops are assembled. You should therefore bring together on the Plains to join our army 1,500 men from the garrison in Québec and all of Bougainville's corps. In this way the enemy will be completely surrounded, and will have no other resources than to retreat towards their left, where their defeat would again be inevitable."

Montcalm never received the letter, if indeed it was written at all.

However, the courier with Vaudreuil's earlier letter to Bougainville arrived at Cap Rouge at about eight. The messenger, riding furiously, had crossed the St. Charles valley and used the back road around Ancienne-Lorette. Though he found Vaudreuil's message somewhat garbled, Bougainville ordered the quick march of most of the cavalry and 900 Grenadiers and militia to the Plains. If he made haste and was not distracted, he could cover the seven miles to the Plains in a

couple of hours. He could arrive at Wolfe's rear with some of
the best soldiers in the French army at about ten o'clock.

Old men, women, children, and all men not bearing arms
lined the streets and the ramparts of Québec watching the
soldiers from Beauport marching through their town, with
flags flying and drums beating. The regulars were all
dressed in their white uniforms, the colonial troops in their
long greyish-white coats, blue breeches, and stockings, and
the militia in their everyday clothes. Among them was an
eighteen-year-old boy by the name of Joseph Trahan, whom
Madame Lefebvre and Father Baudouin recognized. Like the
other militia, he carried his hunting gun and a knife pushed
through his belt. Others saw Montbeillard rushing along
exhorting the men pulling five cannon to make haste and
sending others back to Beauport to fetch more ammunition.
The spectators searched among the army for a father, a husband, a brother, or a friend. Madame Lefebvre's son was not
among them, for he, Mennard, and Mascou were with Bougainville.

The townspeople were not frightened by the Indians even
though they had to admit that *"les sauvages"* looked ferocious. They walked through the town covered in war-paint, a
single feather on their heads, and their tomahawks and
knives among the scalps hanging from their waists.

Montcalm rode by on his black horse, his uniform shining
white, but his face so sad that it brought tears to some of the
spectators' eyes. His coat had large sleeves and when he
raised his arm the white lace of his cuff could be seen.

Meanwhile the rain continued to come and go and come
and go.

Shortly after nine, the 4,500 men Montcalm could count on
were on the Plains. He left the Canadians and the Indians to
harass the English from every conceivable hill, ravine, or
clump of trees. To the far right of his line, near the Chemin

Sainte-Foy, he placed some of the colonial troops along with some militia from Québec and Montréal. Then came the five regiments of regular troops mixed with Canadians: La Sarre next to the colonial troops, the Languedoc straddling the Chemin Saint-Louis, the Béarn in the centre of the line, the Guyenne at the beginning of the left with the Royal-Roussillon beside it, and the militia of Montréal and Trois-Rivières to his far left, closing the line.

Montcalm commanded the centre along with Montreuil; Brigadier Sennesergues, lieutenant-colonel and commander of the La Sarre Regiment, was on the right, and Lieutenant-Colonel Fontbonne of the Guyenne Regiment on the left. Montbeillard remained with the artillery and Dumas with the Canadian sharpshooters. Six hundred yards in front and below him stood Wolfe's army.

As he waited for Montcalm's army to play its role in the drama he had written, Wolfe, in the new uniform he had had made especially for the occasion, was well satisfied with the total surprise he had caused the French. He had landed his troops, climbed the steep precipice of the Foulon, silenced the Samos battery, and chosen carefully the ground on which he was prepared to meet his enemy.

By eight o'clock his entire force of 4,441 men was on the Plains, 387 more guarded the Foulon and the Samos Battery. To protect his rear and to prevent Canadians and Indians from stealing around his left flank, hidden by the brush-wood, he placed Townshend at right angles to the main line, with the 15th Regiment (Amherst's), two battalions of the Royal Americans, and Howe's Light Infantry. Burton, who had just recovered from a serious wound, led the 48th (Webb's), forming a reserve at the rear of the right wing.

To cover a front of some 3,900 feet, Wolfe drew the rest of the men into two thin lines, not having enough for the customary three. The two lines formed three feet apart with about a 120-foot gap between each regiment. To his right, almost on the precipice overlooking the St. Lawrence, he stationed the 35th (Otway's), which made them closest to the Canadian and Indian sharpshooters firing from the bushes by the cliff. To Otway's left were the Louisbourg Grenadiers under Carleton, followed in succession by the 28th, 43rd, the 47th, and Fraser's Highlanders (the 78th), with the 58th closing the line on Wolfe's extreme left. Wolfe commanded the centre of the line; Monckton, as the senior Brigadier, the right; and Murray, the left.

The rain fell intermittently, but not sufficiently to hinder the operation. Wolfe ordered his officers to make sure that all the guns were loaded with two balls in their muskets instead of the usual one. He also ordered that no shot be fired until the enemy was within forty yards of the point of the English bayonets.

While he waited for the French army to arrive, he marched over the field, stick in hand and hat cocked at an angle. One moment he was giving words of encouragement to some young lads who might be seeing battle for the first time; the next he was summoning his runners to straighten the line and instruct where the latest arrivals were to stand. In his many rounds, he comforted the wounded. Once, bending over an officer felled by a Canadian sniper, he brought a smile to the man's face when he announced a possible promotion. Finally the guns arrived, but one had the wrong ammunition. This was quickly remedied, and Howe deployed them against Montcalm's arriving forces.

Skirmishes continued all over the field – the house of a man by the name of Borgia on the Chemin Sainte-Foy changed hands several times before the Canadians set it on fire. At one point, as Montcalm lined his troops in battle formation, the Louisbourg Grenadiers fell back, causing some panic among the soldiers in their rear who thought the general attack had begun. Wolfe walked rapidly through their ranks encouraging and exhorting them. When he came to the Highlanders he was annoyed that they had fallen farther back than the others. He complained to one of their officers, who asked that his men be allowed to hear the pipes as nothing encouraged them more. Wolfe, who had silenced the bagpipes earlier, ordered the officer to "let [them] blow like the devil!" And soon after, the wailing of the bagpipes echoed across the Plains.

When everything was organized to his satisfaction, Wolfe ordered the men to lie down. His troops were by then less than half a mile from the gates of Québec. It was nine-thirty in the morning.

The two cannon the English had brought to the Plains were by then playing havoc with the French troops, and Montcalm rode up and down his lines, not knowing if Wolfe had more reinforcements and guns coming. He did not trust the Indians or the Canadians, both of whom could lose patience and suddenly charge the enemy. He was dubious about allowing the English more time. Montcalm consulted briefly and informally with his senior officers, but came to no immediate decision about when to attack the English. At one point he met Montbeillard delivering ammunition and said to him, "We cannot avoid action; the enemy is entrenching, he already has two pieces of cannon. If we give him time to establish himself, we shall never be able to attack him with the sort of troops we have." He then added with a shiver, "Is it possible that Bougainville doesn't hear all that noise?"

It was impossible for Bougainville not to hear. He had not been able to leave Cap Rouge before nine and was by nine-forty-five not far from Sillery. He still had over three miles to go to reach the rear of the English on the Plains. The road was in a terrible condition, slowing his progress considerably. Then at Sillery he spent over an hour attempting to dislodge the English from the Samos battery. After losing eighteen men in the process, he let the English do what they would.

Montcalm felt that he could not hold the men much longer. He waited only a few more minutes standing between La Sarre and Languedoc regiments. He looked to both sides, raised his sword high above his head, and pointed in the direction of the English. The regimental bearers unfurled the flags and the drummers beat the charge.

10:00 A.M.

With a long shout, Montcalm's soldiers took four steps in quick succession then ran forward, the Béarn and the Guyenne in columns and the rest in line – more or less. The rain stopped and the sun came out from behind the clouds bathing the Plains in light.

10:02 A.M.

A bloody handkerchief wrapped around his wrist, Wolfe stepped into the gap between the Grenadiers and Bragg's 28th Regiment. He looked almost handsome, his eyes playful and his face radiant with excitement. As he saw the French advancing towards him, he ordered the redcoats to their feet and the Highlanders to drop to one knee.

10:05 A.M.

With Montcalm leading, the soldiers rushed forward in three groups, advancing much too fast – many stumbled over the uneven ground. As they charged down the ravine to meet the English, order and symmetry were sacrificed as the Canadian sharpshooters joined the ranks as best they could. The columns weaved erratically; their front lines were too far ahead and the left flank too far back. Before Montcalm could order his troops to fire, a shot rang out, followed by a general volley, which had little impact on the English.

The redcoats remained still, looked straight ahead and took the volley. Here and there a man fell where he was standing or stepped back, wounded. His companions remained as rigid as if they were on parade.

10:10 A.M.

Having fired to their heart's content, the Canadians, as was their custom, threw themselves on the ground to reload and rolled to the right. The regulars tripped over them and became confused. But soon Montcalm and the officers rallied them; the Canadians stood up and the march continued forward. Again the columns moved too fast and unevenly, as if no one knew where they were going and why.

10:13 A.M.

Wolfe gave the command. The redcoats took three steps forward and turned slightly to the right to present the French a smaller target. Montcalm's soldiers were now about forty yards away from their enemy. A moment went by, then Wolfe yelled "Fire!" The soldiers on the right and left of the line shot at intervals, platoon by platoon, while those in the centre, less affected by French bullets, fired simultaneously. Monckton fell wounded and Carleton received a severe blow to the head.

The English volley caught the oncoming soldiers by surprise. They stood fixed in their tracks and soon their corpses littered the Plains. Their right flank no longer existed, its commander fatally wounded and abandoned. But Montcalm held the centre and the right together. At the north end of the field, Vaudreuil witnessed the fatal volley from his *calèche*.

The redcoats took another three steps forward and their front line dropped to one knee. They waited in silence for the smoke to clear. It took seven minutes.

10:22 A.M.

"Fire!" Wolfe commanded a second time. The sound the muskets made was like a single, gigantic cannon shot.

10:24 A.M.

A Canadian sharpshooter, hiding in the bushes along the top of the ridge above the St. Lawrence, aimed and fired. An officer of the Louisbourg Grenadiers close to him saw Wolfe reeling and caught him in his arms. Soldiers rushed to help carry him to the rear of the battlefield. Wolfe was fatally wounded in the chest.

10:25 A.M.

Montcalm's army had disappeared. The regulars were racing off the field towards the town and many of the Canadians scrambled to take cover in the bushes. From there they fired upon the redcoats, as the Highlanders, disobeying their orders, broke rank and rushed to finish off the wounded, the dying, and the fleeing. Soon Montcalm himself became caught in the irreversible flow. With resignation, he let his horse take him where it could.

It was over. The battle of the Plains of Abraham had lasted less than thirty minutes.

During the next half hour

The rout of the French army was by no means complete, as Vaudreuil could see from his *calèche*. When Montcalm's right flank broke, several units of Canadians took position along a wooded ridge to block off access to the St. Charles River. The Grenadiers and others ran as fast as they could towards the Canadians, with the Highlanders, broadswords in their hands, in pursuit. The Canadians managed to hold off the Scots long enough for many of their French comrades to cross the St. Charles. Vaudreuil tried to rally the fugitives, but his presence only seemed to increase the general panic. He followed them to the relative safety of La Canardière.

The habitants kept up their barrage until Murray arrived with reinforcements. Even then, the Canadians held him off for about fifteen minutes, killing and wounding many High-landers, including two officers. Then the militia gave way, inch by inch. Before crossing the bridge over the St. Charles they made their final stand. It did not last long. Within three minutes, five at the most, they abandoned their position and retreated, leaving close to two hundred of their people dead or wounded behind them.

The Canadians who had stationed themselves by the gates of the town to permit the fleeing army to enter Québec fared better. When all the French forces had passed, the gates were closed and locked.

Wolfe lay on his cape, covered with blood. There were no doctors with him and the two Ramezay sent to him did not reach their destination. His aides tried their best to ease his pain and to end the flow of blood, but with no success. After a while he stopped their ministration. "It is needless," he said. "It is all over with me."

In an effort to comfort him, one of the soldiers around him cried out, "They run, see how they run!"

Still not believing his success, Wolfe asked: "Who runs?"

"The enemy, Sir. Egad, they give way everywhere!"

Wolfe roused himself and ordered, "Go one of you, my lads, to Colonel Burton; tell him to march Webb's regiment with all speed down to Charles' River, to cut off the retreat of the fugitives from the bridge."

This long command exhausted him. His breathing difficult, he asked to be turned on his side and then whispered, "Now, God be praised, I will die in peace."

And with that James Wolfe, Major-General in America and commander-in chief of the expedition against Québec, died. He was thirty-two years old.

In the confused flight of his army, Montcalm was swept along towards the Porte Saint-Louis. There he stopped his horse and tried to encourage the soldiers. But it was futile. Most of his senior officers were either dead, wounded or missing and the Highlanders were in pursuit. His men didn't even stop to listen to his exhortations. He rode on.

As he was about to enter through the gate, two shots hit him in rapid succession. Three soldiers hastened foward and held him steady in his saddle. With Montbeillard leading the way, he was taken to the house of André Arnoux, the King's surgeon in Canada. The doctor was away with Bourlamaque on the Ile-aux-Noix, but his brother, also a surgeon, examined Montcalm. The wounds were fatal and Arnoux was of the opinion that Montcalm would not live past sunrise the following day.

With Wolfe dead and Monckton seriously wounded and off the field, the English were leaderless and in disarray. Wolfe's last order to cut off the French retreat by the St. Charles River was not heeded, and Murray, who could have seized the advantage, did not. Finally Townshend, third in command, took charge. He recalled the soldiers and regrouped them on the Plains.

Wolfe's body, wrapped in a grenadier's long coat and draped with the English colours, was put on a stretcher. Preceded by an escort, and with Wolfe's aides in attendance, it was taken to the edge of the cliff, down the path to the beach of the Foulon and reverently placed in one of Chads' boats to be rowed to the *Lowestoft*.

Bougainville was too late. When he got within sight of the Plains of Abraham, the French army had disappeared and redcoats were running all over the Plains.

He began to form a line of defence along the edge of the Chemin Sainte-Foy, but Townshend opened fire, killing two of Bougainville's escort and wounding four more. With no artillery and no communications from anyone in the command of the French army, and with no more than two hundred cavalry and six hundred soldiers at his immediate disposal, Bougainville did not feel himself capable of taking on the English. He sounded the retreat and led his force in good order to the village of Ancienne-Lorette to await both the arrival of the rest of his army and orders from Vaudreuil.

Townshend chose not to pursue Bougainville. He had only one battalion with him and the wrong ammunition for his two guns. Furthermore, as he explained in a dispatch to his superiors in England, it was not his business to chase Bougainville through the woods and swamps of Canada "risking ye fruit of so decisive a Day."

Much ink has been used up in critiques of the generalship on the Plains of Abraham, and historians have used up whole forests debating and analyzing the behaviour and the reasons for Wolfe's and Montcalm's decisions and orders. I could also go on *ad nauseum*, but I will resist the temptation and leave it to you to judge for yourself. I have given you enough clues.

Having said that, however, there are two matters I need to settle.

"Where in the hell were the French supply boats?" I ask Bougainville.

"They had arrived at the mouth of the Cap Rouge River, not far from where the *Sutherland* was. But the boats were leaking badly and so it was decided – "

"Who decided?" I practically yell at him.

"I suppose those in charge. No doubt Monsieur Cadet, the purveyor general, was informed of this predicament and a decision made to bring down the supplies by cart to Québec. Before you ask, I was not told of this, nor, as far as I know, were my sentries informed. Would it have made any difference had we known?"

"Perhaps; perhaps not. It would have made it more difficult, though, for the English to get to the Foulon and climb the precipice. It might also have forced you to get out of bed earlier than you did." I look at him for a while and then I ask as gently as I can, "Where were you that night?"

He walks around and I sense that he does not want to deal with my question and the others that are bound to follow. To encourage him, I say, a little too dramatically, as is my wont, "Many people who have written about the battle of the Plains of Abraham blame you for the French defeat."

He looks at me with pain, shrugs his shoulders, and continues his march around my study.

"Look, you were awakened at five-fifteen, told of the firing from the Samos battery, and you did not investigate. You went back to bed."

He does not answer. So I add, "You went back to bed with your cousin's wife!"

He stops, turns around abruptly, and with an edge to his voice, he says, "Did you make that up?"

"No, one historian has argued that there can be no other explanation for your dilatory performance."

"Well, your historian is a fool. I was in bed alone. I did not hear cannon. I was tired. I had marched up to Pointe-aux-Trembles and back in the space of a few hours."

"A famous Canadian historian," I say, interrupting him, "wrote that the English did not move any ships that day!"

"How does he know, your historian? English barges, boats with sailors manning them plied the water continuously – and September 12 was no exception. So I was tired and I slept. I must also tell you that the sentries were always behaving hysterically. When I received Monsieur de Vaudreuil's messenger around eight o'clock, I left almost immediately for the Plains. The only mistake I made was to attempt to dislodge the English at Sillery. I did it to protect my rear. A good commanding officer does that. Enough of this nonsense. Goodbye."

And he leaves me abruptly to my thoughts about the Canadians.

It is an historical axiom, challenged by few historians, that Wolfe made no errors on the Plains, that Montcalm committed more than his share, and that what defeated the French was the superior calibre of the English army. I disagree with this assessment.

I believe that the way Wolfe planned his landing at Foulon and assembled his army on the Plains proves that he was incompetent, if not insane. What destroyed Montcalm was his pessimism, his paranoia, and his incapacity to act resolutely. As for the English army, it was no better and no worse than the French one – and both were not worth much. That leaves the Canadians.

It is often stated that Montcalm's fatal mistake was to incorporate Canadians into the regular troops. Perhaps this is true, since the two were accustomed to different forms of warfare. However, only the Canadians behaved well and with any semblance of honour on the Plains of Abraham. Left to themselves, it was their courage, their fine marksmanship, and their initiative that made it possible for many of their French comrades to find safety in the trenches of Beauport and behind the walls of Québec. The Canadians – at great cost in human lives – salvaged at least part of the day. Historians, in their frenzy to emphasize only the negative aspects of the Canadians in the defence of their country, have failed to record the habitant's noble act of September 13, 1759.

Now after some two hundred and thirty years, the record is straight.

Plains of Abraham
1:00 P.M.

Townshend, Murray, and other senior officers marched to the head of each regiment assembled on the Plains to congratulate and thank the troops for their victory. Townshend ordered the men to have a meal and take a short rest while he did the same.

While he ate and rested, he pondered the predicament he was in. Wolfe had done only half the job. Should he finish it? He could pursue the battle by crossing the St. Charles River and fighting the French at Beauport. Obviously the French soldiers who had fought on the Plains were dispirited and disorganized, but Vaudreuil might have fresh troops in his trenches who had not yet seen battle, and the English had none. Also, Bougainville was at his rear and the garrison of Québec with all of its guns was in front of him. He decided to resolve his predicament by waiting for another day.

In the meantime he would secure his position. He ordered a road built to the Foulon so that his cannon, supplies, and ammunition could be hauled more easily to the Plains. He devised batteries and redoubts, Mackellar and the engineers having assured him that twelve could be completed by nightfall. Every house and building around the edge of the Plains and those bordering the two roads that ran through it was burned to the ground. He ordered every tree and shrub uprooted, and every fence destroyed. Dugouts and trenches criss-crossed the whole plateau, and sentries were posted in every conceivable location.

Townshend sent some of the wounded to the hospitals on the Ile d'Orléans and at Pointe-Lévy. A few, he learned later, had already been taken to the Hôpital Général, which now lay within the boundary of his battlefield. Thirteen French officers and three hundred soldiers who had been taken prisoner were marched to the Foulon and taken to various transports in the St. Lawrence. The dead of both armies he ordered buried in a common grave.

He congratulated Saunders, who technically was the senior English officer in and around Québec. The navy had done well. Chads had worked miracles and Admiral Holmes' sailors and marines had performed to perfection. In his reply to Townshend, Saunders wrote, "The loss of our friend, General Wolfe, gives me the greatest concern which in some measure is taken off by the great victory of today."

They agreed that Wolfe's body, after being embalmed at Pointe-Lévy, would be brought to the *Stirling Castle*, Saunders' flagship, where it would await transfer to the HMS *Royal William* for the journey home to Portsmouth.

La Canardière
3:00 P.M.

The fleeing soldiers who had crossed the St. Charles hornwork were still disorderly, frightened, and for the most part leaderless. Their officers behaved no differently. No one was capable of restoring order.

Vaudreuil himself was powerless. Senior officers, captains, and even men from the junior ranks forced their way into his headquarters to badger him. Some wanted him to cut the bridge over the St. Charles and stay put, while others clamoured for the army to retreat to Pointe-aux-Trembles. Their voices were shrill, their arguments impossible to follow, and their fear overpowering.

Only a few advised him to return to the Plains with fifteen hundred fresh troops under Poulhariez, the two thousand or so men of the garrison of Québec, Bougainville's force of three thousand, the Canadian militia who could still shoot straight, and the Indians who could still terrify. They argued that the battle of the Plains of Abraham had been indecisive and that Vaudreuil would have to attack almost immediately, before the English defences being built became impregnable. Only by such a course of action would the honour of the King and of French arms be maintained.

But, Vaudreuil asked himself in exasperation, would the army follow him? Would they serve under Bougainville, who was now the senior French officer in and around Québec? And, should he lose the second battle of the Plains of Abraham, would he not have to capitulate for the whole of Canada?

Vaudreuil, not knowing what to do, closeted himself with Bigot and reviewed the Articles of Capitulation Montcalm had prepared before the arrival of the English at Québec. Still incapable of making a decision, he sent an officer to Montcalm's deathbed seeking advice. Montcalm replied that there were only three choices open to the Governor General: to attack the enemy immediately, to retreat to Jacques-Cartier about thirty miles above Québec, or to seek out Townshend and capitulate for the whole colony. Montcalm left to Vaudreuil the responsibility of choosing the course of action that best suited the old man.

Dismissing Bigot, Vaudreuil called a council of war for five o'clock that evening and went into seclusion. After fifteen minutes or so, he had made up his mind. He would buy time. Summoning his secretary, he dictated a letter to Lévis in Montréal. He related the events of the day, emphasizing his role in them. His hopes for victory had lain, he said, in Montcalm not acting precipitously, but "luck was against us, the attack being made with too much precipitation." The battle had cost many lives; Montcalm was among the wounded, and everyone feared for his life. "No one desires more than I that this fear be unfounded."

As for the future, he wrote, "Tonight I shall leave for Jacques-Cartier where I hope you will join me as soon as you have received my letter. It is of the utmost importance that you come as quickly as possible. I shall wait for you with great impatience ... I leave [Québec] to its own devices." Vaudreuil signed the letter at four-thirty.

Half an hour later, at the council of war, composed of military officials and Bigot, Vaudreuil's decision was accepted unanimously. At six o'clock the army was ordered to be ready to leave for Jacques-Cartier by ten o'clock that night.

Québec
That evening

Montcalm was dying, but for the moment he was resting comfortably. After Vaudreuil's courier had departed, he had fallen asleep. Then around seven o'clock, another messenger arrived from Vaudreuil with a letter and documents. In the letter Vaudreuil announced that he and the army were leaving for Jacques-Cartier. He had hoped, he wrote, for a different course of action but "the opinion of these gentlemen [the military officers] being supported by your own I give way to it, though sadly enough." He asked Montcalm to forward to Ramezay the terms of capitulation, which "you will see are the same which I arranged with you."

Marcel replied for Montcalm. "The Marquis de Montcalm entrusts to me the honour of writing to tell you that he approves of everything. I read him your letter and the terms of capitulation, which I have given to M. Ramezay according to your instructions, together with the letter you wrote to him."

In a postscript, Marcel added, "The Marquis de Montcalm is not much better, though his pulse is now a little stronger."

Before relapsing into sleep, Montcalm named Lévis as the guardian of his official papers and asked Marcel to write to his mother, his wife, and each of his children. As well, he dictated a letter to Townshend in which he recommended the sick and the wounded to his kindness. He then turned his attention to the state of his soul. The Chaplain of the Uruslines came to hear his confession and administer the last rites of the Catholic Church.

Vaudreuil's instructions to Ramezay were explicit: Ramezay was left to fend for himself. "We want to state categorically," wrote Vaudreuil, "that Monsieur de Ramezay is not to wait until the enemy storms the city." Instead Ramezay was to capitulate as soon as he ran out of food.

La Canardière and Beauport
10:00 P.M.

Vaudreuil was the first to leave in his *calèche*, protected by six hundred men from the Montréal militia. He took the road to Charlesbourg to the east of the St. Charles River and the English lines. Bigot was not far behind. He left at Beauport hundreds of barrels of flour and pork, some beef, thousands of pounds of bread and biscuits, close to one hundred barrels of brandy and fourteen of wine – provisions for about ten days. The tents were left standing, the ammunition remained in its caches, and the guns sat quietly in their entrenchments. In his haste to escape, Bigot did not send word to Ramezay in Québec.

The soldiers, many of whom were drunk on the alcohol Vaudreuil had distributed lavishly, walked in no particular military order, the only exception being that of the Royal-Roussillon. "It was not a retreat," Johnstone wrote, "but a horrid, abominable flight, a thousand times worse than that in the morning upon the Heights of Abraham, with such disorder and confusion that, had the English known it, three hundred men sent after us would have been sufficient to destroy and cut all our army to pieces."

But the English chose not to hear a sound.

Hôpital Général
11:30 P.M.

Two young nuns carrying hot broth to one of the wards heard the banging at the front door of the hospital. Opening the door, they saw a tall officer wearing "a kind of skirt" standing in the entrance with a large number of soldiers also "without breeches." The officer walked in quietly and closed the door firmly behind him. He asked to see the Reverend Mothers, the Superiors of the three communities of nuns now living in the hospital. When they arrived, he greeted them politely and informed them that he was taking the hospital in the name of his King and would be placing guards outside. The nuns were not to fear for their safety. Wolfe had promised them his protection and his wish would be honoured. The officer saluted and left the three nuns standing in the foyer. Moments later, two hundred redcoats surrounded the Hôpital Général.

The English casualties of that day numbered 658 from all ranks. On the French side, Vaudreuil reported 644 dead, wounded, or missing. However, many Canadian and Indian losses were not recorded.

THE INEVITABLE

September 14–18, 1759

It has been very difficult to reconstruct what happened in Québec during those days. The evidence is often contradictory and, most of the time, unclear. I had to rely on reading between the lines of many documents to arrive at what you are about to read.

September 14, 1759

(Day Eighty-one)

In flight
With the French army

By three o'clock in the morning, Vaudreuil and the army were at Charlesbourg. He gave orders that the 150 men of the Béarn Regiment, whom Montreuil had sent to Québec before the flight, were to join him at Jacques-Cartier. Québec was left with 120 regular troops. He also wrote to Ramezay telling him nothing of importance except that he would "speak highly of you to the Court at Versailles." Then he met briefly with the Bishop and departed for Ancienne-Lorette, which he reached by six o'clock. He had lunch at Saint-Augustin and slept at Pointe-aux-Trembles.

Vaudreuil had a terribly anxious day as his horses put twenty miles between him and Townshend in Québec. For most of that bumpy ride he was exhausted, hungry, alarmed, and in bad temper. He was an old man made even older by the horrible events of the past day and the long siege that had preceded it. He worried about his reputation at Court and the fate that might await him there. He worried about his people in Québec, whom he had left in the hands of the English, unless a miracle happened. Knowing them well, he realized the Canadians were cursing him. When he tried to find an excuse, a reason to alleviate his responsibility, he attributed all his woes to Montcalm, dying in Québec. He even prepared in his mind a letter to the court in which he wrote of Montcalm's ambition, deceit, and his constant conspiring against himself and the Intendant. He described Montcalm as tolerating insubordination and looting when these crimes were committed by the regular troops, but as being harsh with the Canadians, whom he tried to turn against Vaudreuil. As for the Indians, Montcalm's meddling had caused only friction and disaster. It was all Montcalm's fault.

Vaudreuil's army did not behave any better in flight than it had at the Battle of the Plains. At Ancienne-Lorette, they looted a bakery, killing the baker. Shortly thereafter, a courier caught up to Vaudreuil with the news of Montcalm's death.

Arnoux's house
5:00 A.M.

Montcalm took Monsieur Marcel's hand and whispered "Candiac! Candiac!" He smiled. The priest began reciting the Hail Mary: *"Je vous salue, Marie ... ."* With a deep sigh, Louis-Joseph Marquis de Montcalm, seigneur de Saint-Véran, Candiac, Tournemine, Vestric, Saint-Julien, and Arpaon, Baron de Gabriac, lieutenant-général and commander-in-chief of the French regular troops in North America, died.

A few miles away at the Hôpital Général, the nun entrusted with her community's diary wrote, "The remnants of the French army have disappeared. Their tents are still standing along the flats of Beauport; but their batteries and trenches are silent and solitary; their guns, still pointed, are mute. Along the batteries of the Plains, still reeking with gore and covered with the slained, the victors are opening the turf to hide from view the hideous effects of war; bearing off such of the poor victims as still survive and hastening to entrench themselves, to secure their position so fortunately gained."

When the news arrived of Montcalm's death, she cried. Then, with the nuns and the patients who were well enough to attend, she went to the chapel to pray for his soul.

Pointe-Lévy
That afternoon

In the orders of the day, Townshend remembered Wolfe. "We wish," he said, "that our late commander, James Wolfe, had survived so glorious a day, and had been able to give the troops their just reward."

In their best uniforms, the soldiers stationed at Pointe-Lévy and all those who were not needed to man the batteries against Québec lined the path from the hospital, where Wolfe had been embalmed, to the shore. A barge shrouded in black, with twelve sailors of the admiral's ship under Chads, waited near the shore. Men from the Louisbourg Grenadiers, preceded by Murray, who was representing Townshend, and senior officers from the various regiments, and followed by Wolfe's aides, bore the casket draped in the crosses of England and Scotland to the barge. The officers and the aides embarked in five other longboats and the flotilla was rowed to the *Stirling Castle*, where Admiral Saunders, the senior chaplain, and the naval officers received the body. The mournful pipe sounded and the cannon of the fleet fired their salute. The flag was lowered to half-mast, and the body was borne solemnly to a stateroom that had been specially prepared. There James Wolfe would remain until his departure for his homeland.

Québec
Late afternoon

In honour of Montcalm, Ramezay had ordered the flags to be flown at half-mast in Québec. Now he coordinated the arrangements for Montcalm's funeral. Between tasks he found out that the French army at Beauport had disappeared without his being informed. He sent messengers to retrieve whatever food there was, but they returned empty-handed, the place having been looted, no doubt by the habitants of Ange-Gardien, Beaupré, and Château-Richer. Under several flags of truce, the wounded from the Plains who could not be taken to the Hôpital Général were brought to Québec, where Ramezay arranged for their care. Those who went to the English camp to retrieve the injured informed him of the progress of Townshend's entrenchment on the Plains. At two-thirty in the afternoon, Captain Barrot of the Béarn came to bid him farewell and march the regulars out of the town.

The citizens, realizing that they were being totally abandoned, were furious and took to the streets. They more or less rioted, accusing the French army and its officers of cowardice. They openly criticized Vaudreuil, wishing him every conceivable ill, and asked for an immediate capitulation. The principal merchants and citizens met with the officers of the militia to draft a formal request. Later, their rage momentarily spent, they gathered for Montcalm's funeral.

It had not been possible to find a carpenter to make a decent casket and there was no way to procure Montcalm a clean uniform. The *bonhomme* Michel, who worked for the nuns, built him a box from scraps and found a cushion for his head. Marcel scraped some of the blood off Montcalm's garments.

At nine o'clock in the evening, Montcalm was carried slowly through the ruined streets from Arnoux's house to the Ursuline Convent a short distance away. A soldier carrying the processional cross, flanked by two militia men each with lighted lanterns, led the way. Father Baudouin and the two priests left in the town followed, with Ramezay, the chief of police, and other officials behind them. The people, ignoring the bombs that the English still hurled from Pointe-aux-Pères, stood in clumps along the route, reciting the rosary.

At the chapel of the Ursulines, the only church still standing, the body was met by the chaplain of the nuns and by Father Récher, who conducted a simple funeral service. In the candlelight the dignitaries could make out the splintered ceiling, the ruined frescos, and the shattered grill of the cloister, behind which the nuns who had been left to guard the convent knelt to pray.

After the service, the body of the Marquis de Montcalm was lowered into the bomb crater where the altar had been. After everyone had left, the *bonhomme* Michel filled the cavity with earth and stones, then repaired the chapel floor as best he could.

Saint-Thomas on the south shore
Around supper time

Goreham arrived in Saint-Thomas after having burned Berthier, Saint-François, and Saint-Pierre in the past few days. While he ate and rested, waiting for the next day to begin, he wrote Saunders that a French frigate was in the Saguenay River, where it had been for a month. In the evening, a few Canadians, led by the seigneur of Rivière-du-Sud, Jean-Baptiste Couillard, and his son, Joseph, attacked Goreham's detachment. Three Rangers were killed along with the seigneur, his son, and two of their companions. In his week of destruction, Goreham had burned 121 farms.

September 15, 1759

(Day Eighty-two)

In the early morning, Lévis left Montréal in the pouring rain for Jacques-Cartier to meet Vaudreuil, Bigot, and the French army. They had arrived there at about noon after having been considerably delayed between Pointe-aux-Trembles and Jacques-Cartier by a collapsed bridge over the river.

The English continued to strengthen their camp on the Plains of Abraham. While most soldiers dug trenches and built fortifications, some were out looting. Two women were raped and many more abused. On the south shore, Scott was busy destroying the seigneurie de Saint-Roch. During a rest period, Captain Elphistone, the master of the *Eurus*, arrived with news of the French defeat on the thirteenth and orders for Scott to return immediately to Québec. Scott reluctantly complied but delayed his departure.

At eleven o'clock in the morning, twenty-six of the principal citizens of Québec assembled at Ramezay's house on Rue Saint-Louis, which was still inhabitable, to present him the petition they had prepared the night before. Panet, the notary, was their spokesman. Reading in his sonorous, dull voice, Panet reminded Ramezay that the people of the town had withstood a bombardment of sixty-three days, had lived without sufficient food during the seventy-nine day siege, and had suffered great loss of property. Throughout that ordeal, their only concern had been "the safety of Québec and the glory of the King of France."

"Now the situation has changed." The English were on the Plains, and the French army had retreated; there was barely any food left, and Ramezay had no way of successfully defending Québec. The only possible course of action was a "capitulation honorable ... If we submit now [the English] will be conciliatory. On the other hand, if we keep them waiting, they will become frustrated and we shall have to bear the brunt of their anger." In the name of the women, the children, and of all those who had already suffered so much, he begged Ramezay to be compassionate and save the little that was left, *"le peu qui leur reste de l'incendie."*

When Panet had finished, he handed the petition to Ramezay duly signed by the citizens and co-signed by some "gentlemen of the militia." Ramezay thanked them for their concern and assured them that he would follow the instructions he had received from the Governor General. He shook their hands, offered them a glass of wine, and left to assess the strength of his army and the condition of his stores.

Ramezay was aware that he would need close to seven thousand seasoned soldiers to defend the town of Québec properly. If he were lucky, he could count on the 120 regular troops Vaudreuil had left, the sailors manning the batteries, and a few of the militia. Certainly not enough to withstand a siege of any duration. Already many of the militia had left their posts and many more were just waiting for the opportunity to do so. He was convinced that mutiny was inevitable. The town major, Armand de Joannes, had struck two militia officers with the flat surface of his sword, provoking a great deal of anger among the soldiers.

As for his stores, they contained eighteen quarts of flour, twenty-eight hundred kilograms of biscuits, twenty-eight quarts of rice, eighteen of lard, thirty cattle, fifty-nine barrels of wine, forty of olive oil, eight of plums, sixty cases of candles, three casks of butter, and thirty quarts of salt beef. The food caches of the citizens of the town were all empty. Ramezay needed food to feed 2,200 soldiers, sailors, and militia, 2,600 women and children, 1,200 officials, clerks, countless others who were sick, infirm, or wounded in various makeshift hospitals, the few priests and nuns remaining, and prisoners of war. And Vaudreuil had not sent any instructions further to his letter of September 13.

At ten o'clock in the evening, Ramezay summoned a council of war, which was attended by fourteen senior officers, four of whom were Canadians. Ramezay began by reading to those present Vaudreuil's instructions and then proceeded to a careful review of every aspect of the defence of Québec, particularly the food supply. He then asked each one of the officers a simple question: Should he capitulate if he were able to obtain honourabe terms?

Twelve officers were in favour of immediate capitulation. Joannes eventually agreed with them after further discussion, but the commander of the town's artillery, Louis-Thomas Jacau de Fiedmont, dissented, arguing that it would be more honourable to reduce the rations even further and defend the city to the last extremity than to capitulate. Each member of the council gave the reasons for his vote in writing and signed the minutes. Ramezay, the last to do so, stated, "Given the instructions which I have received from the Marquis de Vaudreuil and given the grave shortage of food corroborated by official statements and the inquiry I undertook, I conclude that I must try to obtain the most honourable capitulation from the enemy." But he waited before hoisting the white flag.

September 16, 1759

(Day Eighty-three)

Bougainville was at Pointe-aux-Trembles when, early in the morning, le Chevalier de Saint-Rome brought him Vaudreuil's latest orders. Le Chevalier was on his way to Saint-Augustin to procure carts and take provisions to Québec. Bougainville was to provide an escort, Vaudreuil considering "the cavalry ... best suited for this purpose, for the main object now is to save the town from want, and keep the enemy outside it." Bougainville gave the necessary orders and sent a messenger to Ramezay that some supplies were on their way, also informing him of possible caches in the town.

When Bougainville's messenger arrived a couple of hours later, Ramezay dispatched Joannes and another officer to find Vaudreuil, or, failing that, to ascertain what exactly the Governor was proposing to do – if any one of Bougainville's officers knew. Joannes and his escort were to return that night.

While he waited for Vaudreuil to make his intentions known, Ramezay had the town searched once again for food, but nothing was found. By midnight, Vaudreuil had not sent word and the supplies from Saint-Augustin had not arrived.

When Joannes returned, he reported to Ramezay that he had travelled about nine miles when an officer from Bougainville's advance guard told him that Vaudreuil was at Jacques-Cartier but that the soldiers were still dispirited and could not be counted on. It would be best, Joannes was told, if Québec did not expect much relief from this source. Nevertheless, before he rode back to Québec, Joannes wrote to Vaudreuil telling him that the town would have to capitulate unless supplies and reinforcements arrived by ten o'clock the next morning. But, as he told Ramezay, there was no way of knowing if his letter had reached Vaudreuil.

Meanwhile on the south shore, Scott and his Rangers walked a long way that day from Saint-Roch to Cap Saint-

Ignace, burning and looting as they went and destroying Saint-Jean-Port-Joly and L'Islet. Goreham with James Montague and other Rangers marched from Saint-Thomas, where they had been on the fourteenth, closer to Pointe-Lévy. On that journey they found themselves in the village of the de Melançon family. Elisabeth was waiting by the maple sugar cabin.

She knew what the English were doing – rounding up the people who were still around, looting their farms, confiscating their cattle, and while the habitants prayed in front of the church, burning the village. She saw James Montague coming through the trees and met him at the door of the cabin. He smiled nervously, but she did not return his greeting.

"Where is your grandfather?" he asked gently in French.

"He was made a prisoner a few weeks ago," she replied, not looking at him.

He wanted to take her in his arms, to tell her that it would be over soon and that he loved her. But he could not and he sensed she would not hear him. Instead he told her that they had already burned her house. She walked a few feet with tears in her eyes. But she quickly recovered and wiped them away more in annoyance than anger. For the first time she looked at him, and she remembered every minute they had spent together. It was a short-lived moment. She glanced at her house nearby and said, "We shall rebuild it all. We are accustomed to misfortunes. We shall rebuild it."

Then sitting bareback on the horse, she looked intently at him, "I'm going to ride to the second concession to tell the people there of your coming. Please do not stop me. I did you a favour once. I need one now."

She paused, then she added, "I am with your child," and rode off.

September 17, 1759

(Day Eighty-four)

Jacques-Cartier
A little after dawn

Through the rain and mist, the sentry saw a *calèche* with an escort coming his way. It was followed by many men both on foot and on horseback. The guard summoned his lieutenant and the post was reinforced. Soon thereafter, an officer emerged from the *calèche*. Lévis had arrived. He had brought his servants.

Québec
10:30 A.M.

No word, reinforcements, or food had yet come from Vaudreuil, or from anyone else for that matter. Ramezay, faithful to the deadline he had given himself, ordered Joannes to be ready at any moment to proceed to the English camp to arrange for the capitulation of Québec.

Joannes, wanting to buy more time, argued strongly that they should delay longer while he made another thorough search for flour and other supplies. Ramezay agreed.

Plains of Abraham
11:15 A.M.

The weather was wet and unpleasant but Knox, the diarist, found the orders of the day encouraging. Three days after the battle of the Plains, Townshend had finally laid down the law. "I will not permit such act of licentiousness," he stated, "and will take all the necessary measures to ensure the proper discipline which the good of the service demands and the memory of our late General dictates." He repeated his order that under the pain of death no officer or soldier was to enter the Hôpital Général without proper authorization. Knox approved of Townshend's firmness. "The battle is not over," he wrote in his diary. "It has just begun. The country is not ours yet."

Later, at an officers' briefing, Knox learned that sixty cannon and fifty-eight mortars had been brought to the Plains. These would soon be ready to bombard Québec should Ramezay not capitulate. Already Admiral Saunders was moving more of the fleet into the basin in preparation for an attack on the Lower Town.

Jacques-Cartier
Noon

Lévis had come to Vaudreuil's house expecting an earful. Vaudreuil, who appeared frail and aged beyond his years, greeted him effusively and placed the blame for the defeat of the thirteenth on Montcalm's shoulders. Lévis interrupted him.

"Monsieur le Gouverneur," he said, "we must leave Monsieur de Montcalm to rest in peace. I owe it to his memory to stress to you that he believed he was acting for the best. Unfortunately, generals who lose are never right." He stopped for a moment before stating sternly, "If we question the honesty and honour of Monsieur de Montcalm, I wonder if you are aware, *Excellence*, that *Sa Majesté, notre Roi* will not judge as honourable the decisions you and the council of war made after the battle of the Plains of Abraham?"

Vaudreuil reeled under the brutality of the attack, but before he could answer, Lévis went on, "The loss of a battle does not necessitate the abandonment of thirty miles of territory. The retreat of your army – indeed the flight of your army – was an error; it was precipitous and dishonourable. It has caused us untold grief. We were about to see this dreadful siege end in glory; instead we have a battle lost, a flight, the deterioration of the morale of the troops with a loss of confidence in their officers. Everywhere we are surrounded by confusion and a dangerous lack of discipline. The militia is deserting in droves, and the people are discouraged."

As Lévis stopped to take a deep breath, Vaudreuil made ready to speak, but Lévis would have none of it. More softly he continued, "I have no doubt that your courage will enable you to bear the responsibility for the decisions taken and the disgrace which is bound to visit them. You could have rallied the troops and fought the English on the thirteenth or in the morning of the fourteenth. You chose not to do so. We must now do our utmost to repair this outrage."

He paused and announced his plan of action:

"I intend, *Monsieur le Gouverneur*, to march the army back to Québec immediately and there to attack the English. I will risk everything to prevent the taking of Québec, and, if the worst comes to the worst, I will move all the people out and destroy the town. The enemy shall not pass the winter in the capital of New France."

Refusing to acknowledge Vaudreuil's cry of alarm, Lévis went on, "Monsieur le Marquis de Vaudreuil, I will need the full and complete cooperation you assured me of in the two letters you did me the honour of writing to me on the thirteenth and the fourteenth instant. I shall be in total command of all our forces and of the operation. Are we in agreement, *Excellence?*"

Vaudreuil was astounded. No one, except Madame la Marquise, had ever spoken to him so plainly and harshly before. Yet, he saw in Lévis' plan a possible remedy for the mischief his decisions had caused and for which he would be held to account by Versailles. It meant giving up his authority, but he judged it to be a fair price to pay. He replied: "Yes, Monsieur le Chevalier, I am in agreement. You shall have full authority. I myself will remain here at Jacques-Cartier."

Lévis gave orders for the immediate departure of the army, but Bigot could not provision the troops as quickly as that. Lévis had to wait until dawn the next day.

Vaudreuil wrote to Ramezay and to Bougainville. Lévis sent Bernetz, Ramezay's second in command in Québec, a letter that he was on his way. It took a couple of hours before the couriers left. They had to travel over thirty miles to reach the besieged town of Québec.

Behind the English lines
2:00 P.M.

Bougainville was waiting for Saint-Rome and his supplies from Saint-Augustin. But he received instead a message that the convoy of food could not leave because of the poor conditions of the roads. Nevertheless, Bougainville decided to act. He sent the commander of the cavalry, Rochebeaucour, to Charlesbourg with a hundred horsemen to commandeer a hundred bags of biscuits and deliver them to Québec as quickly as possible. At the same time, a small detachment under Captain de Belcourt went to occupy the hornwork on the St. Charles River by La Canardière. As soon as he had reached his destination, Belcourt was to send a courier to Ramezay to inform him that food was coming.

Québec
Between 4:00 P.M. and 6:00 P.M.

The morale of the inhabitants and militia was at the lowest it had been since the beginning of the siege. No help had come at all. Women and children walked through the rubble of the town wailing and begging for food. The principal citizens refused to bear arms. More and more soldiers were deserting the town, some to rejoin the French army, others to return to their homes, and a few to seek shelter with Townshend. Ramezay was even told of a sergeant of the regular troops who had given the key to one of the town's gates to the English. Matters had deteriorated to such a degree that Ramezay could not get his orders carried out.

And the English were making ready to attack. They were setting up more and more cannon on the batteries and redoubts of the Plains. Saunders was carrying out extensive manoeuvres in the harbour of the Lower Town. By four o'clock in the afternoon, he had six imposing vessels poised to attack and more were sailing towards Québec. Soldiers were seen embarking in barges and making for the harbour. Lookouts on the ramparts reported to Ramezay that a large English force was marching forward on the Plains toward the Porte du Palais.

Ramezay ordered the general alarm to be sounded. Accompanied by some senior officers, he rushed to the waterfront, where he found that the militia would not fight and that most of them, along with their officers, were returning their arms to the King's stores, thus reassuming their status as civilians and non-belligerents. They explained that, having been abandoned by the French army, they had no intention of being massacred by the English, who were bound to storm the town at any time.

Unable to defend the city or even to make a show of doing so, Ramezay consulted once again with his officers. They concurred with his decision to hoist the white flag. In writing, he ordered Joannes to proceed to the English camp with the Articles of Capitulation. Another officer, as was the custom, accompanied Joannes to serve as a hostage. Ramezay then went to his house to await the *dénouement*.

Cap Saint-Ignace, south shore
5:00 P.M.

Scott and Goreham had travelled close to sixty miles since the beginning of their mission. They had burned fifteen villages, seigneuries, and concessions, including eleven hundred houses, barns, and other buildings. They had taken over sixty prisoners and had killed five Canadians. Their soldiers had destroyed vessels of various sizes, mills, hundreds of acres of corn, and some fishery installations along the St. Lawrence and other rivers. They had also appropriated a vast number of cattle and sheep, as well as an immense amount of household goods. Scott reported that he had lost seven Rangers, three killed and four wounded.

Now Scott was preparing to board the ship which Saunders had sent to pick up him and his men. He had planned to embark earlier in the day but the tide had not cooperated. As he waited, he had amused himself by burning the sixty houses of Cap Saint-Ignace, including the priest's.

Québec
7:00 P.M.

Belcourt delivered his message verbally: "Do not despair; food is on its way." But Ramezay decided to wait until the food was on his doorstep before recalling Joannes.

English camp on the Plains of Abraham
8:00 P.M.

When Townshend had finished his dinner, he summoned Joannes and read Vaudreuil's document. There were eleven Articles of Capitulation. Articles two to eleven gave him no difficulty: the inhabitants could retain the enjoyment of their property and, upon laying down their arms, they would be free of reprisals for having defended their country; the property of those absent would not be touched; freedom of religion and freedom of movement for the Bishop and the clergy in the exercise of their duties would be granted; the sick and wounded would be protected, and guards would be posted at churches, hospitals, convents, and principal habitations; and Ramezay would be allowed to communicate with Vaudreuil and with his government in France.

The first article, however, proved difficult. Townshend was ready to grant the honours of war to the French garrison but not to allow the officers and the soldiers to rejoin the main army at Jacques-Cartier. Instead, along with the sailors, they would become prisoners of war and be transported to France in English ships and at English expense.

Vaudreuil had foreseen Townshend's reaction and had advised Ramezay not to insist. Joannes, however, to gain more time, asked permission to return to Ramezay and seek his consent to Townshend's proposal. The English general gave his approval but ordered Joannes to be back by eleven o'clock that night or there would be no capitulation. The English would storm Québec.

Joannes had one hour.

On the way to Québec
Late that evening

Vaudreuil's courier to Ramezay somehow lost the Governor's letters and decided not to proceed to Québec. Bernetz did not receive Lévis' message.

Rue Saint-Louis, Upper Town
10:30 P.M.

Ramezay was satisfied. The terms obtained from Townshend were more favourable than Vaudreuil had anticipated. Ramezay saw no reason why he should not sign the Capitulation on the spot and send Joannes back to the English. However, the major pleaded once more with Ramezay to wait until morning; food, and perhaps troops, could be on their way. But Ramezay would no longer contemplate any delay. He signed the agreement and gave Joannes a written order to proceed at once to Townshend's camp.

When Joannes arrived there a quarter of an hour later, with only minutes to spare, Townshend had gone to bed.

Québec
Shortly before midnight

A hundred horsemen, under Rochebeaucourt, entered through the Porte du Palais with soaking wet sacks of biscuits tied to their saddles. Delivering them to Ramezay, Rochebeaucourt said, "There will be no need to capitulate. More food is on the way, I am certain. And perhaps troops."

"You have arrived too late, Monsieur." Ramezay replied. "Major Joannes is presently delivering the Articles of Capitulation, which I have already signed, to His Excellency, the English general."

Rochebeaucourt was startled. He pleaded with Ramezay to withdraw his signature and wait, arguing that he should have confidence in the Governor, in Lévis, in the army, and that delaying for a few hours would permit the honour of France to be preserved. Suddenly Ramezay became quite angry. Unable to control himself any longer, he vented his displeasure on the poor cavalry commander.

"I am a man of honour," he said rather pompously. "I have obtained terms of surrender more favourable than Monsieur de Vaudreuil even contemplated."

He looked at Rochebeaucourt and asked, "What do you think will happen if I do not honour my pledge to the English, as you request? What then, Monsieur?" Inches from Rochebeaucourt's face, he answered his question himself. "An hour after I have withdrawn my signature, General Townshend will storm us from the Plains of Abraham and Admiral Saunders from the harbour. Many in this town are of the opinion that if that eventuality happens, we, the military as well as the civilians, will be executed."

He waited for what he had just said to sink in, then with emotion he asked Rochebeaucourt, "Where is our army, Monsieur? Still at Jacques-Cartier? Well, I am here and I have to decide. This town, with its crumbling walls and rotten palisades, Monsieur, is besieged from all possible angles. The population feels abandoned and betrayed by the army that had been sent to protect it. They want me to surrender, honourably no doubt, but surrender just the same."

Ramezay walked up and down and grabbing hold of some wet biscuits, he snarled, "Is this, these wet, soggy biscuits, all the food we are to have? Where are the troops, the ammunition I have been told are on their way? Where indeed!" Again he came close to Rochebeaucourt, "And, Monsieur, I have held out *alone* for four days. It is more than the army did after the battle of the Plains of Abraham."

He stopped, startled at his own rage. An inner voice told him to quiet down and so, with a smile, he said to the commander, "I am a faithful servant of our King. If the English have second thoughts and change the terms they have agreed to, I will consider the agreement void. But for that consideration to have any meaning, it is imperative that tomorrow, before the day is well advanced, a force of five hundred regular troops with equipment, baggage, and provisions enter the town with food for my people. Upon your departure this night, I will dispatch a courier to His Excellency the Governor to that effect, and if you have any ways and means at your disposal, I beg you to do the same. I thank you. The people of my household will see to your comfort and that of your men. Bonsoir, Monsieur."

Ramezay went to his quarters and prayed for a miracle.

September 18, 1759

(Day Eighty-five)

Jacques-Cartier
At dawn

The rain had stopped at last and it promised to be a sunny day. The army was ready. Vaudreuil inspected the men of the Béarn, Languedoc, Gueynne, Royal-Roussillon, and La Sarre regiments, the militia who had not given up, and the *troupes franches de la marine*. He found them to be soldiers again, standing straight, their uniforms and clothes cleaned, and their weapons at the ready. They walked proudly, the drummers beat a joyous march, and the flags flew splendidly in the wind. With Montbeillard and Johnstone following a few feet behind, Lévis took his leave of the Governor. "We shall be in Pointe-aux-Trembles tonight," Lévis said, "Saint-Augustin tomorrow night, and in Québec on the twentieth. I pray we shall not be too late." The old man certainly hoped so. "Go with God!" he said.

Bigot had stayed in bed.

English camp
8:00 A.M.

The weather was fine on the Plains of Abraham. The army had been drawn up to the sound of drums, pipes, and fifes to form a large quadrangle on the heights. At the centre of the parade ground stood a table upon which lay two copies of the Articles of Capitulation along with pens and ink. Standing on one side of the table were senior officers from both services. From one end of the field an escort of Highlanders marched forward, followed by Saunders, Townshend, Murray, Carleton, and Burton, the last two having recuperated enough from the wounds they had received on the thirteenth to attend. Monckton, who was still ill, was not invited, nor was he shown the Articles of Capitulation. The procession marched slowly and majestically down the centre of the plateau to the table. Saunders and Townshend sat down, Townshend gave a signal, and Major Joannes and his escort, surrounded by the Louisbourg Grenadiers, came forward.

Admiral Saunders was the first to sign the two copies of the Articles. He was followed by Townshend. Since Ramezay had already signed, Joannes was left with nothing to do except watch. At the end of the ceremony, Townshend presented him with a copy of the document. Joannes bowed gracefully, thanked him, turned around, and marched as steadily as he could to his horse. As he rode off towards the town, a great cheer went up.

When the troops were silent again, Townshend began to read the orders of the day. "The capital of Canada having this day surrendered to his Majesty's arms upon terms honourable to our victorious army, all acts of violence, pillage, or cruelty are strictly forbidden. The garrison is to have the honours of war; and the inhabitants will lay down their arms. By the Capitulation, they are entitled to His Majesty's protection. Québec is ours!"

Québec
4:00 P.M.

The townspeople lined the streets of what had once been a proud and defiant town. The armed soldiers of the garrison were stationed at their posts, the sailors at their batteries, and the sentries and their officers were at the three gates of Québec. Ramezay, the senior officers of his command, dignitaries and principal citizens, including Fathers Récher and Baudouin, took their places in the square in front of the Château Saint-Louis. The lilies of France still flew over the Citadel.

Shortly before four o'clock, a lookout announced the coming of the English. Leading the march was a detachment of the artillery and one gun with the British colours flying from its carriage. Then came three companies of Grenadiers to take command of the three gates. A few minutes later, with an impressive escort, the commanding officer of the English, Brigadier-General Townshend, rode with his party into the Place d'Armes to receive the keys to the town. At that moment, on the highest ramparts of the Citadel, a French officer lowered the lilies of France, folded the flag respectfully, and carried it solemnly to Ramezay. An English officer unfurled the British flag and raised the crosses of St. George and St. Andrew above the Citadel. In the Lower Town, Captain Palliser of the Royal Navy, attended by a large body of sailors and marines, hoisted the same flag above the harbour.

With drums beating and artillery salvos saluting the new order, the French soldiers, sailors, and officers filed out of Québec to be conveyed to English transports in the Lower St. Lawrence. They carried with them their colours, their arms, and their baggage. English soldiers quickly replaced them at their posts. Townshend bowed to Jean-Baptiste-Nicolas-Roch de Ramezay and ordered a detachment of Highlanders to escort him to his home on Rue Saint-Louis. After Ramezay had walked away, Townshend entered the Château Saint-Louis, now the official residence of the English Governor of Québec. Capitaine Daubressy left with a small escort to report the news to Vaudreuil.

From the woods around Québec, women and children, half-naked, almost starving, their emaciated bodies bitten by flies and fleas, rushed into the town to beg for bread. The first official act of the English was to set up a kitchen to feed them.

During the first night of English rule, Ramezay rested at his house, certain that no one could reproach him. The Canadian priest, Charles Baudouin, packed his bags and went to the Hôpital Général to convert the English. Lévis, angry at being deprived of his moment of glory, wrote in his journal: "It is unheard of that a place should be given up without being either attacked or invested," and he began to make plans for the winter and the next campaign. Bougainville, about nine miles away, said to no one in particular: "Such is the end of what had been the finest campaign in the world." And Vaudreuil told Ramezay that he could send the Articles of Capitulation to France himself.

Townshend returned to his camp on the Plains, pleased with himself. Since the Battle of the Plains of Abraham, he had been in a precarious position. Now with the English occupying the Citadel, he was certain the French would not attack. Saunders could take the fleet home and Townshend could turn his command over to Murray and leave on the Admiral's ship. It did not matter to him if it began to snow the very next day. Québec was his. He had bought it with a generous capitulation. Others would have to decide if he paid too much.

But on that first night, the Mother Superior of the Hôpital Général began to encourage resistance to the English and in the villages of the south shore for the first time the expression, "Les Maudits Anglais!" was heard. At Beauport and in Québec, Major Moncrief "found 234 pieces of cannon, 17 mortars, 4 howitzers, brass and iron of all sorts included, 694 barrels of powder, 14,800 round shot, 1,500 shells, 3,000 muskets with bayonets, and 70 tons of musket shot, with a good many other articles of less value," but only a small quantity of food. At Pointe-aux-Pères the batteries were silent. There was hardly anything left in Québec to destroy. Besides, what little there was now belonged to His Most Britannic Majesty.

Shortly before midnight, James Montague left his detachment and went back to Elisabeth de Melançon. Madame Lefebvre, who had spent the day in prayer in Notre-Dame-des-Victoires walked through the deserted streets of the ruined town that was her home. Near what remained of the cathedral, a soldier stopped her and in a tongue she found incomprehensible and humiliating told her to go away. Sneaking down an alley behind one of the many uninhabitable houses, she came to an escarpment where she stopped to watch the St. Lawrence flowing by. A new life was beginning, she thought. In time her husband would return from the West and her children from Sorel and Jean-François-Xavier from the army. There would be much work to rebuild Québec and the countryside. It would take fifty years.

At the dawn of the new order, close to fifteen thousand people from Québec to Gaspé, on both sides of the St. Lawrence, living in one town and fifty-nine villages, parishes, and seigneuries were the subjects of the English King.

Aftermath

After a hard winter and before the ice had barely left the St. Lawrence, Lévis marched back to Québec, where on April 28, 1760, he defeated the English at the battle of Sainte-Foy, a battle generally known as the second battle of the Plains of Abraham. The siege of Québec had begun again – this time with the French outside the town's walls. But it was short-lived. On May 15, English ships sailed into the Québec harbour and the next day proceeded to destroy what was left of Lévis' navy. Unable to maintain his position, Lévis retreated to Montréal on the night of May 16 to await the inevitable.

He did not have long to wait. Over the summer, Amherst and three English armies of seventeen thousand men converged leisurely upon Montréal. One, under Murray, came up the St. Lawrence from Québec burning a few villages on the way; another, under Brigadier-General William Haviland, occupied Bourlamaque's deserted fort on the Ile-aux-Noix and proceeded up the Richelieu River; and Amherst's army crossed the rapids at the head of the St. Lawrence.

France had sent no reinforcements, and the Canadians, abandoned, betrayed, and alienated, refused to bear arms. At the beginning of September, Lévis was left with an army of about two thousand soldiers. Vaudreuil sued for peace, but the terms Amherst granted were much harsher than Ramezay had obtained a year earlier. Lévis, having been refused the honours of war by Amherst and permission to continue the war by Vaudreuil, retreated to the Ile Sainte-Helène, where he burned his colours so that they would not fall into English hands.

On September 8, 1760, Montréal and the northern territories of the French empire in America were handed over to the English. All of Canada belonged to George II. The French officers, and soldiers, officials and some Canadian merchants and businesmen, sailed for France. But the 76,172 "souls" Amherst found in Canada stayed in their three towns and their 108 parishes – and survived.

Bougainville arrives for the last time, he tells me. He needs information.

"I know that le Marquis de Vaudreuil was imprisoned at the Bastille upon his return to France but later exonerated," he says. "But what happened to Bigot after he was found guilty of fraud and banished?"

"Toward the end of his life he was allowed to visit the Péans at Blois in Touraine in 1771," I inform him.

"Ah! La belle Lélie! I heard she died at age seventy, still beautiful, energetic, and desirable. And Monsieur de Ramezay?"

"He sailed for France in October 1759 and spent twenty years vindicating himself. In the end he had the satisfaction of receiving Vaudreuil's apologies and a pension from the King."

"A victim of circumstances," Bougainville suggests.

"He was, like the rest of us, betrayed," I correct him with some anger. After a while, he tells me about Lévis.

"He became a marshal of France and a duke. He was lucky to die before the French Revolution, but his widow and two of his three daughters went to the guillotine. His son managed to survive and witnessed the mob desecrating the tomb of his father."

"What about you, Monsieur?" I ask.

"Oh, I did fairly well. As you know I sailed around the world, helped the Americans free themselves, survived the revolution of 1789, married at age fifty-two, had four sons, became a *comte de l'Empire*, and on September 3, 1811, they placed my mortal remains in the Panthéon."

He looks pleased with himself. He pats the dogs and then asks me to tell him about *"les Anglais."*

"Amherst continued to fool everybody." I reply. "The rest of Monckton's career was not spectacular, unless one considers the conquest of Martinique and Grenada significant. Murray spent the last thirty-five years of his life fighting with everybody and did not amount to very much – on the other hand there are some people who say he was one of our friends. Saunders died of gout, and Townshend served as Lord Lieutenant of Ireland and, like all aristocrats of his day, lived a leisured lifestyle."

"And your friends Major Scott and the man from your Nova Scotia, what was his name?"

"Goreham. Scott went with Monckton to loot Martinique and Grenada, and Goreham found his salvation in liquor and debts. What else do you want to know?"

"Father Baudouin?"

"Murray kicked him out of the Hôpital Général. He died in 1761."

"You admired him, n'est-ce pas Monsieur LaPierre?"

"Yes, very much. And before you ask, Madame Lefebvre died doing what she always did – helping others; Mascou went off to the Canadian West and lived to a ripe old age; Mennard became a priest; Jean-François-Xavier returned to the Séminaire for a while, but I lost track of him."

"What about Elisabeth de Melançon and James Montague?"

"They lived happily ever after."

"Unlike your people."

"My people survived and did so, eventually, with quality. No thanks to any of you on the Plains of Abraham."

"You judge us harshly!"

"No, I do not. All of you, les Français comme les Anglais, were cruel in your dealings with my people and indifferent to our plight." He looks at me perplexed.

"You do not understand, do you?" I ask him more with pity than annoyance. "We, the Canadians, meant nothing to either of you. We were just pawns in your relentless and obsessive search for la gloire and in settling the score in Europe. We had built something of value here, in the St. Lawrence Valley and in the lands of the Great Lakes; even in Louisianna and Acadia. But you, the French, betrayed us, had us pillaged and killed, and left us here in the rubble. The English did not behave any better, but at least they stayed on, helped us to rebuild, and when it became time to choose between us and their colonies in the south, they opted for us. We owe you hardly anything. We owe the English a survival of sorts."

After an embarrassing silence, I say, "*Adieu*, Monsieur Louis-Antoine de Bougainville!"

"*Au revoir*, Monsieur Laurier Lucien LaPierre."

He walks to the door, but before he opens it to leave, he says, his back to me, "Will you write my biography?"

I laugh.

Notes On Sources

Most of the original documents referring to the siege of the town of Québec, the battle of the Plains of Abraham, and the capitulation have been published extensively in French and in English and can be found in any reliable library in Canada. I have made extensive use of these sources.

I am particularly grateful to Professor C.P. Stacey for his precise scholarship in *Quebec, 1759*, published to coincide with the two hundredth anniversary of the battle of the Plains of Abraham. As well, Monsieur le Professeur Guy Frégault in his work *La Guerre de la Conquête* (1955) provided me with an historical perspective not available anywhere else. I am grateful for it. Also, Professor W.J. Eccles, whose knowledge of Canada prior to 1760 is phenomenal, has inspired much of the social and cultural comments I make. I have always been in his debt.

For your purposes, I have added a short bibliography of sources that are easily accessible.

Beer, G. L., *British Colonial Policy, 1754–1765*. New York, 1922.

Bird, Harrison, *Battle for a Continent*. New York, 1965.

Bonnault, C. de, *Histoire du Canada Français*. Paris, 1950.

Bradley, Arthur Granville, *The Fight with France for North America*. Toronto, 1908.

Brunet, Michel, *Les Canadiens Après la Conquête. 1759–1775*. Montreal, 1969.

Casgrain, H. R. ed., *Collection des Manuscrits du Maréchal de Lévis*. 12 vols. Montréal-Québec, 1889–1895.

Casgrain, H.R., *Montcalm et Lévis*. 2 vols. Québec, 1891.

Chapais, Thomas, *Le Marquis de Montcalm*. Québec, 1891.

Connel, Brian, *The Plains of Abraham*. London, 1959.

Donaldson, Gordon, *Battle for a Continent: Quebec 1759*. Toronto, 1973.

Doughty, A.G. and Parmelee, G.W., *The Siege of Quebec 1759.* Toronto, 1973.

Douville, R., et Casanova, J.D., *La Vie Quotidienne en Nouvelle-France; le Canada de Champlain à Montcalm.* Paris, 1964.

Eccles, W.J., *Canada Under Louis XIV, 1663–1701.* Toronto, 1964.

Eccles, W.J., *France in America.* New York, 1972.

Eccles, W.J., *The Canadian Frontier, 1534–1760.* New York, 1969.

Findlay, James Thomas, *Wolfe in Scotland.* London & New York, 1928.

Frégault, Guy, *La Guerre de la Conquête.* Montreal, 1955.

Garrett, Richard T., *General Wolfe.* London, 1975.

Gibson, L.H., *The British Empire before The American Revolution.* 8 vols. New York, 1939–1954.

Graham, G.S., *Empire of the North Atlantic: The Maritime Struggle for North America.* Toronto, 1950.

Grinnell-Milne and Duncan William, *Mad, is he? The Character and Achievement of James Wolfe.* London, 1963.

Groulx, Lionel Adolphe, *Histoire du Canada Français.* 40 vols. Montreal, 1950–1952.

Groulx, Lionel Adolphe, *Lendemain de Conquête.* Montreal. 1920.

Guenin, Eugene, *Montcalm.* Paris, 1898.

Hamelin, J., *Economie et Société en Nouvelle-France.* Québec, 1960.

Harper, John Murdoch, *The Greatest Event in Canadian History. The Battle of the Plains.* Toronto, 1909.

Hart, Gerald, *The Fall of New France.* Montreal, 1888.

Hatheway, Warren Franklin, *Why France Lost Canada, and other essays and poems.* Toronto, 1915.

Hibbert, C., *Wolfe at Quebec.* London, 1959.

Lanctot, G., *Histoire du Canada du Traité d'Utrech au Traité de Paris, 1713–1763.* Montréal, 1964.

Mahen, Reginald Henry, *Life of General The Hon. James Murray, a Builder of Canada.* London, 1921.

Martin, Felix, *Le Marquis de Montcalm et les Dernières Années de la Colonie Française au Canada.* Paris, 1879.

Martin, Félix, *De Montcalm en Canada*. Paris, 1867.

Mitchell, John, *The Conquest in America between Great Britain and France with its Consequences and Importance*. New York, 1965.

Nish, C., *The French Canadians. 1759–1766. Conquered? Half Conquered? Liberated?* Toronto, 1966.

Parkman, Francis, *Montcalm and Wolfe*. London, 1962.

Reilly, Robin, *Wolfe at Quebec*. London, 1963.

Robitaille, George, *Montcalm et ses Historiens*. Montréal, 1936.

Roy, P.G., *Bigot et sa Bande et l'Affaire du Canada*. Levis, 1950.

Samuel, S., *The Seven Years' War in Canada. 1756–1763*. Toronto, 1959.

Stacey, C.P., *Quebec, 1759 – The Siege and Battle*. Toronto, 1959.

Stanley, G.F.F, *Canada's Soldiers, the Military History of an Unmilitary People*. Toronto, 1959.

Stanley, G.F.F, *New France. The Last Phase, 1744–1760*. Toronto, 1968.

Waddington, Richard, *La Guerre de 7 ans. Histoire Diplomatique et Militaire*. 5 vols. Paris, 1899–1914.

Waugh, W.T., *James Wolfe, The Man and the Soldier*. Montreal, 1928.

Warburton, George, *The Conquest of Canada*. 2 vols. London, 1857.

Williams, Smith, *First Days of British Rule in Canada*. Kingston, 1922.

Willson, Beckles, *The Life and Letters of James Wolfe*. London, 1909.

Wood, William Charles Henry, *The Passing of New France*. Toronto, 1915.

Wood, William Charles Henry, *The Fight for Canada*. Boston, 1906.

Wrong, George McKinnon, *The Fall of Canada*. Oxford, 1914.